Master of Disaster

FRANK KRAKE

Master of Disaster

WHEN GIVING UP IS NOT AN OPTION

FRANK KRAKE

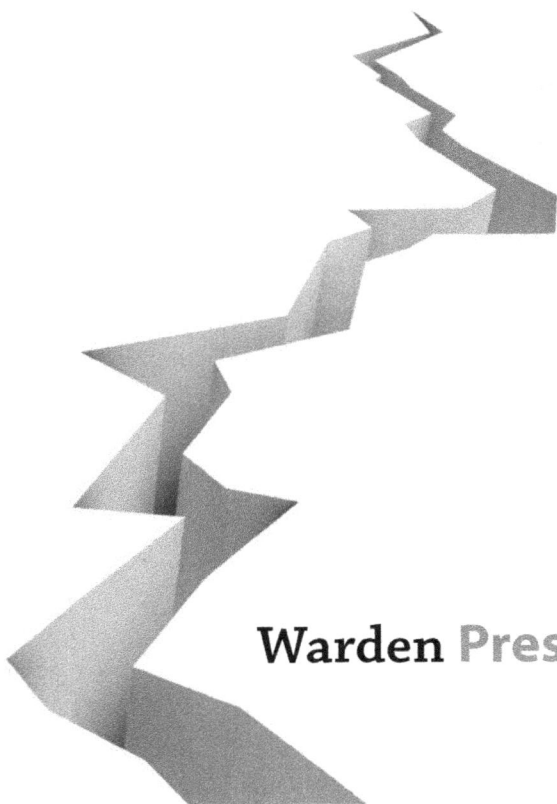

Warden Press

© 2017 Frank Krake

ISBN:
Paperback: 978-94-92004-48-2
E-book (Epub): 978-94-92004-49-9
E-book (Kindle): 978-94-92004-50-5

Original title: *De rampondernemer. Overwinnen als alles tegenzit*
(Amsterdam: Pearson Benelux, 2013)

Editor and advisor: Enno de Witt
Translated from the Dutch by Allison Krüter-Klein
Editor English translation: Andrea Thornton
Cover design: Studio Pearson
Cover illustration: Shutterstock/Kruglov_Orda (legs), Shutterstock/hkeita (crack),
Shutterstock/Jiang Hongyan (firecrackers), Shutterstock/Brian Kinney (airplane)
Interior design and lay-out: Philip de Josselin de Jong, Haarlem

You can contact the author at frank@rampondernemer.nl

This edition published by Warden Press, Amsterdam (wardenpress.com)

For Sven, Esmee and Peep

'Listen to the beat of your own drum
and make your dreams come true'

Acknowledgements

My first book; a momentous occasion. Time to stop and think about the rollercoaster ride that thundered on at dizzying speeds for 13 years of my life. Climbing high peaks and dipping down through very deep valleys. I wouldn't have survived it all without support from the home front. And this is why I owe a special word of thanks to my wife, Edith. I thank her for her unceasing support, and mostly, the freedom that she gave me to embark on my adventures.

I would also like to thank my father Henny for his continual support and his ever-encouraging words.

I thank my mother posthumously, for the warm home she created and sense of independence she instilled in me. The day I ended up in a jail cell in Washington, D.C., as cruel fate would have it, was the day she would receive the omen signaling the end of her life.

I never could have written this book if I had not had such wonderful co-workers, both those at Unimeta as well as Bukatchi. I am not only referring to the office staff, but especially those people working in the plant, on the assembly line and the cushion filling line. And to everyone else involved in these activities, a heartfelt thanks for your unbridled dedication and amazing team spirit.

A special word of thanks to my co-director at Unimeta and personal advisor at Bukatchi, Ruud Kuipers, who advised and assisted me for 18 years in the patio furniture industry.

I would like to thank Johan Schreur for making video material available from his personal archives. Parts of these may be viewed using the Layar app in this book.

Last but not least, a huge thank you to the people who helped me realize my dream: Kees Schafrat for helping me get started in the wondrous world of this book, Enno de Witt for his critical notes and help in keeping the text readable, Rick van der Ploeg for writing the wonderful foreword, and John Numan and his team for believing in this project.

Frank Krake
frank@rampondernemer.nl

Contents

Foreword

by Rick van de Ploeg

My father had fled from prison in Scheveningen to England, and like so many other Dutch at the time, joined the Royal Air Force. While stationed in Manchester, he met the love of his life, a woman with whom he brought four children into the world. As a businessman from Rotterdam with a boundless love for entrepreneurship and England, he was always looking for lucrative business, mostly between the Netherlands and England.

Under the name "House of Holland", he started a chain of stores dealing in wares such as sleeping bags, tools and patio furniture. This business eventually grew to become 150 stores located throughout the United Kingdom. He also had an advertising agency, New Trend Advertising, which had 150 employees. During those years, we often accompanied my father on vacation at the British holiday camps owned by his RAF buddy Billy Butlins, where we were allowed to ride the rollercoaster and watch the rock band Slade play for free, and my father could visit the stores incognito.

In the late 1960s, when the opportunity arose to start a patio furniture factory in Enschede in the Netherlands, he seized it with both hands. He bought Unimeta from Hartman in the year of the hippies. While everyone was getting their fill of marijuana, flower power and free love, my father was starting a patio furniture factory. The frames were made from metal tubes, and then fitted with canvas seats and backs. Some 300 people worked there. Those were also the years that our family went to Boekelo to frolic in the saltwater wave pool in the middle of the forest in Twente. My older brother John worked at Unimeta for a while under the CEO at the time, Meerdink.

Thanks to my father's business, at the age of 15, I developed an interest in the theory of foreign currencies and exchange rates. I couldn't understand why patio furniture was made in one country where people paid for purchases with guilders, and were sold in a country that used pounds sterling if the pound was losing value every year. It is possible to hedge some of your risk on the futures market, but at that time, the Netherlands was expensive (even though it boasted high-quality industry) and England was inexpensive. I understand it all a bit better now, but I still don't know why vertical integration is such a good business model, since a third party might be better at making products sold in stores.

Ultimately, my father got cancer and died two years later in the spring of 1975. I now realize what an accomplishment it was to build up such a business empire in such a short period of time. My father was furious when he heard I wanted to study math and physics. Because of his illness, he wanted me to go into his business. We compromised: I would study in England because that was only a three-year program in the 1970s. In addition to math and physics, the arrangement was that I would also do the SPD business administration program and part of the NIVRA accountancy program. My father ultimately died too soon, during the first year of my studies. I got hooked on science, went to Cambridge for my doctorate degree, and rebelled by turning my back on the business world. As a result of the sky-high inheritance tax and lack of a successor, things went downhill pretty fast at House of Holland. Eventually, the heirs (including 12 children) sold Unimeta to Mr. Meerdink.

In spite of my career in politics as a social-democrat, thanks to my father and all of his business partners who would often come to visit us at home, I have always had a tremendous admiration for entrepreneurs. As the Red Queen in *Through the Looking Glass* explains to Alice, where she comes from, you have to run twice as fast if you want to get anywhere. The technological progress and the rise of offshoring to low-wage countries such as India and China means that entrepreneurs must constantly stay alert in order to survive and realize a growth in their profits.
Metal tube and canvas patio furniture had to make room for the much cheaper plastic patio furniture the company Hartman became so famous for. Plastic later had to make way for high-end, high-quality furniture that could be made a lot more cheaply in China.

It is easier to write an intriguing novel about the adventures of an entrepreneur than those of a scientist. This is why I was really happy to hear that the relatively young Frank Krake had taken over the helm at Unimeta at the time. Frank is a quintessential businessman and works in an environment that is very different from the safe world of science. Frank has also proven himself to be an excellent writer, and his book is impossible to put down. It is a fascinating, informative and often hilarious picaresque novel. The book doesn't just cover all the highlights he experienced as helmsman of Unimeta, but also provides an account of the often unexpected low points that you can't predict. One such low point is the American adventure that unfortunately fails when the attacks of 9/11 and the economic crisis cause the market for high-end patio furniture to collapse. Another involves the plan to conquer the German market that gets nipped in the bud as a result of the Enschede fireworks disaster. Learning to cope with new situations and reinventing yourself time after time is therefore the recipe for becoming successful in business, even if it means that you might go bankrupt along the way. A good entrepreneur is someone who learns from failure and starts over again.

Frank explains in detail how hard you have to fight to keep a company going in a world of globalization and international competition. This is why this amazing book should be required reading for every business administration student and every entrepreneur just starting out. However, I can also highly recommend this book for every other type of reader, not only because of the captivating story and the many lessons it has to teach, but also because of the multimedia approach the book uses.

Rick van de Ploeg
London, September 2013
Professor at the University of Oxford and the VU University Amsterdam,
Former State Secretary for Education, Culture and Science

Prologue

Bang! The barred door of a cell in the jail below the Washington, D.C. police station slams shut with a loud clang. Frank doesn't notice that he's not alone in the cell until he looks around him. A tall, dark man is lying stretched out on a metal plate which is kept in its horizontal position by chains bolted to the wall.
Frank extends his hand in greeting. The man introduces himself as William and tells him he was arrested for having run too many red lights. Frank can only hope that the man is telling the truth. On his way to his cell, he has already noticed he's the only white person here.
The other prisoners call out to him. He can't shake the image of the angry look in their eyes. He shivers.
   There is another metal plate hanging from the wall about three feet above the traffic violator. Frank pulls it down and climbs on. There aren't any chairs, just a steel toilet with a small sink above it. The cell is no larger than six by nine feet. Frank lies down, using his shoes as a pillow.

After completing his studies, he worked for three months at a summer camp in upstate New York with children from shelters in the Bronx. Their parents were either addicted to drugs or dead, or were in prison. A special bus brought the children to Camp Lanowa where, for three weeks, they could forget their troubles, in the middle of the woods at the edge of a large lake.

In exchange for the work he did there, the camp gave him a plane ticket and some spending money. An unforgettable experience, the folder had promised. Staring at the ceiling of his cell, he smiles in spite of everything and thinks back to his time there.

After the three months were up, Frank boarded a bus to explore America. Travelling on a Greyhound pass, he headed south along the East Coast, towards Florida.

Without any indication of the trouble he will quickly find himself in, he stands in the line of people waiting to tour the White House. He doesn't have to wait long; after half an hour, he's already inside. All he has to do now is go through a gate equipped with a metal detector. The next thing he knows, an alarm is going off, making a tremendous racket, and a huge rotating light is flashing through the hall, scaring Frank out of his wits. The guard tells him to empty his pockets and lay his possessions on a belt. He quickly discovers the cause of all this: as always, Frank has his jackknife with him. The guard returns it to him without a fuss. Relieved, Frank gathers his things together again.

After the White House, he goes to Capitol Hill, the seat of the U.S. government, and an absolute must-see for anyone visiting the city. Once again, Frank has to get on the back of the line. As he nears the front, he sees the exact same type of gate as the one he went through at the White House. To prevent the alarm from going off again, he empties his pockets and lays his things on the belt. He walks through the metal detector without a problem. A security guard has removed all his things from the belt, and from that moment on, everything happens very fast. Frank holds out his hand to retrieve his possessions, but the officer grabs his hand and pins his arm to his back. In one swift move, he also grabs Frank's other arm, and before Frank has time to react, both his wrists are in handcuffs. Frank looks at him in surprise and asks,

"What's going on? All I wanted to do was tour the building. Would you please uncuff me, sir? I would like my things back."

Without saying a word, the guard pushes Frank ahead of him into the building, through several corridors until they reach stairs leading outside. After a few minutes, a police car pulls up. A policeman gets out of the car, stands in front of Frank and reads him his rights.

He is then shoved onto the hard plastic back seat of the police car and they drive off, sirens screaming. The handcuffs are cutting off his circulation, and the hard back seat makes every turn painful.

Frank vows to never sit on another plastic chair again, as long as he shall live.

They stop in front of a building where he sees *Washington Police Department* in giant letters on the façade. Two minutes later, he's led into a detention room, where he's told to sit on a bench. An officer unlocks one of the handcuffs. Although he can now stretch his left hand, he doesn't even get the chance. Before he realizes it, his wrist is clicked into a new handcuff, and this time it's chained to the wall. The officer leaves the room and a man in a nice suit comes in.

He doesn't introduce himself, just gives Frank a stern look.

"You're in big trouble. You're being charged with being in possession of a jackknife. This weapon is prohibited by law here in Washington, D.C."

"But I walked around with it in my pocket for three months in New York, sir," Frank says, and talks about the summer camp for homeless kids.

"They let me into the White House with it a little while ago."

"We'll tell all this to the assistant district attorney," the man says. "Everything you say now will be written down, and that report will be going to him. Until that time, you'll remain in custody. You can make one telephone call and then you'll be going to a cell in a different complex. After that, we'll decide if you'll have to appear before a judge."

Frank realizes that arguing is pointless, and wonders who he should call. Not his parents or girlfriend; this will only scare the daylights out of them. He decides to call the Dutch embassy. The man looks up the number for him and dials. Frank's hands remain in the handcuffs and the telephone is put on speaker, and placed a few inches in front of his face. The people at the embassy listen to his story and remain incredibly cool.

"We have made a note of it all, young man. This might take a couple days, but we expect that you'll be released after that."

"A couple days? I'll never last that long," Frank shouts.

"I'm afraid you'll just have to wait it out. We'll contact the Department of Justice in three days to find out if you're still there."

In a special room, they remove the shoelaces from his shoes. He also has to hand over his belt and his pockets are emptied. When he is brought to the jail complex, he is told to hold up a sign with a number on it in front of his chest. They take photos from all sides, and after taking his fingerprints, they put a blue band around his wrist. *Washington Detention Services*, he reads.

Frank closes his eyes and tries to clear his head. It's now four o'clock in the afternoon, two hours after his arrest. In spite of the stressful circumstances, he manages to doze off. At around six, two plates with sandwiches are slid under the bars.

Frank doesn't touch his; he can't swallow a bite. At ten o'clock, he awakens with a start when a guard slides the cell door open.

Bang!

"Krake, dismissed," he barks. "The charges have been dropped. You're free to go."

1

A NEW MILLENNIUM

Ten years have passed and the new millennium has just begun when Frank starts his new job as the CEO at Unimeta, a manufacturer of patio furniture in Enschede. This enormous company employs 300 people and has sales of over 20 million Euros. The manufacturing site is as large as three football fields. When Frank wakes up on the first day in his new position, the responsibility briefly seizes him by the throat, but he quickly gets a hold of himself. This is what he has always dreamed of, and now he can enjoy the results of all his hard work at Unimeta over the past six years, when he came to work here after his previous job at Wehkamp. Although he had been responsible for purchasing at Wehkamp, here he's sitting on the other side of the table and he's only just turned 31. When he realizes what's in store for him, he is briefly overcome by doubt yet again. He wonders if he projects enough authority, and whether customers will take him seriously or not. As he puts on his suit and ties his tie, he shakes off all these worries.

"They'll just have to accept me for who I am," he says to his cleanly shaven image in the mirror.

This almost took quite a different turn six years ago. In his cover letter, he had written that he was eager to work for Hartman, the patio furniture manufacturer in Enschede who was making major inroads in the Netherlands at the time. Even though Frank was from the neighboring Twente, he had no idea that there was another factory in the city where they also made patio furniture, and that it was located right next to Hartman. The name "Unimeta" indicated that they made all sorts of metal products, but he had never heard of them. The company was only known in Enschede, but the majority of people looked up to Hartman, with its popular chairs made entirely of plastic. Thanks to a faux-pas like that, his life could have taken a completely different turn, but Unimeta was very eager to have him, and were willing to overlook it. Frank started out as a commercial manager, and quickly worked his way up.

He gradually developed a passion for the products they made. He loved strolling through the factory and breathing in the scent of manufactured metal. He delighted in watching dozens of people attaching component after component to a basic frame, until finally at the end of the assembly line, the contours of a real patio chair became visible, ready for further processing. In the large warehouse, you could hear the shrill sounds of industrial saws and grinding lathes; music to his ears.

As Frank sits at his director's desk this particular morning, he first looks around critically. The furniture has actually been in need of replacement for years. His distant predecessor, a man in his sixties, had decorated the office a long time ago, and this was painfully apparent. The heavy, dark-brown furniture with its rough, beige upholstery was actually quite outdated, but they didn't have money for new furnishings; the company wasn't doing well enough for that.

Planting the typical three Dutch kisses on his cheeks, his secretary wishes him all the best for the new millennium. He's known Marion for years, he knows what she's capable of, and has high expectations for working with her. She is about six years older than he is, and much more conservative in her ways. This tends to balance out his naturally casual and informal manner.

She has completely filled his schedule for his first day, from meetings with the works council up to the New Year's speech the director always gives the staff in the cafeteria, and in which he, also according to tradition, will announce the plans for the new year. It is also a much-appreciated custom for him to personally wish everyone a Happy New Year, a tradition that will involve shaking 300 hands. He has a brief moment to relax before he sinks his teeth into the future of the company.

The first hurdle he has to overcome is the works council. As always, the council has doubts about the course the company is taking, and concerns about the retention of jobs. The bicycle racks will also undoubtedly be a topic of conversation; this issue has been a regular item on the agenda for years now. If it were up to Frank, the staff would all come to work on foot or by car, at least then they would be done with all the complaints. The racks are always the cause of problems. This time, someone has slipped and fallen on a metal connecting strip. If the works council had its way, management would free up some of the budget for better lighting. Better lighting would apparently be helpful for employees who had had too much to drink the night before, so they could spot where danger is lurking, even when suffering from a hangover.

Although these things can be irritating, Frank still manages to summon sympathy for the people who fight for the items on their co-workers' wish lists. These are very devoted employees, many of whom have been working for the company from its inception, over 30 years ago. These men were here from the very beginning, old-school, and always there when they were needed. They had experienced the time when the company was growing and blossoming in the 1980s, when the railroad cars used to drive directly into the company's forwarding warehouse, where they would be loaded up with patio chairs for the foreign market.

Those times were over. The railroad connection was no longer profitable for the Dutch Railways, and had been closed.
Since that time, the patio furniture has been transported by trucks. The end of an era, but also a necessary change. These days, they ship nearly everything by container. Most are destined for the English market, with hundreds of thousands of chairs per year, "relaxers", a model that they can't even give away for free in the Netherlands.

Before going to the cafeteria, he makes a quick stop to see his production manager. Ruud Kuipers is his great supporter and ally. In his late fifties and loyal to the core, perhaps even more importantly Ruud is in favor of innovation. Kuipers applauds every change, as long as it represents an improvement.

Frank also gets along very well with the man who is set to take Kuipers' place, and who now leads the textile department. Frank Pet is only in his mid-thirties, yet is taking over more and more of Kuipers' duties. The company's controller, his contemporary Erwin Hoge Bavel, makes the management team complete. Four very different men, each with his own strong character, all working together to achieve a single goal.

All four know that the task they have been charged with is not a simple one. The numbers aren't exactly encouraging, to put it mildly, and they have been teetering on the edge for years now, but each time they manage to land on the right side of the bottom line. The important thing now is to generate a good level of profit for a few years so that they have some room to breathe again.

At the New Year's breakfast, Frank sits in the middle of the cafeteria. He's known most of the people there for years, but there are also a few tables filled with unfamiliar faces. This is the group of temporary employees they have working there. During peak periods in production, there may be more than 100 of these employees, some of whom return year after year, helping out during the busy spring and early summer periods.

The foreign contingent of these employees eat at separate tables; this is how they want it. Although Frank thinks this is a shame, he gave up the fight for more integration in the cafeteria years ago. In the factory however, everyone mixes and works well together, and during the breaks, they gravitate back to their own little groups. Most of the men are in their fifties and are first-generation immigrants, the majority of whom come from Turkey. A smaller group comes from Morocco, and then there are a few Surinam-Dutch as well.

After Frank has once again wished his co-workers a healthy and successful new millennium, he starts his actual New Year's speech.

"Over the past year, we have taken major steps to increase efficiency in production. In order to survive the fierce competition, the processing time per chair has to be brought down even further. The goal is to achieve a further 10% in time savings in two years."

He sees a few people frown. He realizes that they have just completed a whole phase of implementing measures designed to increase efficiency. But it has to be even faster, even more streamlined, since they're earning next to nothing on all these hundreds of thousands of chairs.

"We also have to increase sales," he says, "and we need better distribution of our sales. We are currently dependent on the English market for 60% of the sales of our relaxers. Germany represents 20%, and most of the sales there consist of metal chairs with synthetic mats clicked onto them. There are opportunities in Belgium and Scandinavia. Our export managers are focusing on these markets. I will continue to personally handle sales to the American market, working closely with Bart. We are already doing well there, but there is definitely room for growth."

Frank starts feeling more comfortable in his new role, and is getting more and more enthusiastic. He tells them that they are going to put major efforts into the sales of the Preston collection for the top segment of the market in the Netherlands. This furniture line is made from aluminum frames, combined with teak slats, arm rests and table tops. They started with the line three years ago, and sales are already at nearly one million Euros. The products are distributed to 50 dealers, most of which are garden centers and patio furniture stores.

"The Preston collection is our showpiece, and proves what we are capable of in terms of technology and design. Our customers really love it. Although it's an expensive line of patio furniture, consumers can see how much craftsmanship and dedication go into them."

Smiles appear on the many faces in the cafeteria. Frank knows how proud these people are of this new collection. They are lining up for the chance to be able to work on the Preston assembly line. Since the level of quality is incredibly high, only the most skilled workers are chosen to work on this line. When they first started production, they had no idea that Preston would be such a huge boost for the company. It was a dire necessity to come up with new ideas, and this was one of the reasons Frank was brought on board.

They had needed two years to prepare. Ruud Kuipers and his development team had done everything they could to come up with an innovative idea. Frank had applied all of his marketing expertise to develop a plan they could use to launch this new line on the market. He had decided to market directly to the potential points of sale using a special salesman, and not limit themselves to distribution through the usual wholesalers only. This meant that they had more control over the entire process. It also meant that they had to produce inventory since the customers would have to be able to receive their orders within 48 hours of placing them. Frank had had to revamp the entire system of logistics to accomplish this. This was a major undertaking, but the people who had made it a reality were the ones sitting in the cafeteria, listening to Frank's story, with a smile on their faces.

He arrives at the most important part of his New Year's speech.

"We have solid plans for marketing to the middle segment of the market. The relaxers target the lower end of the market, the Preston the upper end, but we don't have a good, commercially priced collection for the middle segment. This is what Sombrero is designed to achieve: chairs, tables, chaise lounges and ottomans that are only ideas on paper at this point. We will be applying part of the techniques from the Preston series for this line, but will be focusing on large production quantities, with simplified designs. This will allow for semi-automated production and the cost price will be a bit lower than it is for Preston. In the coming months, we will be working hard to produce the prototypes. We will introduce the collection at the large international patio furniture show in Cologne in September of this year."

Frank now has his audience's undivided attention. You can see them all thinking that this was just what the company needed. This is what will ensure a bright future. All of the market segments covered, all of the products made in Enschede, all with a steel or aluminum basis. This was also the only material that Unimeta could process. For years, they had watched their neighbor Hartman in envy, a factory that churned out many thousands of plastic chairs each day. The production machinery was fully adapted for this purpose. Enormous, fully automated injection moulding machines spit plastic chairs out of their molds. In the 1990s, those things were impossible to get a hold of. The former director of Unimeta would have never dared to take on an investment of millions of Euros for a production line like that, and that's why they still made these old-fashioned metal chairs. This has all changed now thanks to Preston.

"This does not mean our problems are all solved," Frank says, "but there is a light at the end of the tunnel now."

As he gathers up his notes a moment later, a ripple of applause cascades through the room. From now on, things can only get better.

2

BAPTISM OF FIRE

Groaning and perspiring heavily, Frank relocates his work area a yard or two to the left. This part of the border is in the shadow of a birch tree and it's a lot cooler here. It's impossible to work in the sun on a day like this, and he still has a lot of weeding to do in the garden. Earlier that morning, he brought a trailer full of garden waste to the garbage dump, and now that the grass is short again, everything looks a lot neater. Frank can't remember a time when it has been this warm so early in the spring in the Netherlands. After all, it's only the 13th of May, and the mercury on the outdoor thermometer has already reached 84 degrees.

The strenuous physical work-out is a welcome distraction. Those first few months, his days consisted primarily of meetings, writing reports and brainstorming about missions, visions and strategies. All are incredibly interesting of course, but draining in terms of his mental energy.

The start of the season has gone well, and that makes everything that much easier of course. The good weather in the spring of 2000 has meant an automatic increase in the demand for patio furniture. The sales staff's telephones have been ringing off the hook for weeks. They have stepped up production even further, and the warehouse is packed full of inventory. A large group of production and warehouse employees have worked overtime without protest. Everyone knows that the company has to earn money now, so no one takes vacation during the spring. They will have time to rest during the summer and the months afterwards; for now, they have to work really hard. People are even working today, a Saturday, under the command of Jules Lumens, the logistics manager. He is working with a few people to sort and prepare orders that will have to be sent out on Monday.

This is all happening about half a mile away from the factory, in an extra warehouse that they have rented at the Bamshoeve, a former textile mill in Enschede, just outside of the city center in an old working-class neighborhood. For the residents of Enschede, the Bamshoeve is a household word. It is a surviving icon from the 1960s and 1970s, when Twente still had numerous textile mills, bleaching facilities and spinning mills. Like so many of the manufacturing complexes that have fallen into disuse, the Bamshoeve is also awaiting rezoning for residential construction. Until that time, Unimeta uses part of the facility to store old machines and steel frames for relaxers, the basic line of chairs they sell shipping containers full of, primarily in England. These have already been produced in the winter, and will be finished in the spring with the addition of thick cushions, ready for shipment to customers. The entire Preston collection is also stored there.

Later that afternoon, as Frank is emptying the next bucket filled with weeds into the wheelbarrow, he feels the ground tremble slightly. He hears a dull rumble in the distance. He has no idea where it's coming from, but doesn't pay it any further mind. It is around 3:30, and time for a cup of coffee. He wipes the perspiration from his brow, and has barely sat down when he hears another boom, louder this time. Once again, a shudder seems to run through the floor.

"Edith, am I going crazy, or did you feel that too? It feels like the ground is moving."

"Maybe it's an earthquake?" his wife says.

"Highly doubtful. You don't hear a dull boom before an earthquake, do you? It felt like something huge landed on the ground really hard. It couldn't be another F16 that's crashed, could it? It did come from the general direction of the air base. Very strange."

Frank doesn't give it another thought, downs his coffee, and picks up his gardening gloves. Ten minutes later, when he looks to the south, he sees a huge dark cloud there, quickly growing larger and darker. It is obvious something is really wrong over there. The smoke cloud rises up into the spring sky like an inverted funnel. As Frank stands and watches this strange spectacle, export manager Gerrit van Gils walks into his garden. Frank is startled when he sees the serious look on Gerrit's face.

"Our factory didn't just blow sky-high by any chance, did it?" he jokes.

"No, it didn't, but I guess you haven't heard what *did* happen?" Gerrit asks, surprised. "Don't you have the television on? And you're not answering your phone either. Johan has been trying to reach you, but since he couldn't get a hold of you, he called me. That's why I'm here."

Frank shrugs his shoulders and mumbles something about working in the yard today. The area where the dull booms have come from is now pitch-black.

"It looks like a solar eclipse," Frank says. "But if it's not the factory, what is it then?"

"They think a fireworks factory has exploded."

"But there aren't any fireworks factories in Enschede, are there?"

"You better believe there is! Or rather, there was one, right next to Bamshoeve. Johan told me that everything has been blown sky-high."

"You mean...the entire fireworks factory?" Frank tries again.

"No, man! The entire Bamshoeve! Johan didn't see it himself, he couldn't get close enough, but he heard that there's nothing left."

"Unbelievable, this can't be happening. I'm going to make some calls straight away," says Frank. "I'm going to see who I can reach."

Once Gerrit has left, Frank turns on the television. The regional network is broadcasting live coverage of the disaster. Edith watches over his shoulder now and then, but is mostly preoccupied with their children. The youngest is just three months old and the oldest just over two. They're adorable, but right now, Frank can't focus on them. He calls one co-worker after the other and tries to get an idea of the damage. He uses his landline since the cell network is for the most part either down or overloaded.

A reporter on television is talking about multiple fatalities and this number is rising as time goes on, as is the number of injured. An unrelenting flow of ambulances, fire engines and all sorts of emergency service vehicles from the Netherlands and Germany flashes across the screen. If you didn't know any better, this could be coverage of events in a war zone. He hasn't heard anything about the Bamshoeve.

After many attempts, in the early evening Frank finally manages to get Johan Schreur on the line, the man from the technical department.

"I was still at the Bamshoeve at two this afternoon. We had gotten all the pallets with furniture ready for the shipment on Monday. After that, I turned on the alarm and closed up, but I was barely home an hour when the emergency center called. I drove back right away, but didn't get very far. The police stopped me and no matter what I told them about Bamshoeve and the warehouse, they wouldn't let me through. When I got out of the car, a policeman came running by and all he was shouting was, 'Get out of here! Everybody out!' He had a gaping wound in his head and his shirt was covered in blood. He was in a total panic. I couldn't believe my eyes. All the windows have been blown out of the houses and cars, as far as half a mile away."

"Have any of our people been hurt?"

"No, I don't think so. No one was left when I was closing up, and I don't think any of them live close by."

Frank spends the rest of the evening watching the news on television and calling key employees in the organization. Slowly but surely, a picture of the catastrophe starts forming in his mind, but he can't comprehend it. The disaster has hit the company at its very core. They are right in the middle of the delivery season. The entire warehouse was full, and if the initial reports are accurate, there's nothing left. He finally goes to bed at around one o'clock, his stomach aching from the stress, but doesn't sleep much beyond a few catnaps. He keeps waking up with a start, the images of the disaster burned onto his retina.

The next morning, Frank gets in the car at 8:00 and heads towards Enschede; he wasn't able to sleep anyway. It takes a great deal of effort to even get to the office. Most of the access roads are closed, and he repeatedly has to explain to police officers that he is on his way to a crucial emergency meeting. On the way, he sees some of the tremendous havoc the explosions have wreaked, even miles away from the disaster site.

When he finally parks his car at the Unimeta parking lot around 9:00, he sees a few bicycles there, and Johan's car. One window on the side of the building has been shattered, and the shards are inside. Jules is nailing a sheet of plywood over the smashed window. He had been working in the warehouse until a couple hours before the fatal explosion, but because he had some odd jobs to do at home, he stopped working at 1:30 in the afternoon. That decision ended up saving his life.

As they walk towards the conference room on the second floor, they see the stairs are littered with tiles from the modular ceiling. The shock wave had lifted the entire roof up briefly.

"I saw pieces from containers lying on the Singel yesterday," Jules says. "They were shot over 500 yards through the air. Unbelievable."

The emergency meeting starts that Sunday morning at 10:00. It quickly becomes clear that none of their staff are among the dead or injured. The priority now is to ensure that customers experience as little inconvenience as possible from the disaster, because before you know it, they'll go to the competition and then you'll have lost them forever. They decide to step up production even further, and as soon as possible.

They are going to be working nights and weekends after this, but even then, they won't be able to get the inventory of the entire product line back up to where it needs to be. Part of the inventory that was destroyed in the explosion is produced in China. It will take at least three months to replenish that stock, and by that time, the season will be over. The customers will not be happy at all about this, but there's nothing they can do about it. Frank will send them a letter to explain the situation, and beyond that, all he can do is hope for the best.

On Monday morning, Frank schedules a meeting with the insurance company that is doing everything it can to pay out the benefits for the millions worth of damage. This is all he can do. Frank turns on the alarm, and is the last to leave the building.

Three weeks later, Frank and two insurance adjusters are standing in a special portable building on the site where the Bamshoeve once stood. A white suit hangs on a peg for every person there. Next to the suit is a face mask with a respiratory compressor to prevent them from breathing in any asbestos particles that might have been released during the explosion. Wrapped up and hermetically sealed, they walk onto the disaster site. Looking around, Frank is shocked by what he sees. Although these are images he's already seen dozens of times, it only seems real to him now that he is right here, in the middle of the disaster area. Literally everything is destroyed.

There are pieces of steel and concrete everywhere where a proud textile mill once stood. It takes them some effort to get their bearings simply because nothing has been left standing. Frank has the feeling that they must be standing right around the spot where the containers would be loaded, and there used to be a large storage warehouse about ten yards to the right, but all he sees now is a massive ruin. The insurance adjusters are walking around with lists in their hands, but can see that every attempt to figure out what used to be here is a waste of time. On the way back, they drive past dozens of charred carcasses of cars and structures that used to be houses, past a church without a roof, and mostly, past a trail of misery and sorrow.

Second only to Grolsch, Unimeta suffered the most damage. Fortunately, everything was well-arranged in terms of their insurance, and the company immediately transfers an advance payment of three million Euros. It's just a start though; the total damage is over ten million, but for the time being, it's enough to get the ball rolling again. It takes a Herculean effort, but they manage to deliver all the products that were lost in the explosion within three weeks. They have found and set up an alternative warehouse space. It may only be temporary, but it works. They get back to work with renewed enthusiasm, but what continues to bother Frank is the reaction from a handful of customers who can't seem to sympathize with his situation. They scream into the telephone.

"*Wo bleibt meine Ware!* (Where are my products?!)"

Even when they tell them about the 20 fatalities and thousands of injuries, the customers are not interested.

"*Ist mir scheissegal!* (I don't give a damn!)"

During this period, Frank has to calm his co-workers down on more than one occasion, and also explain that these angry customers have absolutely no concept of what is going on. Frank would actually be happier to lose these customers than keep them, but the company absolutely cannot afford for this to happen. Their position on the German market is awkward as it is, and now the German wholesalers are buying their patio furniture from the competition. The insurance will also cover the consequential damage during the first year, but if they lose important customers, it could mean their downfall in the years after that. Frank can't help but have the sinking feeling that the explosion will continue to rumble on much longer than anyone realizes.

3

EXPORT TO AMERICA

The summer of 2000 has just ended, and Frank is in a good mood as he gets into his rental car, a one-month-old silver Cadillac Deville. The beast swings and banks around curves the way one would expect from a real American machine. The dashboard is worthy of criticism, thus confirming all the preconceived notions about America. They'll just never learn, over there on the other side of the Atlantic, Frank thinks, but he refuses to let this spoil his mood. Americans are starting to recognize and appreciate European quality and design more and more, and this is why he's been so successful with the Preston collection here.

Having arrived at the Cincinnati/Northern Kentucky airport last night, where he picked up this huge boat of a car, he is now whizzing over the state line into Ohio. Frank looks around and likes what he sees. The highway is eight lanes wide, and everywhere he looks he sees cars that you seldom or never see in Europe.

The speed limit is relatively low here, so he has plenty of time to take in his surroundings. He passes a few enormous trucks, their powerful noses full of chrome, with airbrushed paintings on the hood and sides of the cabin. Behind the driver's seat he sees what appears to be a complete temporary home, large enough to easily house an entire family.

Along the way, he sees small towns that all proudly promote themselves with huge water towers. Topped with round water tanks, these typically American structures tower proudly in the air. The name of the town is painted clearly on the water tank, confirming for Frank that he's on the right road.

Everything here is colossal and overdone. It started early this morning at breakfast, where he was served a cup of coffee containing nearly a quart of the black liquid. On second thought, calling this cup of colored water "coffee" was a bit of a stretch. Accustomed to strong, aromatic European coffee, Frank was amazed at how these Yanks could guzzle this hot liquid early in the morning with a straight face. And this was nothing compared to the huge hamburgers that he saw entire families devouring at seven in the morning. He escaped this fate by ordering a bowl of cereal which was fortunately served in a sort of soup bowl this time, and not the dreaded salad bowl from his last trip here, over a year ago.

Frank presses the gas pedal down a bit further. At ten o'clock, he has an appointment at the head office of Frontgate, a company that has been Unimeta's customer for the past three years. Frank remembers the first meeting as if it were yesterday. He first met them at the international patio furniture trade show in Cologne in 1998. Unimeta was introducing the then brand-new Preston collection, and two men appeared at their booth. Frank could see from how they were dressed that they were American, and rushed over to them. He had harbored the hope that the Preston collection could also be a success in the U.S.

These men were Frontgate CEO Peter Johnson and one of the company's buyers. After they had introduced themselves, they asked Frank if he had ever heard of their company.

"No, I've never heard of it," Frank answered honestly. "But please, have a seat. I'll get you a cup of good Dutch coffee."

Johnson told him that he had started Frontgate 10 years earlier as a mail-order company for well-to-do customers.

"Our catalog reaches the upper 5%, the richest Americans. We always publish a special garden catalog in the spring, full of luxury outdoor items."

He showed Frank the latest edition of the catalog. The cover featured a giant inflatable movie screen, with a large slide at the side, for sliding into the swimming pool. Flicking through it, Frank saw photos of backyards featuring huge trampolines, and inflatable play islands floating in swimming pools. There was even a complete popcorn cart on wheels with real spokes, as if it had just been driven off the fairgrounds, and a colossal pool table specially made for outdoor use. Everything was typically American.

Frank looked at the two men and realized that this was his chance. This was the moment he had been waiting for all these years.

"I have a fantastic patio furniture collection for you," he said as enthusiastically as he could. "It fits in perfectly with your concept, and is something I don't see in this beautiful book of yours."

In his last job at Wehkamp, he had learned how mail-order companies work, and which products were suitable for a catalog like this and which aren't. But that was in the Netherlands, and the question was whether or not it worked the same way in America. He quickly continued.

"You have to tell a story in a book like this. You have to take the reader by the hand, and using the right photos, explain how unique the product in question is. The goal is to create an almost greedy sort of feeling in the consumer, making him feel like he just has to have the product in his backyard then and there. And you can do this!"

"What did you have in mind?" the Frontgate buyer asked.

Frank knew he had them right where he wanted them.

"Our new Preston collection! Here, have a look. An adjustable chair with armrests you can set to any position you want. Not just five or even seven positions, but a thousand."

Frank knew that Americans loved exaggeration, but Kuipers and his team really had created a work of art with this chair. They had inserted a rod in the wooden armrests, which contained a mechanism they had developed to clamp onto this metal rod in any desired position. Ingenious.

Frank went and sat down in one of the chairs to demonstrate what he had just described to them. The buyer's mouth fell open. His boss was more restrained, and said in a cool tone:

"Nicely done."

Frank then went and stretched out on the matching chaise lounge.

"Your customers enjoy luxury, and want to be pampered," he said. "You have to tempt them by offering them something that they really want and can't buy anywhere else. When you can do that, you'll hit the jackpot." And so will we, Frank thought.

"Imagine you're lying there sunbathing at your own swimming pool," he said, "and you want to adjust the back of the chaise lounge, to read the paper for example. Normally, you have to get up out of the chair, adjust the bar at the back, and then lie back down again. In the meantime, your towel has blown away and your newspaper is at the other end of the yard. A really annoying and amateurish situation. We have the solution."

He reached under the chaise lounge and lightly pressed a bar. The back of the lounge slid noiselessly down.

"All you have to do is stop when it gets to the position that's comfortable for you. And you do the same thing to silently raise the back up again, until you're sitting up straight."

This time, Peter's mouth also fell open.

"Wow! That's great!"

They quickly got down to brass tacks, and the next spring, the Frontgate catalog containing the Preston collection landed on the doormats of seven million rich Americans. The chaise lounges even made the cover of the catalog. The effect was exactly what Frank had predicted with a healthy dose of bluffing: Americans fell in love with them. Consumers in the U.S. really love convenience, and this is exactly what he was able to offer them.

The news of Unimeta's success in America even made the papers in the Netherlands. The national newspaper *De Telegraaf* dedicated a full-page article to the news in their home and design supplement:

"DUTCH COMPANY CONQUERS AMERICAN BACKYARDS AND PATIOS."

Since that time, Frank has been flying to America a couple times a year to visit Frontgate and a few other customers. All the attention in the Frontgate catalog got the ball rolling there. Gary Ecoff, the owner of Carls Patio, a chain of patio furniture stores in Florida, had ordered a set back then and figured out where it came from. He invited Frank to come see them, and two weeks later he was sitting in their head office in the upscale beach city of Boca Raton, on the east coast of Florida, about 60 miles north of Miami.

The weather's always nice in Florida, a state full of retirees who have money to spend. With nine stores in Florida, Carls Patio is the market leader in the higher segment, making it precisely the type of customer Unimeta needed in order to take the next step in its quest to conquer the American market. They had made a careful start with an order of one container, filled with €50,000 in products. One year later, their sales had increased to several hundred thousand. After his visit to Frontgate, Frank would fly to Florida to meet with Gary and discuss their future partnership.

He parks his rented Cadillac at the Frontgate visitors parking lot, right in front of the entrance to the huge building. He is amazed at all the pomp and circumstance and concludes that Frontgate is obviously doing well. Once at the reception desk, Frank is greeted by a large screen flashing the words:

"*We welcome today.*"

After a few minutes, Ron Solstein, the buyer who had visited Unimeta's booth at the trade show in Cologne, comes walking towards him. He has since become purchasing manager, and spends most of his time on matters such as strategy and expansion plans. As busy as he is, he always makes time for Frank when he comes to visit.

"Hey Frank, how you doing?" Ron asks.

"Great, just a little groggy from the time difference, but otherwise everything is fine. I brought you some of those yummy treacle waffles from the Netherlands. All you have to do is provide the coffee."

A bit later, they are engaged in an animated conversation about sports, vacations, the weather, and Ron's new female co-workers. Frank takes great pains to avoid every reference to religion. This part of America tends to be populated by very conservative and strict religious groups. Ron has never discussed his own convictions, and Frank also prefers to avoid the topic. This way it can never result in a discussion. Before you know it, you've said something offensive, and sales are more sacred than any religion.

The two men get along well, and Ron once told Frank that he owes his promotion to purchasing manager in part to the success of the Preston collection. He had been the one who had insisted on taking a look at the Unimeta booth. The line had also been one of the greatest successes for the company in recent years.

After half an hour, the topic of patio furniture comes up. Frank pulls several drawings from his briefcase, ideas for new furniture products in the Preston collection, in which the teak slats in the frame are replaced by Textilene, a sling of synthetic fibers. Textilene is a fabric that has been popular in America since as long as anyone can remember, but it is still relatively unknown in Europe. This is actually strange, since it is a weatherproof fabric that allows light and water to pass right through it.

"Our development department has taken a good look at the American market," Frank says. "We have created a series of proposals for products, based on the most successful models using teak, but then produced using a Textilene sling. There are a few adjustable chairs, a really gorgeous chaise lounge, stackable chairs and an ottoman. Frontgate will have the exclusive rights for the mail-order market!"

"Beautiful," Ron says. "A great addition to a collection that is already selling well. We'll enlarge photos of the new chairs and use them for a two-page spread, and put the existing chairs in a frame below them."

They talk a bit longer about other ideas for the products in the new catalog. Ron furiously takes notes, jotting down all Frank's ideas. After an hour, he closes his notebook.

"Well, I'm done," he says. "This is going to be another great year. We will definitely be buying even more from you, at least 50%. We are also increasing the circulation of the catalogs to nine million. Peter has bought two smaller mail-order companies in the past year, and we're adding their mailing lists to ours. With your new furniture, we're really going to score big."

Frank does some quick calculations in his head, and if Ron's right, they will shoot way past the one million mark in sales to Frontgate. This is something he can definitely write home about. The factory has been having some difficulties for a while now, and this will be a welcome boost for morale. They still haven't recovered completely from the fireworks disaster. The company had lost several million in sales for the 2001 season. All the customers that had been forced to buy their products elsewhere never came back to Unimeta. In this industry, you're only as good as your last achievement. Fireworks disaster or not. Now, there's at least some light on the horizon.

After lunch with Ron, Frank drives back to the Cincinnati airport to catch his afternoon flight to Miami. Before he boards the plane, he makes a quick call to Ruud Kuipers to tell him the good news.

"Go ahead and step up the production!" Frank tells him.

The flight to Miami takes about three hours, and on the plane, Frank leafs through the American trade show magazine from the month before. For years now, Unimeta has had a booth at the Chicago Casual Show, the leading trade show for patio furniture and accessories in America, which is held every September. Most of the visitors are representatives from larger garden centers and patio furniture stores who come from all over the country.

The trade show magazine contains a picture of Frank and his export man, Bart, sitting on the new bar set from the Preston collection. Smartly dressed in their suits, they've got big smiles on their faces, and authentic wooden shoes peeking out from under their trousers. The heading over the photo reads: *Dutchies are back in town.*

Last month in Chicago, they were referred to as "the crazy Dutchmen" by their friendly colleagues, with a mix of admiration and jealousy. After all, simple or not, the advertisement had had a fantastic effect. The booth was always packed, and Bart and Frank were writing one full-container order after the other. Americans love European style and quality, and "Made in Holland" was a strong selling point.

It was also a nod to their personal approach, and one they had actually used from the time they started exporting to America. They were not a large, impersonal multinational like most of the American companies selling products, but a small and dedicated Dutch company, where the director personally gave product demonstrations at the booth. This really appealed to the American visitors at the show. They had written a lot of orders that year, and it looked like they had managed to score a million in total sales to the American retail outlets as well; assuming Carls Patio also placed a few orders.

Actually, things had gone really well from the very start on the other side of the Atlantic. After meeting the people at Frontgate, and the interest from Carls Patio, Frank had approached the owner of Unimeta with a proposal.

"I'll create a complete sales and marketing plan for the American market," he had suggested. "To realize this plan, I'll need a budget of a couple hundred thousand so I can develop new furniture products and set up a sales organization."

It was exactly the type of thing they had hired Frank to do at the time.

It wasn't a problem to free up funds for this in spite of the company's tight financial situation. They did it step-by-step, the first of which was participation in the trade show. Frank was determined to make it a success. He knew more than anyone that Unimeta was fizzling out with its metal chairs for the German and English markets. Preston was the key to leading the company into the new century with new momentum.

To prepare for their participation in this trade show, Frank had planned a trip to the U.S. in the spring of 1999. He had contacted the 30 largest potential patio furniture customers by telephone. During those conversations, he had explained who he was, what he could offer, and asked if he might visit them. Not a single one of them had a problem with that. Even a few of the larger retailers, such as Fortunoff, told him he was more than welcome, and that was more or less the fanciest department store in America.

Frank then cut the list down to about 20 companies, spread all over the country. He wanted to take the new Preston chair with him to demonstrate it during these visits. The chair that could be adjusted in a thousand different positions would sell itself. It was a challenge though to take it with him everywhere and get it there in one piece. In the airplane, off the airplane, and in and out of taxis and buses. It was a major ordeal each time. He had gotten the idea to have a flight case made just for this purpose when he saw these cases being used for instruments at concerts. Besides, a black case like this with aluminum strips on the edges and corners looked sharp.

Once the case was finished, Frank was startled at the size, almost six and a half feet long and three feet high. In spite of this, it worked incredibly well. Frank took it with him on his flight to New York, where Fortunoff was the first company he visited. They had seen the products in the Frontgate catalog and wondered where they came from.

An order in his pocket, Frank flew on, from Minneapolis to Philadelphia and from Houston to Detroit. And no matter where he went, it was always the same ritual. Frank would come in with this giant flight case on little wheels. Perched on top of this was his huge suitcase with the personal items he would need for a two-week trip. And at the very top of these two cases was his small briefcase. When Frank then told them that he was the man who had called them a few weeks back, and that he had come from the Netherlands just to see them, they would always make time for him. They offered him coffee (their version of it), and were all ears.

After his second visit, Frank noticed that most of the customers would always be looking over his shoulder, curious about what was in the huge flight case. As he told the story of the company and the special reason for his visit, the customer's attention was always already on the second step. The longer he put off opening the case, the more restless they would become. It was almost like a game for Frank. If it started taking too long, they would ask Frank if he had brought his mother-in-law along. Americans definitely had a sense of humor.

Those two weeks were made up of very long days, getting up before the crack of dawn to be on time for his first appointment, and arriving at the next hotel very late in the evening. And carrying all that luggage, that no taxi driver wanted any part of. In spite of all this, the plan worked incredibly well.

After that sales trip, Frank and Bart headed to Chicago in September

1999, for their first time as exhibitors at the show there. They set up their stand at the gigantic Merchandise Mart, the second largest building in the world. Frank had rented a booth of over 500 square feet on the seventh floor of this concrete giant. They filled the stand with Preston furniture in a variety of colors.

It was an instant success. On the first day, there was barely any room for all the customers coming to see the booth, and they were spilling out into the aisle. Frank and Bart talked until they were hoarse, and took many orders. The demos they gave made a particularly good impression, and throngs of people remained in their booth to watch.

They had never seen anything like these infinitely adjustable chairs and chaise lounges with a pneumatic lift. Everyone coming to the booth was amazed.

Of the 20 companies Frank had visited earlier that year with his "mother-in-law" in tow, 14 placed their first full-container order with Unimeta. In addition to these, they also picked up seven truly new customers. After four days at the show, they flew back to the Netherlands, tired yet satisfied, with orders in their briefcases worth half a million Euros in sales. The production department could get started immediately.

The American Airlines flight attendant asks Frank if he would like anything to drink. He lays his trade show magazine on the empty chair next to him and orders a Coke. Not long afterwards, the plane starts its descent towards Miami International Airport, and before he knows it, he's waiting in line at Hertz to pick up his rental car. This time he rents a Ford Mustang convertible. The weather's perfect for driving around Florida in a convertible. Fall has already arrived in the Netherlands, but here it's a balmy 82°F.

Frank is happy to leave the hotel the following morning. He didn't sleep well, and although jet lag was partly to blame, the grubby hotel room wasn't exactly conducive to a good night's sleep. And as icing on the cake, the air conditioning unit was incredibly noisy. Turning it off was not an option in those temperatures and humidity.

Still groggy but in good spirits, Frank drives to the Carls Patio headquarters in Boca Raton. Driving into the parking lot, he can already see Gary's Porsche Boxter S. A cool car, but much too small for someone like him with his long legs.

Gary gives him the warmest of welcomes, and they slap each other on the shoulder and exchange a few polite words. This is followed by Gary's usual sarcastic remarks.

"You're not getting any younger, are you?" he says with a twinkle in his eye.

"No, and you're not getting any taller either," Frank says to Gary, who can't be more than five foot five. They then move on to more serious business.

"It's about time you Europeans started thinking about lounging," Gary says. "Just look at these gorgeous lounge sets we have in the store." Frank's gaze slides past a few lounge suites, aluminum frames with wicker latticework. Further away, he sees teak couches with fat, inviting pillows. He had seen the same models the last time he was here, and had walked past them, shaking his head. Those crazy Americans; it was if they had just dragged their couches outside. And when you went to sit down on one of them, you were so low to the ground that it took some effort to stand up again.

"No Gary, that's still in the future for us," he answers. "If we ever get to that point at all. I still have to see it to believe it. Let's see if we can sell these adjustable chairs with the Textilene slings first. We still can't get them interested in those in Europe."

The year before, Gary had told Frank that they should develop a new line for the Preston collection, one with Textilene instead of teak slats. Frank pulls the new drawings from his briefcase with a flourish.

"We listened carefully to what you said, and have created a beautiful design with a Textilene sling, just like you want here in America. The wooden slats have been replaced, and the only part still made from teak are the armrests."

Gary smiles from ear to ear. He gives Frank a spontaneous hug and three firm smacks on the shoulder.

"This is it!" Gary cries out. "This is exactly what I mean. We can score big with these."

"Good," Frank says coolly. "How many containers do you want?"

Gary gives a low growl.

"Damn Dutchmen. All you think about is sales. What percentage do I get in royalties for giving you the idea?"

Frank suddenly realizes that he has to tread very carefully now. Gary's got commercial blood flowing through his veins.

"Ah, everyone in America has sling chairs," he says, "so it's not such an original idea. And if you hadn't insisted on it, we would have done it ourselves anyways."

Just a harmless little white lie. No way is Frank going to pay Gary for the range he just sold to Frontgate the day before.

"If you order six containers this year, I'll give you a 4% discount," Frank says with a deep sigh. He had built an extra five percent margin into the price list just in case of stunts like this, and knows exactly how much wiggle room he has. After a bit more haggling back and forth, Gary agrees and the men shake hands.

"And you will do that promotion one more time," sneaky Gary says as he still has a firm grip on Frank's hand. Frank doesn't have a problem with this.

"Deal!" he says.

The past two years, they have held an annual Preston sales promotion, and not because they just loved doing it. No, it had become a dire necessity. The 50 or so salesmen working at Carls Patio don't get a fixed salary; they work on commission-only basis. If they don't sell anything, they don't earn anything. It's that simple. They don't receive the payment for their commission until the customer has paid for their patio furniture, and this usually takes about a week. The order is entered in the computer, and the customer pays a deposit. A message is then sent to the warehouse and the planning department. The planning department then decides on the most economical way to deliver the furniture to the customer. The customer then pays the balance due at delivery, and only then does the salesperson receive their commission. That's just the way the American system works.

The faster the products get to the customer, the sooner the salesperson will have his or her commission.

Frank figured that out during the first year, and sales were really disappointing that season. He didn't understand any of it because Frontgate had been so successful. But that was a mail-order company and this was pure retail. He visited several of Carls Patio stores and talked to the salespeople.

Little by little, he gained a better understanding of the reason behind the disappointing sales. After he had toured the warehouse, it all became crystal clear. The salespeople didn't know that all the products from the Preston collection were in stock in Florida, in their own warehouse of all places, and were therefore immediately available. All they had heard was that the furniture came from the Netherlands, and assumed that the products first had to be manufactured or would at least have to be shipped to the U.S. in a container. That would take months, and all that time, they would have to wait for their commission. So they figured it would be better to sell patio furniture that was made in the U.S.A. Besides, that would also be good for their country's economy.

With this information in the back of his mind, Frank had come up with a strategy for taking the sting out of this situation. He presented his plan to Gary.

"We will send all the salespeople a letter, introducing our company with a clear explanation that although our factory is in the Netherlands, there are two containers full of Preston furniture being stored in the Carls Patio warehouse, available for immediate delivery. And to stimulate sales, we will offer the two best salespeople a trip to the Netherlands. We will monitor sales for three months or so, and the two people who have sold the most Preston furniture during that period will get an all-expenses-paid trip. This will put the spotlight on the collection and where it will stay for a longer period of time."

Gary loved the idea straight away; after all, it wasn't going to cost him anything. For Unimeta, the costs were manageable. The effect was nothing short of spectacular. The two winning salespeople had sold a few dozen sets and the total sales shot up, nearing two hundred thousand. And, just as importantly, all the salespeople knew that the Preston furniture was available from stock.

Americans love competition, and this promotion hit the bulls-eye. It was such a huge success that it paid for Unimeta's investment twice over, which was why Frank had no problem running the promotion a second time. And it had actually been a lot of fun to boot. Last summer, Gary came to the Netherlands together with his sales manager, Paul, and the two winning salesmen. Frank had put together a four-day program, including of course a tour of the Unimeta factory. A tour of the Grolsch brewery was naturally also on the agenda, as were a few garden centers and patio furniture stores. After this, the group went to Amsterdam for the highlight of the trip: a night out on the town in the Red Light District, including a professional Red Light Tour given by none other than Rob van Hulst, a Dutch soap opera star. Oh, the fun and laughs they had with the Americans seeing the Red Light District for the first time!

The sales doubled during the second year, thanks mostly to the efforts of the two salesmen who had won the first time. They really stirred up interest with their enthusiastic and wild stories about Amsterdam. Everyone at Carls Patio was dying to go to Amsterdam. Frank never heard another word about products not being in stock.

Frank flies back to the Netherlands, satisfied. All in all they could expect sales of one or two million in America for the upcoming season. Thanks to the very favorable margins, these sales should be enough to compensate the revenue they missed out on after the fireworks disaster. He is fully aware of how important this is for Unimeta.

4

EMERGENCY LANDING IN NEWFOUNDLAND

Frank flops down into an armchair with a deep sigh. He has a two-hour wait in the business lounge at Schiphol Airport. Later that morning, he will be flying from Amsterdam to Chicago on United Airlines. Marion has taken care of everything; it's a lot cheaper than the KLM flight on the same day. Frank doesn't care at all either way. He is just happy to finally be sitting down and that he can leave the past few hectic months behind him for a little while.

For months, he has been working hard to move forward an IT project that had run aground, which meant that he barely had time for anything else. He inherited the IT problem from his predecessor, who had invested a lot of time and money in a system that could never become operational. The meter is now at 500,000 Euros, and the end is far from being in sight, but even worse is that Frank has no idea whatsoever about the status of the project.

This goes against every aspect of his personality; he always has to know the ins and outs of everything, and now he has to blindly approve an additional investment of 150,000, even though no one seems to be able to explain exactly what it's for. Not only is it gnawing at him, it is taking him away from the work he was hired to do. Even though it goes against his nature, he ultimately decides to turn the whole matter over to someone else, and hires an outside expert, who comes with the crushing reply:

"It's never going to work; it's a bottomless pit."

The expert's report is reason enough for Frank to cancel all payments to the IT company and hire a lawyer. This does not mean the end of the drama however, since the lawsuit in which this all culminated only drains him of more energy, and even ends in an extremely unsatisfactory manner for Frank. They are given permission to tear up the outstanding bills, but they can say goodbye to the 500,000 that had already been paid, forever. A bitter pill and not the last one Frank will have to swallow when it comes to legal circuses. For now, he is focusing his energy on a new IT project that does work, and on the trade show in Chicago where Bart and Toon have already arrived, and are setting up the booth.

Right on time, at 11:30 in the morning, United flight UA967 takes off. A friendly woman in her 60s is sitting next to Frank on the plane, on her way to visit her daughter in Chicago, and talking a mile a minute. Frank is only half listening to her story, and falls asleep immediately after take-off. Hours later, he awakens with a start as the pilot's voice rings out from the loudspeakers with an unpleasant announcement.

"Ladies and gentlemen, the Chicago airport is closed. We are going to have to land at another airport."

Frank checks his watch. They have been in the air for about four hours, and are about halfway through the flight. Suddenly, he is worried. Not about the fact that they have to land at another airport, but about the consequences, since he has no idea where they will land and whether or not he will make it to Chicago on time. He asks the flight attendant, but she doesn't know any more than what the pilot just announced.

Once again, his fate is in the hands of others, and there's nothing he can do about it. He grits his teeth and curses to himself. The buzzing which had started in the cabin has quieted down again. The passengers read or watch a movie, but an hour later, the peace and quiet is brought to an end. The crackling of the intercom system signals a new report from the pilot, and this time, the news is even more disconcerting.

"Ladies and gentlemen, you might see kerosene running down the windows in the next five minutes. This is completely normal in this situation. We have to dump fuel in preparation for our emergency landing at the airport in St. John's, Newfoundland. Please follow the instructions from the cabin personnel closely. And please don't panic; we are going to get you on the ground safely."

Newfoundland, Frank thinks, that's Canada for crying out loud! He quickly looks at the map in the United Airlines magazine. St. John's is located at the very end of Newfoundland, at the easternmost tip of the North American continent, closer to Greenland than the United States. Chicago seems farther away than ever. His gaze is drawn to the woman sitting next to him. She is as white as a sheet and her breathing is ragged. A few tears run down her left cheek. Frank looks at others around him, and notices that people are remaining amazingly calm. Parents reassure their children, and the flight attendants clear away everything that is not secured in the cabin.

He doesn't get a lot of time to think. All of the passengers are instructed to bend forward, and place their heads between their arms. Everyone does what the cabin personnel tell them to; no one protests or makes trouble, as if the seriousness of the situation has paralyzed them. A few minutes later, they are safely on the ground, where according to the evacuation procedure, they will have to leave the aircraft as soon as possible, leaving their carry-on luggage behind. The only door that opens is at the front of the plane. Frank finds his sunglasses and wallet, and at the last minute, also grabs his camera.

As he stands in the doorway at the top of the stairs, he is first blinded by the bright sunlight. Once his eyes become accustomed to the light, he sees passenger planes as far as the eye can see, parked in disarray beside one another, planes from every conceivable airline, at an airport that doesn't seem much larger than his own local airport in Twente. The only aircraft that normally land there are a few vacation charter planes, which is probably more or less the case here too.

He descends the staircase to the runway, and walks with his fellow passengers to a grassy area where they are told to assemble. All around him, all he can see are parked jumbo jets, but what he also notices is that there are no people. The airport seems deserted, and the planes are just far enough away that he can't tell if there are still passengers on board. It seems like the only passengers who had to deplane were the ones on his United flight, but Frank has no idea why they would be the exception.

So here he stands, in only his jeans and thin shirt, no carry-on baggage, in the middle of nowhere. He can't call anyone since the only cell phone he has that can be used on the American network is the one he gave to Bart, and he has been in Chicago for a few days with Toon.

Other passengers do have working telephones, but hardly anyone has reception. The lines are overloaded so there is no way to get through, but behind him, a man about his age manages to place a call. Frank picks up parts of the conversation, and as he walks around, he can also hear snippets of the conversations of other people who have also managed to get through. The wildest rumors start circulating in no time. "The American president has been assassinated," Frank hears next to him. "The Empire State Building and World Trade Center have been bombed," another passenger says. The Dutch man behind Frank has hung up and is frantically pushing all sorts of buttons on his phone. Frank introduces himself and asks him if he has found out anything.

"Jacques," the man answers. "It's like World War III has broken out. I just talked to my colleagues at the office in Holland, and they're not sure either. They don't have a television at the office, but they told me that two planes have flown into the World Trade Center. I mean that's just crazy, isn't it? They've watched too many Star Wars movies. Right when they were about to tell me more, the line suddenly went dead, and now I can't reach them anymore."

"That may all be true," Frank says, "but the fact that we're standing here in Newfoundland next to a pasture full of cows, with dozens of planes parked all around us, isn't science fiction at all."

Frank borrows his telephone and after a couple of tries, miraculously manages to reach his wife. She hasn't heard anything yet; she has been working in the garden all day, in between taking care of their children. All she cares about is that Frank has landed safely in Canada.

Frank ends the call and asks the people around him what they have heard. Everyone is telling a different story and no one seems to know for sure what's going on. Suddenly, someone calls out that the Pentagon has been blown to smithereens. An older gentleman says that a plane full of passengers was shot down. It is starting to sound like all-out war, but no one is sure and now the phone lines appear to be completely dead.

Seven airport buses pull up next to the pasture, and three people wearing orange vests get out of each bus, helping the passengers on board, 50 per bus. Frank asks one of them what is going on, but doesn't get an answer. The look the woman gives him is so cold that he decides not to ask again.

"I guess they're not allowed to tell us," Jacques grins.

After half an hour, when everyone's finally seated on the buses, a Canadian Red Cross van drives up, followed by a large truck with a trailer bed. Four mobile toilet units have been loaded onto the trailer, which are then moved to the runway by a crane. The Red Cross employees get on the bus, and pass out bottles of water. The passengers ask them for information, but the only thing they say is that it is a huge disaster, and that's all they can tell them. A few hours later, employees from the Canadian Salvation Army bring sandwiches, snacks and fruit. Frank's only opportunity to get any fresh air is when he walks to the latrines, chaperoned and closely supervised by the Orange Vests.

After five hours on the ground, three of which are spent on the bus, a large, blue armored car parks next to them, with RNC Tactical Unit in white letters on the side. Two men get out of the car, one of whom has a professional television camera hoisted on his shoulder. The other is carrying a long pole with a microphone on the end. They are followed by policemen with semi-automatic weapons slung over their shoulders, walking German shepherds on leashes.

The doors of the bus open, and an officer addresses them.

"Hello everyone, we are really sorry you've been stranded and we are doing everything we can to get you all out of here as soon as possible. We need your cooperation to do this. Our colleagues in America have asked us to find out who you all are and what you do for a living. They also want to know what your final destination is, and the reason for your trip. Our camera team will record your answers, and after that, we have to wait for a green light from the U.S."

First the policemen walk through the bus with the dogs, which doesn't really tell Frank much, since these dogs can be trained for anything, sniffing out drugs, for example, but also weapons, ammunition and money. As far as Frank can tell, they haven't found anything in any of the seven buses.

Next, it's the camera crew's turn. Frank does what they ask, without complaining.

"My name is Frank Krake. I am the CEO of the patio furniture company, Unimeta. I am from Oldenzaal, which is in the Netherlands. I am now in Canada, but I should have been in Chicago a long time ago."

He would have loved nothing more than to tell them how important this is for him, but bites his tongue. He is at their mercy, and if everyone cooperates, they'll be out of here as soon as possible.

"This is ridiculous," he says, once everyone has been interviewed. "Who do they think we are anyway? Terrorists or something?"

Dusk has already fallen when a driver boards the bus and sits down behind the wheel. For a brief moment, Frank hopes that they will be allowed to reboard the plane and continue their journey to their final destination, but he quickly realizes that they don't need to take a bus to do that. After all, the plane isn't even 100 yards away; everyone can easily walk that distance. Yet another man in an orange vest addresses the passengers on the bus:

"Ladies and gentlemen. Thank you for all your patience during the long wait. Your bus will take you to the airport arrivals terminal, where you will go through customs and receive further instructions from there."

Going through customs means entering Canada but Frank has no desire to go to Canada. He has to go to Chicago to sell chairs. Unfortunately, he doesn't have a choice, and after waiting two hours on the grass and seven hours in the buses, they finally enter the small airport's arrivals hall. The entire process easily takes more than an hour, after which an incredibly tired Frank is led with the others to the exit. An officer tells them to walk outside, where all they have to do is follow the route between the cordons, to the buses that are waiting for them.

"More buses," Jacques sighs.

In spite of his exhaustion, Frank has to laugh. They walk outside together, into the dark Canadian night, where throngs of people are gathered. Suddenly huge searchlights switch on, illuminating an entire group of press photographers, camera people and journalists. They pester Frank and his fellow passengers with questions, wanting to know if they were scared, and how they spent all those hours at the airport.

None of the members of the press realize at that point that the passengers from the UA967 flight still have no idea what exactly is going on. They haven't gotten much information beyond the brief announcement "terrorist attacks". It does, however, quickly become clear to them that the other 26 airplanes at the airport are still filled with passengers. They are the first to get led through customs, and the remaining passengers waiting on the runway have yet to do this.

"What a nightmare," Frank says to Jacques. "If it only takes half an hour per plane, then that would be fast. This still means that the last passengers will have had to wait 12 hours, sitting on the plane that whole time. When you think about it, we have nothing to complain about."

In 20 minutes, the bus takes the group to a large building, Mile One Stadium. This time, they are welcomed by a woman wearing a yellow vest, who tells them they can register with her, so "their families will know where they are."

It's really chilly inside; the stadium appears to be the home of the local ice hockey team. The registration goes quickly and in an orderly manner. There is more than enough food; everything is free and you can take as much as you want.

More passengers slowly trickle into the stadium, including those from the other flights. After they wait around for an hour, an announcement is made asking the passengers from UA967 to go to the exit. When they get there, they see more buses waiting for them. Upon seeing this, Frank and Jacques burst out laughing. Another bus! They still can't stop laughing, even once on board. The tension from everything that has happened, combined with a feeling of relief that they are safe here in Canada, has resulted in the inability to stop laughing, much to the chagrin of the other passengers who really can't see the humor in any of this.

The next stop is at an even bigger building, the Memorial University of Newfoundland. The driver tells them they have arrived at the place they'll be staying for the night. They are met by the dean of the university. Once everyone has arrived in the auditorium, he gives his guests a warm welcome. He says he sympathizes with them for all the stress and uncertainty that they have had to put up with, and thanks them for their patience during the many long hours they have had to wait.

"An informational meeting has been organized for tomorrow morning at 9:00. You will be spending the night in the gym, and will be given packages with soap, a toothbrush and toothpaste."

In a hall as big as a football field, Frank sees hundreds and hundreds of army cots all lined up. Frank can't believe his eyes. Did the Canadians arrange all this that fast? Unbelievable. In the locker rooms, the passengers can splash some water on their faces and brush their teeth.

It is one o'clock in the morning, on September 12, 2001, Canadian time. In the Netherlands, it's 4:30 a.m. Frank tucks the only possessions he was able to take with him off the plane, his wallet, sunglasses and camera, under his pillow and stretches out on one of the cots. He is fast asleep in no time.

At around 8:00 the next morning, he is awakened by the hum of voices in the gym. On his way to the auditorium for breakfast, he runs into Jacques. He is watching one of the many television screens that had been set up the night before in the corridor of the building. Jacques looks tense and edgy. "You have to see this Frank," he says. "This is unbelievable: terrorists flew

49

two planes into the World Trade Center and both towers have come down. Unbelievable! Thousands of people dead."

His mouth open, Frank watches the screens and shivers run up and down his spine. Years before, during his first trip to the U.S., he had stood at the top of those very towers, a few days before his arrest.

"And here," Jacques continues, "a plane that flew into the Pentagon."

As he watches the coverage, Frank realizes how lucky they are that they are safely on the ground. Not at their destination perhaps, but still, in good hands. The airplanes full of passengers that the terrorists used as weapons were also United planes, the same airline he was flying on. Frank has mixed feelings about it all. He's confused for a moment, and so many questions run through his mind.

"Have you eaten yet?" he asks, back in practical mode. "Why don't we start with that?"

The Canadian volunteers have prepared breakfast packages for all the stranded passengers. How they managed to do all this so quickly is a mystery to Frank, but the little bags contain sandwiches, a box of yoghurt drink, and even a croissant. He savors his breakfast and a little while later, the dean of the university is standing on the stage, a microphone in his hand. It suddenly gets so quiet in the auditorium you could hear a pin drop. He summarizes what happened the previous day and during the night.

"After the terrible disaster that took place in America yesterday, we did our best to be a good neighbor. Once the Americans closed their national airspace, the Canadian government decided to allow all incoming trans-Atlantic flights to land here. There are 136 jumbo jets parked at the five small airports in Newfoundland alone. This means a total of 17,000 stranded passengers. Now accommodating 27 planes, the airport here in St. John's is completely full. We had to house a total of 4600 passengers and crew members. Naturally, we don't have this many hotel rooms, so all the public spaces that are suitable to be used as shelters are being used, including this university. Classes have been called off, and all the students have joined the ranks of volunteers. You will recognize them by their orange vests. They will do everything they can to make your stay here as comfortable as possible.

"Since all the available public facilities are now full, over 400 families in St. John's have opened their homes to house stranded passengers. Our volunteers are providing as much food and beverage as you need. We have telephones set up in the room next door which you can use free of charge to get in touch with your loved ones back home. We will provide you with updates on the situation every day at 9:00 in the morning and at 5:00 in the afternoon. We have no idea how long you will be delayed here in St. John's, but we hope that in spite of these difficult circumstances, that you will enjoy your stay here in our beautiful city."

As a roar of applause rises up from the audience, Frank has to swallow a couple times; this is how moved he is by the hospitality of the Canadian people.

That morning, he walks into town to pick up a few things, buying a sweater, shirt and the necessary underthings at a hypermarket. He also buys a toiletry bag and the contents to go with it.

Back in the auditorium, he decides to make another attempt to reach Bart and Toon.

This goes surprisingly well, and Bart answers immediately, pleasantly surprised when he recognizes Frank's voice. He had already heard from the office that Frank was stranded in Canada, only he had no idea where, or how he was doing. Frank updates him in a couple sentences, but is much more curious how things are going in Chicago.

"It's a ghost town," Bart replies. "You can't believe your eyes. No one is on the streets, and the trade show here is completely deserted. I followed everything on television yesterday, and everyone is completely freaked out."

"That's what I was afraid of," Frank says.

"None of the people here want to talk about patio furniture, all they want to talk about is the attacks. 'Nine-eleven' they're calling it here, that's all you hear."

Frank can't hide his disappointment.

"That really sucks, Bart. Right when we're about to score big in the U.S."

"How do you think we feel here? We have killed ourselves for two days setting up the booth, making sure it's perfect, and then no one shows up. Not a single person!"

After getting off the phone with Bart, Frank calls the office, where they listen to his story in disbelief, and finally, he calls his wife, who is mostly just relieved that he is doing okay under the circumstances. She has been able to follow everything going on in America, but remains down-to-earth about it, as usual.

"You were supposed to stay there for a week, right? So nothing's really changed; they'll be flying again in a week, and you'll be home again in time, just like you originally planned."

Frank has no response to logic like this.

"So just try and enjoy yourself there on that peninsula!" she says before hanging up. Frank quickly makes room for the next person; behind him is a long line of people waiting to use the phone.

That afternoon they hang around the university campus, waiting for news or information on what will happen now, to no avail. The only certainty they have is that it doesn't look like they're going to be leaving any time soon. The Canadian and American airspaces will be closed for at least another 24 hours. Jacques and Frank decide to make the best of it. Together with other Dutch passengers who are also tired of sitting around and waiting, they take a walk through St. John's the next morning, a beautiful town that reminds Frank most of the Norwegian villages that he once saw on a television program.

Everywhere they go they are welcomed with a friendly smile or words of encouragement, or are even asked if they need help with anything. People are genuinely interested in their personal experiences, and everyone does what they can to make sure the thousands of stranded passengers enjoy their stay. By noon, they have more or less seen the entire town, and it's time for lunch at one of the many seafood restaurants. They are in no hurry at all, and decide to enjoy themselves. The owner of the restaurant, James, asks if they have any plans.

"Maybe take a look around the area," Jacques answers.
James offers his services as a tour guide, and as they walk around St. John's that afternoon, he tells them in great detail about the town. After walking for an hour, they arrive at some kind of look-out point. Frank really takes in his surroundings, inhaling the fresh sea air. He has the distinct feeling he's in Greenland; a beautiful bay off in the distance framed by enormous rocky cliffs pounded by the waves from the Atlantic. Colorful wooden houses dot the coastline, and he wonders how they ever managed to build them. They enjoy the gorgeous views of the bay on which the city was built. James tells them that there is a unique spot a bit farther away. It was here, from Signal Hill, that Marconi sent and received the first wireless signals between Europe and the North American continent.

"Hey, James," Jacques asks once they are walking again, "do you have any idea why we were the only passengers who were allowed off our plane, and all the other passengers had to stay on theirs?"

James looks at Jacques in amazement.

"You guys really don't know?"

"No," they answer in unison.

"I do. The sheriff told me yesterday. I thought that someone would have explained it to you by now. The American aviation authorities had received a bomb threat for your plane. You were flying United Airlines, and two of the planes used in the attacks were also United planes, and that's why they took the threat so seriously. For all they knew, there could have been terrorists on board the plane, so they didn't want to take any risks. That's why people thought that the plane you were on might have been used for another terrorist attack. Since your final destination was Chicago, they were thinking it could have been targeted to use in an attack on the Sears Tower. You probably know what that is."

Jacques and Frank nodded; of course they knew what the tallest building in the U.S. was.

"Since they didn't trust it, they had your plane parked in a different location at the airport," James explained, "as far away as possible from the other stranded planes, just in case."

Frank starts laughing.

"And then they have us sitting on the grass, 20 yards away from a plane that might have had a bomb on board. Great!"

"Okay," James says, "but you can imagine things were pretty chaotic at the time. Normally we get one Boeing per day here, at the most. Then we suddenly had 27 of them. They weren't so sure what to do with all of you. First they wanted to be certain that there were no terrorists on board. They checked that out thoroughly before allowing you all to go anywhere. That's why our police and the FBI watched the videos of you. As you can imagine, that took them a while."

Before they say goodbye, they have to solemnly swear that they will all go to Trapper John's, the most popular bar on the island, which James says is always a great time. They will have to wait until the next evening though, since everyone is so tired after the long day and is dying to get into their makeshift beds.

In the auditorium they hear that progress is being made. The Canadian airspace is open again, and the first flights are scheduled to fly out the next day. Unfortunately, the only flights that will depart are those of the non-American airlines; these will fly back to Europe, to the airports they originated from. The American airspace is still closed, and it remains unclear when it will reopen; it might be another few days. No one knows for sure. All the planes from the American airlines must stay on the ground as a result, since they will be continuing on to their original final destinations.

The next day, Frank says goodbye to a few people who are going back, people whom he had gotten to know in this short yet intense time. He buys a memo pad and kills the time writing a story for the personnel magazine. At five o'clock, the dean comes with good news: they will probably be able to go to Chicago the next day. This announcement is met with great relief, but this feeling is short-lived for Frank; his worries return, about how they should now proceed in the American market. Jacques sees the look of concern on his face, pats him on the shoulder and says with a grin.

"Chin up, Frank. You'll have plenty of time to worry tomorrow. If we want to keep our promise, we have to go to Trapper John's tonight. A promise is a promise. Let's go into town first, grab a bite to eat, and then go party."

As they arrive at the bar, they see that it's in the middle of a main street, surrounded by other night spots. Sort of like the main square back home in Enschede, but in Canada. Many of the 80,000 residents there are students. Friday night is a big night out, and it doesn't take long for Frank to forget his cares and get swept up in the high-spirited atmosphere. The relief that he has survived this adventure is slowly but surely gaining the upper hand, and his cares have nearly completely disappeared as he walks into the bar and gets immersed in the commotion and the loud music from a live band that is playing.

As Frank is enjoying his third beer, the bartender gets up on a chair. It is time for the "Screech-In", the traditional ceremony in which the locals welcome out-of-towners. A sort of initiation, Newfoundland-style, mandatory for anyone who has never been to the island before. After his explanation, the bartender puts on an enormous fur hat with a tail, a sword in his hand. This is when the spectacle really starts.

When it's Frank's turn, he goes to stand at the bar with the rest of the group, where small glasses of alcohol are lined up. The bartender performs a ritual in which he first says something and Frank and the group have to read out a text that is written in big letters on a sign. Next, the bartender lightly taps everyone on the head with his sword, and lets out an unintelligible primal shriek. Now they have to toss down the contents of the glasses in one swig. Then they all have to kiss a stuffed bird, a puffin, the symbol of Newfoundland. Finally, loud cheering rings out through the bar. According to tradition, they are now "honorary Newfoundlanders."

Well, okay, Frank thought, when in Rome…

On Saturday afternoon, four days and five nights after Frank landed in Newfoundland, there is a short line of people waiting at each customs window. Frank gets his passport stamped and then finds his own suitcase from a giant pile of baggage which is being set aside by a Canadian customs official. A bit farther away, he is asked to point out his carry-on bag, and then walks to a waiting area. He is still a bit foggy from all the alcohol he consumed the night before, but he sure did have fun.

He had reported to the airport earlier that morning, and they have been working on the departure procedure for hours now. In the late afternoon, they are finally allowed to go to the plane. With a wistful feeling, Frank casts one more glance back at St. John's before he steps on board. He has deep respect for everything the Canadians did for him and the other stranded passengers. No favor was too great. They went way out of their way, putting their own interests second, for people they didn't even know.

It is after midnight when Frank checks into the House of Blues Hotel in Chicago. Bart and Toon are already asleep when he arrives, but they meet up at 8:00 the next morning at breakfast. A firm handshake, a pat on the shoulder, and then come the stories. Toon can hardly believe what has been happening all around him in such a short period of time. Bart says that they did end up having some visitors to the booth during the four days, but that no one bought anything.

Frank has arrived just in time as today is the last day of the show; he can witness the catastrophe with his own eyes. It is even worse than he thought; exactly zero visitors come to the booth. On the way there, he already suspected that they wouldn't be doing much business. Chicago is like a ghost town now; the streets are empty. There is no sign of the lively metropolis Frank had gotten to know over the last few years.

He realizes that this is fatal for sales in America, but doesn't tell his colleagues this. They're having a hard enough time as it is. At the end of the afternoon, they tear down the booth in silence.

That night, Frank flies back to Europe. He had actually wanted to go to Birmingham the day before, where Unimeta has a booth at a patio furniture trade show, but this is the first possible flight to England.

It's still chaos at all the airports, and Frank is thankful that he was able to leave America as quickly as he did.

The English market is Unimeta's largest sales market, and in a historical sense, practically their domestic market. He is curious how they have done at the trade show there. After an uneventful flight of just over six hours, Frank lands in England the next morning, lightheaded from jet lag, but he doesn't have time to pay it much mind. He takes a taxi straight from the airport to the exhibition complex in Birmingham. His colleague John, Unimeta's sales rep in England, has already been at the trade show for two days.

John is happy to see him, but immediately says that things are not the same. It seems like the whole world is on fire. The faith is gone, and not a single Unimeta customer is buying what they normally do. Everyone is being careful, not knowing what lies ahead.

Just what we need, Frank thinks. First they lose sales in Germany over the past year because of the fireworks disaster, a setback from which they still haven't fully recovered. Then the attacks from just a couple of days ago cause all the sales in America to dry up. And now they have very wary customers in England, their biggest market. "This will cost us another couple of million." runs through his mind. With a deep sigh, he takes another sip of his coffee. In the meantime John staggers to the little kitchen in their booth; it almost seems like he's drunk.

5

COPYCATS AND BOOZE

Frank's suspicions are confirmed in the months that follow. It seems like no one wants to spend any money, and they definitely don't want to spend it on patio furniture. All of the larger customers have backed out. The company has no choice at this point but to make major cutbacks. Together with his board, he tries to come up with one plan after the other, anything to save money, as long as it doesn't mean having to fire anyone. It does mean bad news for the temporary employees that they normally hire to work in the spring. Now that business is going so badly, they can manage with 50 fewer employees.

One ray of hope is the success they've been having with the Sombrero collection, which covers the middle segment. Garden centers and specialty stores in the Netherlands and Germany are buying massive quantities of these products, but the question remains whether or not this is enough to turn things around. It is clear that 2002 will be a transition year, and that they should actually start setting their sights on 2003. Ruud's development team is working hard on these plans, and the first prototypes are already finished.

In the meantime, Frank is struggling with the problems with John. He would love nothing more than to give him one final warning, but Marion thinks it would be better to just drop the matter for now and allow time to heal this particular wound. Frank is happy to take her advice; after all, the cause of all the problems is tragic enough. John deserves the chance to sort it out himself.

A year and a half ago, John, his wife and their three daughters went to a horse show. The girls were all huge horse lovers, and John would always tag along. He sometimes complained to Frank that he was always the one who had to do the dirty work, like cleaning out the stable. This would really make Frank laugh.

"You should get the ladies to do that then."

"You wouldn't say that if you knew my ladies."

For seven years, Frank and John have been a good team when it comes to the market in England. John was a real people-person, a warm-hearted salesman with a personal approach who will do anything for his customers. Frank, on the other hand, was passionate when it came to defending Unimeta's interests. Negotiations with English customers were always like walking a tightrope. John was the one who was quick to agree to the customer's wishes, but Frank was the one who would set the boundaries. He was the one who would say, "This is as far as we will go. And if it costs us the order, so be it." If it were up to their English customers, the company would get completely fleeced. John and Frank spoke on the phone every day, sometimes as many as ten times a day if necessary. Frank flew to England every other week to accompany John on his visits to customers, or to coordinate current business.

That horse show in the summer of 2000 would change all that. John was walking with his wife and middle daughter Cheryl past horses that were ready to compete in the show. The loud sound made by a door that suddenly blew shut scared the horse so badly that, in a complete panic, it tried to break free from the metal fence it was tied to with a rope. The fence was thrown yards into the air, and landed right on the head of John's daughter Cheryl. The poor girl was seriously injured, and was rushed to the hospital, her life in the balance. She died from her injuries several days later; she was only 11 years old.

John survived the initial months afterwards by throwing himself completely into his work and focusing on the settlement with the insurance company. After six months or so, Frank started to notice that John sometimes had a hard time getting his words out when they spoke on the phone. That Monday morning in Birmingham, he saw with his own eyes how John had lost control. This was the only possible conclusion. He has to talk to John about it, openly and honestly, because this can't go on any longer. Marion tells him to be careful, and Frank bears this in mind.

All he has to do now is wait for the right time.

This will take a while; Frank has other things on his mind this spring. In order to keep all the employees as busy as possible, they have spread the production out between the months of January and May. Thanks to back orders for Preston and Sombrero, they're also able to keep the regular employees working their normal hours during the month of June. A new building next to the factory and the rental of a warehouse in Hengelo helps them solve the storage problems caused by the fireworks disaster.

Somewhat reassured, but with a heavy heart, Frank flies to England for a meeting at Homebase, their biggest customer on the other side of the North Sea. Normally, John comes to pick him up at Gatwick Airport. As always, this time he's also waiting for Frank outside, but he has someone else with him, a man who then gets behind the wheel of the car. John introduces him as Ken. He drives the Land Rover to Croydon, a suburb of London, where Homebase has its headquarters. John doesn't mention it at all, or offer any explanation, acting as if it's perfectly normal for him to suddenly show up with a driver. Frank decides to wait until they've had their meeting with their most important customer before bringing it up.

The Homebase buyer is an incredible sourpuss, someone for whom nothing is ever good enough. He always finds something to complain about, and on the rare occasions he can't find anything, he makes it up. Frank is well aware that he has to be polite and professional no matter what. Unimeta is extremely dependent on sales from Homebase, and they simply can't do without their business.

"Next season, you're going to have to drop the price 10%," the buyer says, opening the meeting.

"Who doesn't want that?" Frank replies. "But that would mean that you will have paid 10% too much this season."

"Okay, I get that, but I'm talking about next year, 2003. You will just have to make up for it with higher efficiency or come up with something else. Your competition has made us an offer that is 10% lower than yours."

John starts talking about the high quality and excellent service Unimeta can offer. The buyer doesn't give him a chance to finish.

"If you only knew what kind of pressure I'm under to generate higher profits. I have to find a way to get a full 5% increase across the board, over the entire product range we sell. The days are long gone that I can allow quality or reputation to play a major role. Everyone makes the same product, and there are no bad relaxers these days. I get the required test certificates and standards qualifications from all the suppliers. It's up to you to go with the flow or just give up the fight. I'm just telling you now, before the new season starts. This way you can prepare and calculate whether or not it's worth it for you. I want the final offer from you within 45 days. I assume you're going to make us an interesting offer."

The proverbial steam was coming out of Frank's ears. They earn next to nothing on those relaxers as it is; taking another 10% off is just not feasible. Before you know it, they'll want even more. He's also annoyed with the buyer's arrogant attitude, sitting there with his laptop in front of him, doling out commands, as if he's the one calling the shots, which in fact, he actually is, a fact Frank can't argue with. He has no choice but to take it.

"We're going to take a serious look at this," he says with a straight face, "and will get back to you within 45 days."

That afternoon he gets a few extra orders that they can start working on immediately, but it's still bothering him, putting a loyal supplier under pressure like that; it's just not done. In the car, he brings up the topic with John who seems to have resigned himself to the situation.

"I'm feeling this pressure everywhere. Don't forget that Homebase is a publicly traded company. All they care about is the figures for the next quarter. They really don't give a damn about the rest. And if you can't or don't want to give them what they want, there's plenty of others who will."

Frank is all too aware of this; he knows the market like the back of his hand. Apart from Unimeta, there are a handful of other manufacturers in Europe who also make competing metal relaxers. There are two in Spain and one in Italy, and then there's an Irish cowboy who buys his frames somewhere else and has the cushion covers made in Poland. They stuff the covers and then add the cushions to the pre-purchased frames in a single packaging. The final product is then sold for a ridiculous price. They had also approached Unimeta about buying their frames, which Frank had categorically refused. He wasn't going to give his own competition a boost, but those naive Spaniards did business with anyone, as long as they could keep their production line running.

"What a crappy market," Frank sighs. "They won't even allow us to earn a decent profit. How will I ever make Unimeta profitable if people take this attitude to products and their quality?"

Before John even gets the chance to answer, Frank continues.

"Let's stop at that restaurant just outside of town, John. We need to talk, just the two of us. Have the driver wait in the car somewhere."

Once they are seated at a table, Frank asks John about this driver.

"Who is this guy? Why aren't you driving?"

John takes a deep breath and looks Frank straight in the eyes.

"The driver, well, he's here because I lost my license. I'm not allowed to drive anymore, so that's how I've solved the problem. I'm an alcoholic, Frank, an addict. I crave alcohol, all the time, every minute of the day. And night. I can't go without it. But I'm fighting it. I've joined an AA support group."

"I really respect you for being up front and honest with me about it, and I hope you're going to get through this. Everyone at Unimeta realizes what a horrible time you've been through, and we will support you however we can. But what has been going on lately is really not okay. Suppose you are drunk while you are talking to customers on the phone?"

"I'm doing my best, also for my other daughters, but the old John, he's gone for good. He's never coming back; it's just not possible. When I lost Cheryl, I also lost part of myself."

Tears are streaming down his face.

When Marion hears the whole story the next day at the office, she covers her eyes with her hands.

"Oh, how awful," she stammers.

"It definitely is," says Frank, "and I have a feeling we haven't seen the last of this, not by a long shot."

There isn't much time to worry about John's fate, however; the next meeting is coming up soon. Preparations are being made for a new exhibition right after the summer vacation, and that means everyone has to work like the devil. This year, Unimeta will once again be putting in an appearance at the exhibitions in Cologne, Birmingham and Chicago. And they'll be doing all of this within the span of two weeks in September. Not only do the new models have to be ready on time, but they are also working on a new booth for trade shows.

"It's going to be spectacular," says Carsten, the young salesman Frank has hired for the German market. Both the Preston and Sombrero lines are doing well there. Sales are not growing as fast as they are in the Netherlands, but they are steadily gaining ground. Frank has figured out that in order to achieve success in Germany, you need a German salesperson. Carsten was born and raised there, and speaks his customers' language, literally and figuratively.

In a week, the factory will be closing for five weeks for the annual major maintenance work on the machinery. This will mark the home stretch before a well-deserved vacation, but before he can enjoy it, Frank has one meeting left with Marion. Thirty-three and quite a bit younger than his predecessor, he does a lot more of his own work. Thanks to his laptop, he actually doesn't need a secretary anymore. He has been looking for a solution for a while, when suddenly the head of personnel announces he is leaving. Frank puts two and two together, and asks Marion if she wants the job. She will have to take a class, but as far as Frank's concerned, that's not a problem. He also immediately arranges for an external personnel specialist with a lot of experience to come in and support her. Fortunately, Marion is very enthusiastic about this new challenge. Finally, he can pull the door closed behind him and focus on his well-earned vacation. For just a little while, he won't have to think about patio furniture, complaining customers, or production, sales, collection, or works councils meetings. Two whole weeks of doing nothing.

The first Sunday of his vacation, he's sitting in his back yard in shorts and a polo shirt when the phone rings. It's John's wife.

"John passed away last night," she says, her voice broken with despair.

Frank has no idea what to say; he is completely dumbfounded.

"Died? So suddenly?" he says softly. "Yes, and the funeral's on Wednesday."

"I'll be there," Frank answers. "My sincerest condolences for you and the girls."

He wanders about his backyard, stupefied. He never could have suspected that John was in such poor health. The next Wednesday, Frank travels to Hereford in England to pay his final respects to John. The church service is heart-wrenching, and the funeral cuts Frank to the bone, all the more so since Frank is so familiar with the background of this family's tragedy.

There is one image that is indelibly imprinted on Frank's mind. John was crazy about his faithful German shepherd, Rush. That dog was for him what the horses were for his girls. After John had been laid to rest and everyone had walked past the grave, Rush remained seated next to the freshly dug hole into which the casket had just been lowered. Like a faithful shepherd, waiting for his master who would never return.

Although John's death continues to haunt Frank, he sets about dealing with the practicalities of the matter, and starts looking for a replacement straight away, working from his vacation cottage. He calls Unimeta's wholesaler in England a couple of times. Frank knows that things aren't too great at that company, and has a sneaking suspicion that they might be carrying a few staff members too many. He gets along particularly well with one of their salesmen, Hugh. Hugh would be the perfect person to take John's place. Frank realizes that he has to act fast, and still on vacation, he gets the green light from England to talk to Hugh about coming to work for Unimeta. Hugh thinks it's a great idea, and right after Frank gets home, they sign the new employment contract. Frank is incredibly relieved. At least this way, business will be able to continue in England.

Several days before the start of the big trade show in Cologne, he gets a call from Bart, who has gone ahead to Germany earlier with three engineers to supervise the set-up of the booth. They have hired a professional booth builder, but are handling the details themselves. They are the ones who decide the ultimate image the booth will project.

A team of employees has prepared everything down to the most minute detail. When Frank hears why Bart is calling, all the alarm bells start ringing. Bart has seen chairs at a competitor's booth that look incredibly similar to the Sombrero models. This is reason enough for Frank to rush to Cologne; this is the first time that a competitor has copied their products, but then again, they were never as unique and innovative as these chairs.

Before he leaves, Frank calls an attorney who specializes in intellectual property. He gives Frank the name and phone number of a law firm in Cologne that has more experience with this type of situation. Their office is near the exhibition complex, so should it become a serious problem, they can be on the scene quickly.

At the very last minute, he gets another phone call, this time from Hugh, who is calling to update him on the situation in England. He has personally notified all the customers about what happened to John. They were incredibly shocked. Suddenly, they realize that there is more to life than business alone. The realization is short-lived; after all, the negotiations for the upcoming season are in full swing. Hugh has not sat still, and dives right in with vigor.

"There are at least 12 English customers coming to the show in Cologne," he says. "With a little luck, maybe even 15."

For the first time, Unimeta has had a booth built with a second storey on top, with staircases leading up on the left and right side of the booth. The customers can tour the second floor, where they will be able to see the complete new cushion collection. The decision for this booth was preceded by intense discussions. Not everyone was convinced that they could afford the additional costs. Frank understands better than anyone that they have to be really careful about their spending, but if they want to get past all the setbacks, they have to generate more sales, and that can only happen if they up their presentation game.

The booth does look fantastic. Less fantastic is the news Bart gives Frank when he arrives in Cologne.

"You're not going to believe it. At first I thought they had stolen the chairs from our booth, but if you get closer, you can tell from the color of the plastic caps that they're not ours. They look nearly identical to one another. The only differences are in a couple of small details."

As Frank walks around with Bart, he sees at least six competitors' booths throughout the enormous exhibition complex where these same chairs are on display. They do in fact bear a striking resemblance to one of the best-selling chairs from their Sombrero collection: the Tornado, an adjustable chair with an aluminum frame, and a sling-fabric cover stretched over the frame. They had made at least 30,000 of these during the last season, and now he is seeing imitations everywhere.

Once back at the booth, the first thing Frank does is call the German law firm. They understand the urgency of the situation immediately, and in no time, a lawyer is standing in their booth. A respectable man, dressed accordingly, he introduces himself as Herr Mahler.

"We do a lot of this type of work," he says. "We can keep two people working on these cases full-time, and it is particularly rampant at exhibitions these days. Just two weeks ago, there was a major bicycle show here. We had five cases at that show alone. It's always Chinese manufacturers copying European products."

"But now I'm also seeing these chairs at our European colleagues' booths," Frank says.

The lawyer starts laughing.

"That may very well be the case. China is often the source, and there are

European customers or importers who offer the same products. But they all do come from a Chinese factory."

"So what can we do about it?"

"Easy," Herr Mahler says. "We walk around and I make a note of all the companies that have copied your chair. Then I'll draw up a document that is known as an *Abmahnung* here in Germany. I have my printer with me; it will only take a second. In this *Abmahnung*, or official warning notice, we tell them that they are in violation, and must remove the offending products from their booth. If they fail to do this, they risk getting an *einstweilige Verfügung*."

"An *einstweilige* what?" Frank cries out impatiently. The lawyer starts laughing again. Frank isn't sure whether this is because of his strong reaction, or his ignorance of these topics. Herr Mahler patiently explains it all again.

"In Germany, we simply take our case to court, and ask the judge for what is known as an *einstweilige Verfügung*, or preliminary injunction. If our case is strong enough, he'll grant this. It is a sort of order demanding the removal of the products in question from the booth."

Frank's face brightens immediately. Having the chairs removed from the competitors' booths will be a spectacular stunt. The patio furniture world is small, and the news of something like this will spread like wildfire. Within no time, everyone will know that the Tornado chairs belong to Unimeta, and that copying them is prohibited.

"You do need to be absolutely certain about your case," Herr Mahler warns.

"If one of your competitors doesn't agree with you, it can lead to a real lawsuit, and then we have to have a solid case backing up our allegations. If the judge does not find in your favor, you will be liable to pay all the damages and costs associated with removing the chairs."

Frank's smile disappears from his face just as quickly as it appeared.

"But they're copying us, not the other way around!"

"You never know for sure with judges. There is a massive difference between being right and proving you're right. I'm sure this is the case in the Netherlands, and Germany is no different."

Frank decides to take his chances. There is just way too much riding on this. If he doesn't take action, half the world will be copying his furniture. And if that happens, they may as well pack it in in Enschede. He and Herr Mahler walk around the exhibition together. Mahler takes note of all the names and types up the *Abmahnungen* on his laptop. When he is finished, he looks at Frank.

"Are you ready?"

"Let's do it!"

The first company they approach, a German importer, offers a sportsmanlike response when Herr Mahler hands him the document.

"I had actually expected this," the director of the company says. "I just thought we would try it and see what happens. But it's true, these chairs are almost the same as the ones at your booth. I'll take them out of my booth."

"Where did you actually buy them?" Frank asks.

"From the YenZhou factory, a company near Shanghai. They've got a booth here too."

The next booth they approach belongs to a company called JIP, a Dutch importer. This company is known for having products copied in China, and selling them below market price. The people at JIP give them a markedly less friendly welcome.

"Oh, what are you getting all worked up about?" the manager in charge growls. Frank knows him; he is known in the industry as being a real cowboy who always pushes the boundaries of what is allowed and what isn't. They have to be careful with this one. Herr Mahler once again clearly states that if they don't remove the chairs, he will petition the court for a removal order, and all the costs and consequences of this will be for JIP's account.

"Yeah, good luck with that," the manager snaps. He turns around and goes back to setting up his booth. Herr Mahler leads Frank out into the aisle.

"There are always people like him in these situations," he says. "We'll just slap him with an order."

Frank starts realizing more and more that the problem is a lot bigger than he had initially thought. Herr Mahler has his work cut out for him. He is walking around doing his thing, a "thing" he does for 200 Euros an hour, and the end is far from being in sight. In the meantime, Frank is trying to figure out how the people at JIP have managed to do this. The only solution he can come up with is that they have bought one of his chairs, sent it to China, and told them to use it as an example for their illegal copies. The thought alone infuriates him. All the hard work they have put into this collection, all the hurdles they have had to overcome, all of this is at stake now.

As YenZhou's booth looms up in front of them, he can't believe his eyes.

Although the two companies they first visited didn't have more than a couple of the copied chairs, here the booth is completely full of them. An arch at the back wall displays at least 20 copies of the Tornado. He has no idea what price they are asking for them, but it is almost certainly lower than what they charge for their own chairs. This is going to cost them sales and they are not talking about negligible numbers here. If this news gets out, they may as well just close the factory in Enschede.

They walk into the booth and look around. About 10 Chinese employees are unpacking products and polishing chairs. Frank and Herr Mahler approach the one closest to them and address him in English, but he gives them a surprised look, and starts chattering away in Chinese.

Suddenly, someone stands up who can actually say "Hello."

"Do you speak English?" Herr Mahler asks him.

He seems to be trying to say that he can speak a little English, but they're not entirely sure this is the case. It remains limited to unintelligible babbling. Herr Mahler tells him that he has to remove the copies from the booth, that otherwise they will be removed for them by court order. The man looks as if he doesn't understand a word, but Frank has his doubts. He looks very tense, and Frank has the idea that he knows darn well what is going on. It is also strange that the only language spoken by the personnel a Chinese company sends to an exhibition in Germany is Chinese. They hand him the letter and tell him to take it to the exhibition organization's interpreting service.

They visit another three European importers' booths. These companies at least understand what is being asked of them, and, after some urging from Herr Mahler, finally remove the copied chairs from their booths voluntarily. Frank notices that they're finding the same copies everywhere. The only logical answer is that they all come from the same factory, and that just has to be YenZhou's.

Herr Mahler has called the right people at the Cologne District Court. He has managed to get two short hearings on the list the following morning, during which he will petition for an *einstweilige Verfügung*. He talks about it like it's just another day at the office, but Frank still can't comprehend what has happened to him. All he can really do now is wait until tomorrow.

As Herr Mahler had predicted, they get the petitioned orders from the court without a problem. This will allow them to have all the copied chairs removed. Herr Mahler asks Frank if he wants to go with him, but Frank decides against it. His body is so full of adrenaline, he doesn't feel it would be a smart move. He still hasn't been able to get rid of his anger.

"It would be better for me to stay here; if I go with you, things might get too personal. Besides, I'm expecting important customers to show up, and I'd rather focus on that for now."

"*Verstehe ich*," " Mahler says, "I understand," and sets out with the ever-important *einstweilige Verfügungen* in his pocket. After half an hour, he's back at the booth.

"It was actually really easy. They both knew exactly what was coming. I even think that they had been in contact with each other. At that Chinese company's booth, they already had other chairs ready, and have now hung these up on the arch instead. This means we don't need the court to intervene to have those copies removed."

Good news, but for some reason, Frank thinks it's a shame that it was all so easy. He would have loved to see the police come in and pull the chairs out of the booths of those criminals, JIP and YenZhou. They obviously took the easy, safe way out; acting at first like they didn't understand, and meanwhile being sneaky and playing along with the game the whole time. Frank and Herr Mahler quickly exchange telephone numbers so they can reach each other during the weekend of the exhibition, just to be on the safe side. The first customers start arriving.

At the end of the day, spirits are low at Unimeta's booth. Although they have heard very high praise about their beautiful collection, they have also received some disconcerting reports. It appears that even though the copies have been removed, that doesn't mean that their competitors have stopped offering the products to the trade show visitors. Customers tell them that photos of the chairs are being shown to visitors, and that the competitors are saying that the chairs are being modified to avoid any more trouble with the design rights. An extra bar between the chair legs and a slight curve to the chair back, a different color frame and fabric cover, and it already looks like a completely different chair.

JIP takes the cake in this regard. They apparently have a copied chair standing in the little walled-in kitchen in their booth. First they show their customers a photograph, and if there's interest, they ask them to come with them to see the actual chair. Frank cannot believe that someone would lower themselves to these tactics.

He would love nothing more than to give these cowards a piece of his mind, but the problem goes even farther than he thought. After 9/11, the Chinese manufacturers saw their flow of orders from America dry up, and thus the risk of forced factory shut-downs. They have also started accepting production runs of a few thousand units or even less, whereas in the past, they wouldn't even turn on the production line for orders under 10,000 or 20,000. They were used to producing for customers like Walmart, K-Mart, Costco and Sears. In one of the Chinese factories, Frank had even seen an order of 120,000 rocking couches being produced. They have lost this business as a result of the copper strike in America, and as an alternative, they are setting their sights on Europe, including the smaller quantities that are typical of this market, and which had been non-negotiable in the past.

And this is all music to the ears of many of Unimeta's customers, particularly when the price of the copied chairs becomes clear. The costs of producing a Tornado at Unimeta are around 60 Euros, for materials, labor and overheads. Add to that their profit margin of 25%, and retailers are paying 75 Euros for the chairs that they are then selling to consumers for 149 Euros. He needs this margin to cover his costs and pay sales tax, and then have a little bit extra left at the end of the day.

The Chinese chairs, on the other hand, cost between 33 and 38 Euros wholesale, depending on the supplier. This is slightly more than half of Unimeta's cost price, and that also even includes freight. The price in the stores ends up being around 70 or 80 Euros, and he realizes that he can never compete with that. Dutch quality may be the highest there is, but customers aren't stupid, particularly when they can buy a chair for a lot less money, and the quality isn't really all that bad. It looks like 2003 is going to be another difficult year.

6

TOUR OF TWENTE

Foreign customers come to visit Unimeta in Enschede now and then, and these trips can create a lot of healthy excitement, even though things don't always go the way Frank expects. He has put together a whole program for the upcoming visit of the English company Co-op. They are currently buying their relaxers from a Spanish competitor, but together with his English representative, Hugh, Frank is slowly but surely working on bringing them into the Unimeta fold. The fact that the buyer and his immediate supervisor are coming to the Netherlands is a good sign. If they make a good impression on them, that could be the deciding factor.

It means the pressure is on in the factory, where everything has to be in tip-top shape. They make special frames in a variety of colors, which stylist Gineke puts together with matching cushions. Nothing is left to chance; they need the extra sales too badly. The cleaning lady has given the showroom an extra thorough working over this week, wiping down all the tables and chairs with a damp cloth.

Frank has gone through the program in detail with Hugh, who is accompanying the people from Co-op on their journey from Manchester to Schiphol Airport. They will take the train from the airport to the Enschede station, and Frank will pick them up there. He will first take them to the factory for a guided tour, and he has made reservations for that evening in a top restaurant just outside of the city. He has a presentation planned for the next morning, and a tour of the showroom, and after a short lunch, Frank will put the visitors on the train again for their trip back home. If everything goes according to the tight schedule, that is.

It starts out well; the train rolls into the Enschede station at three o'clock on the dot. A few minutes later, Frank sees Hugh's dark shock of hair in the distance. Two men are walking alongside him; one is tall and thin, and the other is quite a bit shorter and somewhat stocky. The tall man introduces himself as Cliff while the stocky man is called Terry. The latter extends a limp, sticky hand to Frank and shakes it. Frank has always hated those kinds of handshakes, but he doesn't let it show. You are supposed to pamper customers, particularly important ones like these.

Frank has made sure his car is spic and span, inside and out, and it's sparkling like new, and smelling fresh. As he drives out of the parking lot, Hugh informs him that the plans have changed. They will visit the company first thing tomorrow morning instead, seeing and evaluating everything at once, but first, they want to go to their hotel. The men are in the middle of a very hectic period and need some rest. Frank looks at Hugh. He gives him a big wink and keeps talking.

"Don't ask any questions, Frank, just go with the flow," he says after the men have checked in and have gone to their rooms to freshen up. "Just make sure they enjoy themselves, and the rest will be fine."

Frank isn't convinced. He looks at his watch.

"Can't we just go to the factory now, really quickly? If we hurry, everything will still be running. Then we can take a quick tour through production."

"No way. Just relax man. Let it go."

Once the English guests have come back downstairs, Terry tells them that they've been to Enschede before. They had gone to see Hartman. It must have been 10 years ago, but he can still remember the city center, particularly the outdoor cafés. A bit later, the men are enjoying a beer at one of these cafés, but Cliff isn't happy about the small glasses.

"At home in England, we only drink pints. And they fill them all the way up to the top with beer. This here is just a sneaky way to make money. Three-quarters of the way filled with beer and the rest is foam."

This doesn't stop them from ordering another round though, as they provide loud commentary on the women passing by. Frank looks at Hugh, but he only nods in approval. No one has said a word about patio furniture or relaxers.

In the meantime, it is quickly approaching seven o'clock, and the men are still drinking beer. Frank makes the wise choice to stick with soft drinks, but he notices that the time of their dinner reservation is rapidly approaching. When he suggests they make a move to go to the restaurant, Terry looks at him incredulously.

"I am really enjoying myself here," he says.

Hugh jumps in to offer his help.

"Frank, can't we just grab something to eat here?" The men seem pleased with this plan.

"But it's really an excellent restaurant," Frank tries again, to no avail. While a beautifully set table waits for them a mile away, they sit here at this café, giant plates of steak and French fries in front of them. All that food naturally makes them thirsty, and what with the small glasses, the waiter is rushing back and forth to their table to keep their glasses filled. At around nine o'clock, Frank decides he actually wants to call it a night, but his guests have other plans.

"The men would like to see a bit more of Twente, Frank," Hugh says with yet another wink.

"Sure, no problem," Frank says, relieved. He's just happy that an end seems to be coming to what has become a real drinking spree. "Where would you like to go? We have beautiful farms and country estates. They're really gorgeous at night. Unfortunately, the museums and so on are all closed now."

The men chuckle.

"Frank, we were thinking more along the lines of natural female beauty, to be honest."

"Ohhh..."

Frank feels unusually green and naive.

"Terry can remember being in the right places, shall we say, both in the city center and also outside of Enschede," Hugh says.

Frank gets the message. After paying the bill, he walks ahead of his guests, heading towards the other side of town. He once saw a name on the front of a building for a club that he had heard many stories about. Terry lumbers along at a fairly slow pace. As they walk to the club, a variety of dirty jokes are exchanged, the punch line of which Frank doesn't always get. English humor. They finally arrive at Club Carrousel. Hugh knocks on the door, and the bouncer lets them in. It takes a while for their eyes to adjust to the faint light. Six or so attractive and scantily clad hostesses are hovering around the bar. They men take a seat and order drinks. Frank pulls Hugh aside.

"This is really getting out of hand. Is this necessary?"

"Frank, if you want us to have a shot at that order, you have to let them do what they want. Don't you worry, I'll pay for everything and put it on my expense account."

Frank feels extremely uncomfortable, and hopes that he doesn't run into anyone he knows. He goes and sits at a corner of the bar, out of sight and hiding behind a cold glass of Coke. After half an hour, Hugh comes over to him.

"Cliff and Terry are asking if we can go somewhere else. Terry says there's supposedly one in Hengelo too, but he's forgotten the name."

"He's probably talking about Eva," Frank says.

Hugh raises his eyebrows, his lips form a smile, and he gives Frank a knowing look.

"It's not what you think," Frank says quickly. "The building is used as a point of reference in the city. When people give you directions, they often say that you have to go right or left at Eva."

"Take it easy Frank, I believe you" says Hugh, but Frank has his doubts. Once they get to Eva, things only get worse. He recognizes the only other patron as one of the fathers who, like him, also may be found on the sidelines of the soccer field every Saturday. The man makes a show of acting as if he doesn't see him, and is gone within five minutes. The quality of the women on offer here is visibly lower than in Enschede, but the British trio is still enjoying the taste of their beers and have quickly become engaged in a lively conversation with several of the hostesses. Frank starts getting impatient; it is eleven o'clock, and he tells Hugh that he's calling it a night. His guests, however, have other plans.

"There is supposed to be another place like this outside of Enschede," Hugh says. "Do you know anything about it?"

"Doesn't ring a bell, Hugh. Can you be more specific?"

"I was there once ten years ago," Terry says. "It was on a main road, and outside of town."

Now a light goes on in Frank's head. "Do you mean Bunny Bon?"

"Yes, that's it! Bunny Bonnnnn," he says with a giant grin.

"I don't know, Terry," Frank says. "That club doesn't have the best reputation."

"Doesn't matter, we have to go there."

Frank gives in for the last time.

"Okay, I'll take you there, but then Hugh has to arrange a taxi to take you back to the hotel."

Half an hour later, Frank follows them into Bunny Bon. Terry walks ahead, as if he is in a hurry. What Frank sees inside surpasses even the wildest stories that have made the rounds about this place. As far as he can tell, anyway; it's unusually dark in here. The dark-brown carpet is completely worn out. An old corduroy couch is too dirty to touch. He doesn't even want to know what has happened on that couch.

The ladies are all South American, and all weigh at least 220 pounds in the altogether. Frank can't suppress a shudder, but Terry and Cliff are clearly enjoying themselves. Terry's entire head has disappeared in the bosom of what must have been a real Surinamese beauty once upon a time. She slaps both breasts against the sides of his head like a professional volleyball player. He purrs like a satisfied tomcat after an abundant meal.

Frank makes an agreement with Hugh that he will pick the group up at their hotel at 8:30 the next morning. Hugh will be in charge of everything else the rest of the evening. "Have fun guys," Frank says as he's leaving, but Hugh is the only one to respond, giving him a thumbs-up. The two other men are too busy discovering the hostesses' various specialties.

As Frank tries to walk away from the bar, his right foot gets stuck, and he hears a strange, almost sucking sound. When he puts his foot down another few feet further on, he feels like something is missing from his shoe. He feels wobbly, a bit out of balance, and when he looks behind him, he realizes what's going on. The heel from his right shoe has broken off, having gotten stuck on the brown carpet.

They agreed to meet the following morning at 8:30. Frank walks into the lobby of the hotel just a few minutes before the agreed time. There is no sign of his guests anywhere. He sits down at the bar, and leafs through the morning newspapers. When, by nine o'clock, they still haven't shown up, Frank starts getting restless. Now their entire program will be thrown off. He asks someone at the reception desk to call Hugh's room. He finally picks up after ten rings.

"Yeah?"

"Hugh, it's past nine o'clock. Where are you all? I've been waiting here half an hour."

"You can easily wait another couple hours; you couldn't wake up those two if even you ran over them with a truck. We just got back a couple hours ago; it was already light out. Come back at 11:00."

"Eleven! I can't do that Hugh; the entire visit will be ruined."

"Don't you worry about that Frank. It will all work out fine. I'll be downstairs at 11:00. See you then."

At 11:00, Frank is once again waiting in the hotel lobby.
Hugh comes walking towards him with a broad grin on his face.

"Great night," he says, noticeably cheerful. "I just talked to the guys. They're awake and need another ten minutes or so."

He sits down next to Frank at the bar and orders a glass of water.
He tells him about the other two men's escapades of the night before, in living color.

"They had a really good time, and pretty much closed down the Bunny Bon this morning. Things might have gotten slightly out of hand in terms of the schedule today, but I'm not worried otherwise."

Frank wants to ask him what he means by that, but out of the corner of his eye, he sees Terry walking towards them. The man is a complete wreck. His eyes are slits and he reeks of alcohol, even three feet away. Cliff's condition isn't much better.

He hasn't even gone to the trouble of retying his tie. His shirttails are hanging out of his pants.

In the car, Hugh is rattling on about the most unbelievable nonsense. The other two men are remarkably quiet. Once at the office, they ask for a glass of water with their coffee. They all sit down in the conference room where Gineke will be giving her presentation. The buyer and his boss are slumping in their chairs, and Frank quickly sees Terry dozing off. He feels bad for Gineke, who is really doing her best at the presentation table. She too can see that Terry has fallen asleep and isn't sure how to handle the situation. Frank gestures to her to just continue with her presentation. Cliff nods politely now and then, but he is also visibly having trouble keeping his eyes open.

When the sandwiches are brought in at 12:30, Terry awakens with a start. He wolfs down two of them immediately. There isn't any time left for a tour; the men have to catch their plane. Frank quickly shows them a Sombrero chair before they leave. You never know. The men don't manage much more than a "nice" in response.

A little less than a week later, Jasper from inside sales walks into Frank's office, holding a Fax sheet.

"Fax from England," he says. "Here, look at this. An order for 1.1 million in relaxers, and another order for 200,000 for Sombrero chairs."

7

"WHEN I COME BACK FROM VACATION, I'LL BE COMING BACK AS ELLEN"

Just a few more days before the Christmas break starts, and then 2002 will be almost over. Although the factory will be closed for two weeks, everyone in the office will still be working during the holiday period.

Frank has just sat down at his desk this morning when Marion comes in.

"I just got a call from Michel. He wants to speak to you."

"Just have him come in now, and I'll do my rounds through the factory after that. Any idea what's going on or what it's about?"

"No," says Marion. "All I know is that he's been working in the raw materials warehouse as a forklift driver for a while. He started out there as a temp. Since he got his permanent contract last week, he's been whistling while he works."

"He probably just wants to thank me then."

Michel is a thin young man in his early thirties who wears his long dark hair pulled back in a ponytail. Marion makes a pot of coffee, puts two cups in front of them, and shuts the door. After Frank has poured their coffee, Michel starts talking, or rather, makes a short announcement.

"When I come back from vacation, I'll be coming back as Ellen."

Frank goes quiet, and gives him a questioning look. It takes a little while before the penny drops. Michel doesn't say anything else and looks at Frank. A silence fills the office.

"As Ellen?" Frank asks, once what he has just heard has sunk in.

"Yes, as Ellen," Michel answers. "I will be wearing lipstick and pantyhose under my skirt."

Frank thinks feverishly; they never covered situations like this during his studies. He had never read anything in any textbook about how to handle these situations. He follows his instincts.

"Is this something you've been thinking about for a long time Michel, this, um, process shall we say?"

"This sex change? Yes, for a couple years now. I have been thinking a lot about my feelings and what I want for the past few years. I have started hormone treatments. In about a year I'll undergo a sex-change operation. Part of this whole process is that starting on January 1st, I will tell everyone who I really am. On that date, I will become Ellen. I feel like Ellen, and will go through life as Ellen from then on."

"But will you still be able to do your job, Ellen? Um...I mean, Michel."

"Sure," Michel says, "according to the doctors treating me, I will still be strong enough to keep doing my daily work. And with the help of my co-workers, that shouldn't be a problem."

"Well, we'll just assume that will be the case, and all I can do now is wish you the best of luck in the coming weeks. I'll see you at the New Year's breakfast as Ellen then, Michel."

Michel shakes Frank's hand and thanks him for his support. When Marion comes into his office a little later, Frank gives her a brief summary of what happened.

"This can't possibly go well," he says. "Our foreign employees in production will never, ever accept this. They view people like this as outsiders; in their culture, they're outcasts. That should really be interesting next year. He never said a word about it. He just got his permanent contract last week, and now this. I really don't like this; it's just not right."

He looks outside and realizes that this is an extra hurdle, and they're already having a hard time of it. His coffee stands untouched on his desk.

The first week of 2003 the management team is hard at work to get the internal organization on the rails. A specialized firm has conducted a risk assessment and evaluation. Thick as a telephone book, this report contains a list of all the areas where the company needs to make changes. Rules, rules and more rules. It's enough to drive Frank crazy. Every change costs more money, and these bureaucrats are critical about even the smallest details. They have to make major investments, particularly in the coating department, in order to satisfy all the requirements. Frank is really annoyed by all of it.

"How are we supposed to compete with the Spaniards, Italians and Chinese if we have to spend all our time worrying about all this nonsense?" he grumbles during the management meeting. "And we don't have a damn choice, not if we want to get a permit from the city."

While they're working on that whole project, at the same time, they also have to present an annual occupational health and safety plan. Pet and the technical manager have taken charge of these projects. Step by step, they are trying to deal with and solve the issues involved in these areas, together with the HR department where necessary. This will free up the time Frank needs to concentrate on outlining a reorganization plan. This will be necessary, since no matter how you look at it, the Chinese will start selling copies of their chairs on the market.

They will have to take two steps at once: clamp down legally on every copy that appears on the market, and adapt the organization to the new situation. This is going to be a major ordeal. The production of the entire Sombrero range is at stake. Over the last few months, he has had two meetings with potential outsourcing partners, factories in China they are already doing business with. They buy pavilions and small folding chairs from them, so-called unique pieces. With one of these factories, Compex, they have already subjected a few products to a thorough review. How they do it is a mystery to Frank, but they can actually deliver a complete Tornado chair for just over 30 Euros. And they can do this even though the prices of steel and aluminum are nearly the same all over the world.

Naturally the wages there can't be compared to the West, but even then, they can't explain the difference. Frank and his co-workers from the costing department have been crunching the numbers until they're blue in the face. In their estimation, it's just impossible. Unless of course there are subsidies from the Chinese government involved, but they can't seem to put their finger on it.

In the meantime, Michel has started his new life as Ellen, and is in fact having a hard time of it during the first weeks of the new year. One of the co-workers refuses to call her Ellen, and yells "Michel!" through the warehouse all day. The Turkish and Moroccan employees are snubbing her, which was exactly what Frank was afraid of.

It is in fact strange to see her driving the forklift around in a skirt and high heels. Heavily made up and with her long hair waving in the air, she whizzes around on the forklift all day, from the warehouse to the factory and back again. She is still just as capable when it comes to unloading the heavy metal components and the rolls of fabric. All Frank can do is to give it time, and hope that a certain degree of acceptance will grow among the staff.

In early February, the inevitable happens. A major Dutch home furnishings chain, Blokker, has released its new patio furniture brochure for the spring of 2003, featuring various models which are direct copies of the Tornado. Leen Bakker, another similar chain, is also selling them, and Kwantum, a home-improvement chain, is offering a model in its collection that varies only slightly. Two other chains, Xenos and Marskramer won't be outdone by the competition either.

The situation isn't much better in Germany. One major wholesaler appears to have continued with the sales of the chairs, in spite of its promises at the trade show to stop. Thanks to this company, the imitation Tornado chairs are being sold in home-improvement stores all over Germany. The disaster is complete a few weeks later when the JIP copies also start popping up at garden centers.

These chairs all have one thing in common: their fiercely competitive pricing in the stores. In the garden centers, they cost 79 Euros, but at Blokker and Leen Bakker, the chair is put in the window for 69 Euros from the very beginning. A price that is just above Unimeta's cost price. Frank's spirits are sinking. They have to switch gears really fast now. During those few weeks in February, he meets nearly daily with his specialized attorney to prepare a few lawsuits. Summonses are also being sent to the various chains that are selling the copies.

In the meantime, Frank flies to China with Ruud Kuipers to discuss an extensive partnership with Compex.

Compex is a publicly traded company that has its headquarters and a factory in Taiwan. About five years ago, they also added a production location in China. This facility is in the Guangdong province, in South China, a two-hour drive from Hong Kong. The people there speak English fairly well, and with their Taiwanese background, they have also had thorough technical training. Frank has been doing business with them for about three years, and they would love to take over part of Unimeta's production.

After the disappointing trade show in Cologne, various Unimeta employees had been to visit Compex. They studied the available technical options, and took a few products with them from the Netherlands, which were dissected and inspected on the spot in China. Every screw, bolt and hinge was measured and recorded in technical drawings by the Compex engineers. Using this information, they generated a cost estimate for producing the Tornado chair. This resulted in a price that Compex would charge Unimeta of approximately 30 Euros.

It is clear that this is the path they must follow. The Sombrero collection will be going to China in its entirety, and the cushion production to Poland. Pet has thrown himself into the latter project. He has it all completely under control, and they don't have to worry about it anymore. Ruud and Frank are taking responsibility for China, and Erwin Hoge Bavel, Unimeta's controller, is calculating and forecasting all the financial consequences.

They have to move fast. The initial calculations have shown that the savings are tremendous, and that Unimeta's financial results thus far for this season are disastrous. They are heading towards a loss of over one million Euros. Frank is fully aware of the fact that this will be particularly hard to explain to the bank.

They already have very little financial cushion as it is, and this could endanger the future of the company. This will definitely be the case if they don't take action now. He will have to come up with a solid reorganization plan to show that Unimeta's future really does look profitable and rosy, and to show how they plan to achieve this. The bank will be extremely critical in evaluating the new credit application.

Frank comes home with his head about to explode on a regular basis these days. Completely drained, he has no energy left to play the wonderful family man for his wife and three kids. This gnaws at him, but he has no choice. He has to grin and bear it for now; hundreds of employees' jobs are on the line.

The negotiations with Compex are now so advanced that a complete outsourcing contact is on the table waiting to be signed. They have established and protected the intellectual property and design and model rights for the Sombrero collection in this contract in every way possible. Unimeta can't just bring all its technical know-how and skills to China and have Compex make a run for it with it all. Compex has indicated repeatedly that this is not their intention, and they sign the contract without a problem. Unimeta also stipulates that at least three Unimeta employees must be present in the factory on a permanent basis. They will live there, and have an office and living accommodations at their disposal. Two engineers will travel there from the Netherlands. They will be assisted by people in China. A few years ago, Unimeta hired Flora, a young Chinese woman who speaks excellent English, a sharp little spitfire. She will work with the two engineers and also move into the factory complex.

This whole operation will save them nearly 1.3 million, and if all goes well, they will be back in the game again. One consequence, however, is that 90 jobs will disappear. Fifty temporary employees are being told that their services are no longer necessary, and 17 annual contracts will not be renewed, but the worst part about it for Frank is that they can't avoid also firing 23 permanent employees. Some of these employees have worked for the company for decades, and it isn't their fault that people in Poland and China earn a fraction of the wages that employees in the Netherlands are paid. He has no choice.

Evening after evening, he sits there working out all the plans, sometimes until long after midnight. Fortunately, his wife doesn't give him a hard time about it.

"You have to do what you have to do," she simply says. "Just make sure that you make the factory profitable again, Frank."

Over the next few months, all the preparations have to be made for the upcoming season. Moving all the means of production to China and preparing for the production of approximately 60 Sombrero chairs is incredibly time-consuming. Frank is fairly sure that six or so Unimeta employees will have to stay on-site in China for a few months in order to realize their ambitious yet realistic objective. If everything goes well, in exactly six months they will be on schedule to produce the first orders for 2004 at Compex. This means that there is no leeway for any problems or setbacks.

The following week it is already mid-March and the next trip to China is coming up. Right now, Frank is eating his sandwich in Kuipers' office. He usually does this at lunch time; it gives him an excuse to get out of his own office. He feels like he has been spending so much time at his own desk. It also gives him the chance to catch up. Even though Frank has finished two lawsuits this past week, he still doesn't understand it.

"These lawyers have gone totally crazy. We file two lawsuits, two cases involving our Tornado versus one of these copies. We win one case hands down, and lose the other, even though the chairs the lawsuits are about are exactly the same."

"Unbelievably frustrating," Ruud says. "It just goes to show you that being right and being proven right are two very different things. Mostly it proves that we have to focus on the future. We have to concentrate on innovation and new developments so that we can constantly remain a step ahead of the competition. Let them trail along behind us."

Frank agrees completely with Ruud, but the frustration is still written all over his face.

"The lawsuit against the German wholesaler is going to court next month. I have done everything I can to prepare for it. I've spent many an evening plugging away at it. And now I have to worry about the outcome too, in spite of the fact that we are completely in the right."

They continue to eat their sandwiches in silence, lost deep in thought.

A week later, Frank is getting ready for his trip to China. It is long after dinnertime as he packs his suitcase. His wife has put the kids to bed, and Frank goes into their rooms to give them a hug before they go to sleep.

"Are you leaving again Papa?" his four-year-old daughter asks as he gives her a big kiss goodnight. Frank sits on the edge of her bed and swallows.

"Yes, honey. Papa has to go to China to have chairs made there. I'll be gone a week. Will you take really good care of Mama?"

She nods bravely and says softly: "Come home again soon Papa," and snuggles down into her bed. Frank tiptoes quietly out of her room and feels tears stinging his eyes.

8

"Give me that drawing a second, GertJan," Raymond asks.

GertJan slides the drawing over to him.

"Look," Raymond says, "this is the problem. They are using the inside measurements on our drawing as the outside measurements for the hinge. That's why it doesn't fit."

Frank watches this scene with a giant yawn. Jetlag has really hit him hard. He arrived in China yesterday, and only got a couple hours of sleep last night. In spite of the fact that it's mid-March, the temperature in Guangzhou has risen to 88°F this afternoon.

Raymond beckons the Chinese engineer over and asks Flora to translate for them. He patiently explains exactly what they are doing wrong with this spare part at Compex. Frank has been sitting in the hot, stuffy little office all afternoon. He wants to learn more about everything involved in the outsourcing of their products. If it's going to be this slow of a process for every little part, he thinks, then we won't even be done by Christmas.

Raymond and GertJan have already been working in China for about 10 days. They've still got a lot to do before the first chair comes rolling off the assembly line. They have to go through it all this way, product by product and component by component. Frank is watching all of this with clenched teeth. This is taking longer than he had expected.

The owner of Compex has lived up to his promises, down to the last detail. When Frank arrived the day before, they spent an hour drinking Chinese tea and voicing their good intentions to one another. Steve Lin tells him that his family is the majority shareholder in the company, but that they applied for a listing on the stock exchange years ago, mostly to finance the new factory in China and all the other necessary investments. Since Compex is entirely dependent on its American customers, they would like to increase their market share in Europe. And they want to raise the level of quality.

Since Unimeta sells primarily to customers in Europe and is known for its high-quality products, they are extremely interested in this partnership. Frank can understand this completely. He knows that many Chinese factories are somewhat envious of their Sombrero and Preston collections, with their beautiful design and the level of technical perfection that has gone into their development. This knowledge now has to be shared with a Chinese manufacturer, something that gives many of Frank's colleagues a strange and sometimes unpleasant feeling. Frank understands this, but also knows that they have no choice.

He leaves the engineers to do their job, and asks Flora to walk with him into the factory. Frank has known Flora for about two years now, and is very happy with her contribution. Since she started working for Unimeta, doing business in China has become a lot easier. They first met her at a Chinese factory that supplies teak products to Unimeta. She stood out thanks to the energetic way she went about her work. Flora didn't beat about the bush about anything, like most Chinese employees try to do; she just came right out with it and told the truth. This was a real breath of fresh air for the Unimeta staff. Frank had already decided that with Flora at the helm, they could continue to expand the Chinese organization in the years to come. She was in her mid-20s now, with a college degree under her belt. She had proven to be a real warhorse.

Now and then, they even had to keep her in check. When a Chinese supplier tried to pull the wool over their eyes, this was when Flora was at her best. She would rake the supplier over the coals in a way that might embarrass people in the West. But in China, this type of behavior is necessary, otherwise they will really try to trick you.

As they walk through the factory together, Frank takes it all in.

Everything here is a million times bigger than at Unimeta. Instead of two welding robots, they've got 20 here. Instead of one powder-coating installation, they've got three. There are 3000 employees walking around in the various metal departments alone. In Frank's opinion, they could have easily done with 1000 less, since as far as he can see, half of them seem to be sitting around doing nothing, but still. The nice thing is that the smell in this factory, the familiar hint of metal in the air, is exactly the same as in the factory in Enschede.

He sees the same thing in the textile department, where there are also at least 500 people milling around. Downstairs in the metal department all the machines are operated by men, but here on the upper level all you can see are women. Actually, they're really girls, most of whom don't seem to be older than 18. They all look alike, with their jet-black hair pulled back in a ponytail. Just like Michel used to look, Frank thinks.

"How is he actually doing right now?" flashes through his mind. "Or should I say, 'her'?"

The women here sit at their sewing machines, in long rows of twenty or thirty that extend all the way to the back of the factory.

"We can never compete with this," Frank says to Flora. "We only have 15 seamstresses, and we have to fire them all soon."

Flora gives him a questioning look.

"Don't tell anyone else about this, Flora. We are working out the plans now, and still have to complete the official procedure."

The question marks in her eyes only grow larger.

"If you want to fire people because you don't have any work for them, then why don't you just tell them that? They'll leave on their own, won't they?" she says, naively.

"I wish it was that easy in the Netherlands, Flora," he answers. "In our country, this is a major procedure, and it can cost an incredible amount of money. It's actually the last thing we can afford right now."

Flora walks down the steps of the cushion department, shaking her head. In the Netherlands, she would be at odds with everyone in no time, with her temperament.

They walk back to the office area next to the production warehouses. Their office is at the very end of a long corridor. Everywhere you look, employees are hunched over stacks of paperwork, or are staring at their computer screens. Frank once again is reminded of his earlier thought that they could manage with a lot fewer employees here too. The costs of labor may be very low, just a couple of dollars per day, but efficiency is nowhere to be found.

A few days later, Frank is the one sitting hunched over a tall stack of paperwork in the little office. These are the initial calculations for chairs and tables, worked out down to the last detail by Compex. The idea they had initially gotten from the very first test calculations appears to be completely accurate. In fact, it is even more positive than they had thought. Or more negative, depending on how you look at it.

The difference in the cost price between this facility and their own production in the Netherlands appears to be even greater than they had initially estimated.

Frank calculates everything twice, and arrives at the conclusion that they must now go full steam ahead with their plans for the reorganization. All the products that they make in the Netherlands cost less than half the price here, including transport to the Netherlands. Sometimes the cost price for Compex is even as low as one-third of the cost price that they apply at Unimeta. A feeling of impending doom overcomes Frank as it slowly dawns on him what the consequences of this could be.

Suddenly, his phone rings. He answers it, identifying himself by his first name only.

With the six-hour time difference, it's already evening in Europe, so it would have to be a good friend calling him at this hour.

"Hi, Frank speaking."

"Hi honey, everything okay there?"

It's Edith, his wife, and she normally never calls him. They had already spoken briefly that afternoon. Frank hears worry in her voice.

"Everything's okay here; is something wrong there?" he asks.

"No, not here, but there might be something wrong with you all, over there."

Frank doesn't understand this at all.

"Why? What do you mean?"

"Well, I've just been watching the eight o'clock news. Where exactly are you in China? What's the name of that big city near you? 'Guanzu' something or other?"

"Do you mean 'Guangzhou'?" Frank asks.

"Do you spell that G-u-a-n-g-z-h-o-u?" Edith asks.

"That's right, we're about half an hour from there."

Nothing but silence on the other end of the line. "What's wrong?" he asks.

90

"They were just talking about really strange things on the news. That some extremely infectious disease has been discovered. They said that nine people have already died from it worldwide. Two Canadians who were in Hong Kong, and an American who had travelled from Shanghai to Hanoi in Vietnam. He died from the disease while he was there. And just now a doctor from Singapore was pulled off a plane in Frankfurt. Apparently, he contracted it because he had been in contact with a sick patient. Now they're saying on the news that hundreds of people have been admitted to the hospital, all over Asia. Mostly Vietnam and Hong Kong, but also in Taiwan and Indonesia."

"But I'm in China!"

"Yes, I know, but let me finish. That's why I asked you about the big city near there, because that's been mentioned as one of the possible outbreak centers for the disease. That's where it apparently started."

"What kind of disease is it? Do you just drop dead all of a sudden or something? Or do you vomit blood or get a heart attack?"

"Supposedly it's a type of pneumonia. It is accompanied by coughing and a high fever."

"Oh, then it's no big deal," Frank says. "I don't have a fever and I haven't been coughing. I feel perfectly fine. Just have a little jetlag, that's all. Do you have any matchsticks for me that I can use to hold my eyes open during the day?"

Edith isn't laughing.

"By the way," says Frank, "no one here in China is talking about this. It's probably just some kind of flu that will blow over. Don't worry, I'm safe here. Besides, we're way too busy for nonsense like this. We have to do all the detailed calculations for sixty products and..."

"Frank," his wife interrupts him, "you're really underestimating the situation. I have been watching footage of overcrowded hospitals in Asia, and nine deaths haven't just come out of nowhere. Please just be careful, okay?"

Frank takes her advice to heart, and thanks Edith for her call and concern.

"It'll be okay."

He puts his telephone back in his pocket and looks at Flora. She naturally didn't understand a word of his conversation, but still picked up on the fact that something's wrong. Frank tells her the same thing his wife told him on the phone, and Flora doesn't understand it either.

"Impossible," she says. "I watched the afternoon news here during the lunch break. No one said a word about it. If it is so major and important as your wife thinks, wouldn't we know all the details of it here? I'll ask around in the factory and among my friends, but I can't imagine any of this is true."

Frank is relieved. If the Chinese don't even know about this, then it must be okay.

"Women..." he says quietly to no one in particular.

That evening, Frank asks a few of his Dutch co-workers whether or not they had heard anything. They look at him, dumbfounded. It is still at least 77°F outside, and they are sitting on patio chairs in front of their sleeping quarters. Frank drinks a beer with them before going back to his hotel, half an hour's drive from the factory.

The next morning, Raymond comes rushing into the office.

"Frank, that disease you were talking about yesterday, that is some serious bad news. My sister just called me. She had heard on the radio that the World Health Organization had issued a global health alert. Three more people have died in Hong Kong, and there are a couple hundred new cases. My sister was saying that the authorities there are trying to put an entire block of houses in quarantine. Apparently, they've traced the spread of the infection in Hong Kong back to that location. But the person who died had just visited his family here in Guangzhou."

"That's right next door," GertJan remarks drily.

Frank joins the conversation and makes it clear that they just have to stay calm.

"There's nothing going on here. None of the Chinese are talking about it, and the factory here is running at full speed. I will ask around and let you know right away if there's any news."

He walks to one of the other offices, where Flora is working at a computer. He looks at her inquisitively, and Flora's look of denial says it all.

"I have called everyone I could think of, Frank. They all think that I'm starting to lose my mind from all the foreigners around me. No one knows what I'm talking about. No one has heard anything or could give me any information."

"Great," says Frank, "then it's just a storm in a teacup. We'll just keep doing our work and wait until the whole thing blows over."

At the end of that week, the large Mercedes 500SL belonging to the owner, Steve Lin, drives onto the property. He gets out of the car, together with his son-in-law, Ryan Tong. Ryan is in charge of the day-to-day management at Compex, leaving Steve free to focus on the big picture. Through the office window, Frank watches them walk toward the main entrance, a doorway surrounded by marble. He immediately decides to check the situation with them.

When he stands waiting for Steve in the doorway of his office, Steve is surprised to see him.

"Are you still here?" he asks. "And your co-workers from the Netherlands are still here too?"

"Yes, of course. We have a huge job to do and have only been working on it for a couple weeks."

"That's not what I mean," Steve says. "That epidemic apparently started here in Guangzhou. We've just gotten back from Shanghai; we heard about it there. They've had quite a few deaths there too. According to the Taiwanese media, there have definitely been a few hundred fatalities in South China. They are also saying that the Chinese authorities are hushing everything up. They are digging their own graves, those stupid Chinese. No one is taking precautions, and this means that the virus can spread like wildfire throughout the country. All the evidence shows that the epidemic originated just a short distance away from our factory, Frank. I would recommend you get out of here as fast as you can."

Frank feels his legs getting weak, and he breaks out in a cold sweat everywhere. He thanks Steve for his information, and walks back to the office, deep in thought. This is really messed up, he thinks. They can't leave at all. If they all leave, the five Dutch employees working at Compex, the outsourcing project will run into huge delays. Financially, this is the last thing they need. And who knows how long this disaster will go on? When would they be able to return to China? If they don't continue working on all these patio chair models, they will be too late for production for the new season.

He decides it's time to call everyone in the Netherlands. First, he needs to call home, then the office.

The decision seems to be quickly made for him when he hears that a travel alert has been issued for Hong Kong and Guangzhou, among other cities, and that dozens of people are dying from the virus every day. If you try to fly to the Netherlands with a cough or mild fever now, they won't even let you in the country. Frank's wife practically begs him to get out of there. Together they decide that he will fly directly back home.

Frank briefly toys with the idea of first moving into the local Van der Valk hotel for ten days, until the incubation period is over. The last thing he wants is to risk infecting his wife or children just in case he's carrying the virus. Fortunately, he still feels fine.

His co-workers are relieved that they at least now know what they're going to do. Frank brings them up to speed, and says that the virus has now also been given a name, SARS. It stands for Severe Acute Respiratory Syndrome, a very serious, acute type of pneumonia. In the meantime, Marion has made arrangements from the office in the Netherlands, and has booked them seats on the KLM flight the next morning, direct from Hong Kong back to Amsterdam.

Together with his co-workers, Frank makes one more round through the Compex factory. Everything is the same as it always is. There's nothing to indicate a new disease. No signs that hundreds of people have died just a stone's throw away. The Chinese workers are just doing their thing, like they always do. They are sawing, drilling, welding and sewing so that another 10,000 patio chairs come rolling off the assembly line again that day. Epidemic or no epidemic.

On the way to the Hong Kong airport the next morning, there are also no signs whatsoever that something is going on. As usual, it's total chaos on the roads. Every Chinese person who has earned a bit of money seems to have bought a car. They probably get their driver's license free with the purchase, like we get a bouquet of flowers in the Netherlands when we buy a new car. Every time he goes to China, it seems to get worse. They have no idea at all whether they are driving in the left or right lane, and they even seem to prefer to drive down the center line, only to be passed on the left or right side. And all that honking.

After an hour in the car, they finally arrive at the Fuyong Ferry Terminal. From there, they will sail directly to the Hong Kong airport, on a nice, clean ferry. It's business as usual on the boat too. Frank and his co-workers have breakfast, and have plenty of room to walk around; it's not very crowded on the ferry.

Slowly, the jetty at the airport comes into view. Once the ferry has moored, all the passengers are taken to a separate area. The airport employees are all wearing surgical masks. It's a strange sight to behold, and they make jokes about it. In the area they are told to wait in, several employees are standing there holding something that looks like a laser gun. Memories of 9/11 flash briefly through Frank's mind. These pistols are harmless, however; they're only designed to measure body temperature. The five of them are able to walk through without a problem, but a bit further back, a woman is pulled out of the line and taken to a separate exit.

A little while later, they are on the bus heading for the main terminal. Frank is shocked by what he sees there. It's completely deserted. Normally this place is crawling with thousands of people milling about like ants on an anthill. Today, peace and quiet dominate. Nearly all the duty-free shops and restaurants are closed, even now, in the middle of the morning. All of the shop personnel, police officers and customs officials are wearing surgical masks.

Frank walks through the airport in amazement. They have their temperature taken again. This time, they have to walk through a security gate with a safety scanner mounted on top. One hour later, when they are allowed to board the plane, he can also see that the KLM crew are walking around wearing surgical masks. It's all very surreal. He feels like he's ended up in the middle of a science fiction movie, really strange.

Raymond has a witty response to this.

"If everyone is walking around with one of these silly surgical masks, we're safe, even if we're not wearing one."

They laugh at his clever remark, but at the same time, Frank senses the enormous tension that dominates the atmosphere.

Once home, Frank tries to keep as much physical distance as he can from his wife and children. It might be pointless, but it can't hurt to try. If he were by chance infected, then that might help at least a little bit to prevent him from transmitting the virus. Although his wife has already explained it to the children, they don't really understand what's going on. Papa is now finally home, and they can't even hug him. Fortunately Frank continues to feel fine, and after a little over a week, everything is back to normal in his family.

Unfortunately, he can't say the same of the situation at work. SARS or no SARS, the reorganization has to go ahead, of that much they are all certain. Even though things have been delayed, they will have to keep producing the

Sombrero line in Enschede a few months longer.

During the months of April, May and June of 2003, he works on the reorganization almost every day, and regularly comes home with a headache. First, the entire plan has to be prepared by the management team, with the support of a good lawyer. Thankfully he has found this individual in Ronald van Gurp, one of the best employment lawyers in the region. The reorganization memorandum then has to be submitted to the works council. The council must then provide a recommendation, which hopefully will be positive.

This will be followed by tough negotiations with the unions. They have sought representation from Toon Verdijsseldonk, the experienced leader from the FNV Bondgenoten, the Dutch Trade Union Federation. He is a sly fox and cunning negotiator who always manages to get the most out of a situation. In this case, and against the will of Frank and the negotiating team, this is a severance payment for the permanent employees, to which a 0.6 correction factor is applied. This costs Unimeta a whopping half million Euros, money that they actually can't afford to do without. This means that the tiny remnant of buffer they had left in their capital is now gone, and they will be completely at the mercy of the bank from now on. However, there is no alternative. If a social plan is approved, an individual dismissal application will have to be filed with the subdistrict court, for every employee. This procedure will take even more time, and with a financial outcome that costs the company more rather than less money.

Frank can hear Flora's words in his mind again.

"Can't you just tell people that there's no work for them? They'll leave on their own, won't they?"

Every now and then he bursts out laughing, when he thinks about it. In late May, Frank is standing in the cafeteria with a heavy heart, acutely aware of how much the situation has changed since he stood on this very spot three years ago. He takes a deep breath and says his piece. After his short speech, most of the employees walk silently out of the cafeteria, their heads down. In another two weeks, they will be having some very heavy discussions, and then everyone will know where they stand.

Disillusioned, Frank drives home that evening. This was not the challenge he thought he was taking on over three years ago. He wanted to help the company grow, not send home employees, some of whom have been doing their best for the company for over 30 years. It feels like a catastrophe.

The situation in the Far East doesn't do much to cheer him up either. They still haven't gotten SARS under control. This means they can't send their engineers back to Compex yet. He is, however, extremely relieved that everything ended well for him and his co-workers. The seriousness of the epidemic didn't become clear until after they returned. In June, they are able to take stock of the situation. The epidemic has essentially been brought to a standstill, and the number of new cases is minimal. With 800 fatalities and a total of more than 8000 people infected in 32 countries, they can consider themselves very lucky.

In the last few months, the world has come to a standstill in Asia. People are still petrified. Airplanes and hotels are still empty, and people are afraid to travel. The most frightening part of this is that the medical community still hasn't been able to develop a vaccine against SARS. This will take many years. They do discover that the disease originated in the rural areas in China, somewhere not too far from Compex. They find out that a breed of cat, the civet, appears to carry both the virus and the antibodies. These animals are traded daily on the markets in South China, where they are considered a delicacy. From there, the infection spread like an inkblot, first through South China, and then all over Asia.

Finally, in early July 2003, the world is declared to be free from SARS, and no new cases of infection have been discovered for 20 days. Taiwan is the last country with a documented case of infection. Only then are Frank's co-workers able to return to China.

Three key months have been lost, and with them, a large percentage of an entire production season. Frank realizes that they will have to produce the entire pre-sale stock of Sombrero products in Enschede, out of sheer necessity. The first products won't come rolling off the Compex assembly line until early 2004. The development of new molds alone will take a few months, time that has vanished into thin air due to the SARS epidemic. The most they can hope to achieve for the coming season is a couple hundred thousand in improved profits, of the 1.3 million that had been forecast.

One sunny summer day, just before the summer vacation period, Frank is sitting at his desk in the office when the phone rings. It's the account manager from ABN AMRO, the company's bank. He wants to make an appointment to visit Unimeta, together with a co-worker from Amsterdam who works at a division of the bank Frank has never heard of, "Special Credits".

9

FROM NOW ON, THE BANK HAS THE FINAL WORD

Frank makes a solemn promise to himself to truly enjoy time with his family during the short summer vacation. The children are still young, but time is flying. During the first week of their vacation in Turkey, he manages to put everything out of his mind. The two youngest can't swim yet, so they have to be watched every second. They spend their days in and around the huge swimming pool at the apartment complex. Every now and then they brave the waves in the ocean, but they actually all hate the sandy beach.

The sand literally gets everywhere. They'd rather relax around the pool on the lounge chairs which are more comfortable, and it's easier to keep an eye on the kids there.

The last few days of their stay, Frank starts feeling restless. He tries to organize his thoughts. They still have so much to arrange, and then there's that man from Amsterdam who's coming to the office, and he still has no idea why. The transfer of knowledge and skills to Compex is in full swing. A large group of engineers is working right through the vacation period.

Something that is a cause for concern for Frank is the situation with Ellen, formerly known as Michel. Within the management team, they have agreed to give her a fair chance. During the reorganization, they kept her position. As long as she does her job well, there's really no reason to take any action. But this is actually where the problem lies. The hormones are causing her strength to slowly decrease, and she has a job that simply demands physical strength.

It is also getting increasingly more difficult for her to do her job well since her co-workers aren't exactly cooperating. The foreign employees won't even look at her, and now they are having to help her move and lift boxes with spare parts and aluminum tubes. They are having a really hard time with this, and they let it show every single day. The situation is eating away at Frank; this is actually the last thing they need right now. What they really need is for all the employees to give more than their 100% effort and dedication, particularly now that efficiency has risen even more after the reorganization.

Frank tries to take advantage of the free time during a few evenings in Turkey to focus on his studies. He still has to take one last final exam, and then he can start working on his thesis, after which he'll have his Master of Marketing Strategy diploma. Four years ago, he had started a part-time degree program at the State University of Groningen, as a distraction from his daily worries and to grow further in his career.

Since it is a part-time program, he can combine classes with work, for better or for worse. This was definitely an unusually difficult challenge during the last two years. In spite of it all, he persevered. He reads as many books as he can during the vacations, and he goes to Groningen to attend classes for two days, four times a year. Other than that, the program is mostly independent study, but Frank really enjoys this part of it. Once he can put aside his work for Unimeta at around ten or eleven in the evening, he enjoys focusing on something else for another hour or two. Friends and family don't understand why, but for him, it's a way to relax. He can switch off everything for a little while and escape completely from his everyday problems.

He has chosen brand management as his specialization, an interesting area that Frank can't quite get enough of. The aspect that really intrigues him is how this works in small- and medium-sized companies. At Unimeta, they don't have a budget of hundreds of thousands of Euros, let alone millions, to build up a brand. The other people in his study group are all managers who work at multinationals like Philips, Coca Cola, and Unilever. These guys talk about amounts in the millions like it's nothing.

All the existing literature on brand management addresses these types of multinationals. Frank can't imagine how an SMB with limited resources could ever develop such a huge brand. He naturally tries to do this with the Preston line in his day-to-day work, but he only has a couple thousand Euros at his disposal for this each year. It can be frustrating sometimes. During this vacation he decides that his thesis will be about this balance.

The appointment with the bank is scheduled for late August. The day of the meeting, Frank has put on his best suit, dark blue with a cheerful striped tie.

Later that day, Frank meets Peter Groeleken, the bank manager from Amsterdam, who is wearing an even fancier suit than Frank. He is sturdily built and extremely tall. Frank is far from short himself, and it isn't often that he is standing in front of someone who can see the top of his head, but this man towers over everyone and everything. He even has to duck to get through the doorway.

Once they are all seated, his extreme height isn't as noticeable. Erwin Hoge Bavel, Unimeta's controller, sits down next to Frank and listens to the conversation. Frank notices that his own account manager from the bank, a man who has been coming to their office for about three years now, doesn't say very much. He leaves the entire conversation to his colleague from Special Credits.

"You are dealing with particularly difficult circumstances here at Unimeta," Peter says, opening the meeting.

"That's absolutely correct, Mr. Groeleken," Frank says. "Do you mind if we dispense with the formal form of address? It makes conversation easier." This guy is only a couple years older than me, it shouldn't be a problem, Frank thinks.

"We can definitely do that, Mr. Krake, if you would prefer," Groeleken answers, "but it won't change the situation."

Frank frowns.

"How do you mean, Peter?" he asks, emphasizing the man's first name.

"Allow me to explain it to you. It's very simple. My associate here from the local account management division has had to transfer your company's account to my division. I work for Special Credits, also referred to as SC, and our office is in Amsterdam, at our bank's headquarters. Although we are also just part of ABN Amro, it is not a good sign when a company has to deal with our division. After all, it means that the company is having serious financial problems. Unimeta has a credit running into the millions with our bank, and we prefer to lend money to healthy companies. This gives us a fair degree of certainty that these loans will also be repaid someday. We are no longer so sure about this when it comes to Unimeta. Your results have deteriorated rapidly, and after the reorganization, your capital has actually become insufficient."

Frank shifts in his chair. He is having trouble finding a comfortable position. Groeleken isn't finished.

"Starting today, we will be in contact with one another. Directly. I want to be kept informed of all the developments that have an effect on the company's results. The status of orders, investments, liquidity forecasts. Everything has to come across my desk. We have an entire department that keeps an eye on things behind the scenes, and which can help if necessary. That's the advantage of Special Credits; we can make decisions on the spot. Credit applications no longer have to go through the whole procedure to which you have become accustomed. It's a much nicer way to work, and it's often necessary in situations like this one. We are used to getting right to the point. I am not going to try to make it sound better than it is. Unimeta is alive, but on a drip, hooked up to the bank. We understand the situation the company is in. Your account manager has brought me completely up to speed about what has been going on in your company the last few years. And it's far from inconsequential."

Frank thinks fast. He doesn't let his irritation with the man's formal attitude show. This is not the time or place for that.

"So if I understand you correctly, Peter, we can just continue with what we have been doing, and the credit application for the coming season is otherwise approved?"

"That is correct. But then you have to make good on your promises. The costs will have to stay under control, sales can never be too high of course, and we want to see the expected positive financial effects of the reorganization. To put it simply, you will have to start making a profit again. Unimeta has to become a healthy company. That is your job and my concern."

"That's clear," Frank answers. He has the impression the man is finally starting to loosen up a little bit. "In that case, we will carry on, full steam ahead. I am convinced we are on the right track."

An hour later, Groeleken and his colleague drive out of the parking lot. Frank looks at Erwin. He is looking a bit pale, and takes a deep sigh.

"We will have to start up the production of Sombrero in China even sooner, Frank."

"I know, Erwin, but we have to be responsible about it. We have to be able to deliver to our customers on time, otherwise we'll never get such great orders again. A few more production runs in our own factory are unavoidable, even if we don't earn anything on them."

They walk together to Ruud Kuipers' office, where Ruud and Pet are going over the production schedules. Frank gives him the run-down on what happened during the meeting, and they talk about the consequences.

"From now on, the bank has the final word," Kuipers says. "That means we will have to make even more cuts in the organization. We have to bring costs down, and get sales up. Show them that we are in total control of the situation. If we don't, the bank's response and our future will be unpredictable."

From the management level to the work floor, everyone senses in their own way that there are no more excuses. The metal relaxers for the English market are produced in record time. In less than seven minutes, a finished, shrink-wrapped chair is standing next to the conveyor belt. The salesmen are also travelling everywhere, visiting customers and writing orders. In Germany, however, Unimeta still hasn't gotten all of its customers back. Several of them have closed their doors unconditionally, claiming they are satisfied with their current supplier. Little by little, they are succeeding in regaining their market share in America. After 9/11, they had to start all over again. That fall, Frank manages to sell a couple hundred thousand Euros worth of products on the other side of the pond, but he hasn't seen the real verve return that they had achieved before the attacks.

At Compex, the first Sombrero products come rolling off the assembly line in those last weeks of 2003. They have to pull out all the stops to do it, but they manage to arrange for half of the necessary production to be handled in China. After the lost 2003 season, 2004 just has to be the year they do a big about-face.

In the meantime, the engineers in Unimeta's R&D department work hard to hammer out new concepts and new products. Frank has been able to limit the dismissals in this department to one out of four employees; after all, they really need these people to supervise the outsourcing to Compex, but also because this department is the lifeblood of the company. They won't manage much longer with the old relaxers. They have to constantly look for innovative ideas. This department has definitely proven its worth in recent years. They had come up with fantastic, successful products, and now they are being secretive about an entirely new discovery. Even Kuipers doesn't want to reveal too much.

"Just wait a couple of months and you'll be surprised. If what we have come up with works, Unimeta will be saved."

Frank has learned that he shouldn't disrupt these geniuses at work, but he is incredibly curious.

In the meantime, he meets regularly with Peter Groeleken. Even after a few meetings, Frank still senses the official position coming from the other side of the table. That might just change if their results improve. Frank has no choice but to wait.

This year, the factory is closed between Christmas and New Year's. This way all the employees will use up their extra days off at the same time, which will also benefit efficiency. Frank takes advantage of the quiet during this period to finish his thesis on brand management in small- and medium-sized businesses. He sits in his office from early in the morning to late in the evening to work out all the details, without kids whining in the background or any disruptions from meetings or discussions at work. He makes good progress, and in early January, he can hand in his thesis. He had briefly considered writing it together with his supervising professor. The professor had offered this after Frank had turned in his first draft. This would mean the professor would be credited as co-author, but Frank had his pride. He would be the one doing all the work, and the professor would have something to show off with. The offer was actually more of a sign for Frank that the quality of the thesis he was working on was good, but once he had decided to decline the offer, the man's attitude towards him had suddenly turned a lot colder.

Frank had once looked into what he would need to do to turn his thesis into an official academic article, that he would then publish in an academic journal. During his research, he found the *Journal of Product and Brand Management*, the leading publication in the field of brand management in America. As he wrote his thesis, Frank took their criteria and preferences into account. After he had finished the article at the end of the Christmas holiday, he mailed it to America, anxious to see how it would be received. He had given the article the title, "Successful Brand Management in SMEs", and as a subtitle, "A new theory and practical hints". Mostly, he was feeling like a practical entrepreneur who was continuously struggling with how to build a strong brand with few resources.

He knows that the article will first be reviewed by two independent experts in this field, with his name hidden in order to guarantee maximum objectivity, a process that will take months. The most likely outcome is that it will either be considered unsuitable for publication, or it will first have to be adapted. Unfortunately, he doesn't have time to adapt it. The 2004 delivery season is just around the corner. He decides they'll just have to accept it the way it is now.

During the first weeks of 2004, in spite of all their efforts, not everything goes according to plan. In China, there are some delays in the production of the first Sombrero products, which means yet another extra production run at Unimeta. If they don't do this, customers will have to wait too long for their first chairs for the new season, and will cancel their orders. This will cost them profit margin, but they don't have a choice. Hopefully it will be a nice spring, weather-wise. This will mean they will get back orders, and they can compensate for the lost profits through higher sales.

One Thursday morning in February as Frank is sitting in his office working, Marion suddenly dashes past his doorway, headed for the factory. Less than two minutes later, the first-aid employee working in inside sales also runs past, heading in the same direction. Frank wonders what on earth could be going on. He quickly finishes a calculation, and just as he is getting up to go take a look, he sees Marion coming towards him with one of the Turkish production employees. His head is covered in blood, and his right eye is black and blue. She sits the man down in Frank's office, and gets him a glass of water. Frank realizes that it is Metlev Gorkan, a well-mannered middle-aged man who has been working in the relaxer production department for years.

"What in heaven's name has happened?" he asks. "Did you have an accident?"

"No," Metlev answers, his voice shaking. "Durhan."

"What do you mean, Durhan?"

"That Durhan hit me in the head with a metal pipe."

"With a metal pipe? You are kidding me. What on earth would make someone do that?"

"I don't know. He fell. A little pushing and shoving because he didn't want to write down my production quantities. Then he grabbed pipe from metal box and hit me on head."

Frank looks at Marion. Marion says that a first-aid employee is going to take Metlev to the emergency room at the hospital.

"We are going to get to the bottom of this, Metlev," Frank says. "First go get yourself checked out and make sure everything is okay. You might need stitches; it looks like you've got a pretty nasty gash on the side of your head."

He calls Pet, the manager of the metal production line in the factory, while Marion walks out with Gorkan.

"We're already on our way to your office," Pet says. "With Durhan."

Marion has just returned when Pet comes walking in with Guslin Durhan. He has also been working at Unimeta for at least five years; his job is to keep the production line going with the supply of raw materials. He must also report the production output to the department manager, but he is off today, of all days.

"Guslin, what is this I'm hearing?" Frank asks. "I was just sitting here with your co-worker, Gorkan. What on earth happened?"

"That Gorkan is crazy. He attacked me, pushed me to ground. I grabbed metal box and grab pipe to protect myself from that idiot. That pipe hit Gorkan in the head."

Now Frank is looking at Pet.

"It all happened in a split second, Frank," he says. "No one really saw what happened. I've already asked around."

"But Guslin, I just saw Gorkan here, in my office. He has a bad head injury and a swollen eye. Something like that doesn't happen by accident, does it?" Frank asks.

"I told you what happened. I had to do it. Otherwise he would have killed me or something," Guslin says.

Frank decides that both men will write down their version of the story and asks Pet if he can ask around again and make sure no one really saw anything.

"Guslin," he says, "we're going to get to the bottom of this. I think it would be a good idea for you to go home now, and come back to work on Monday. We can decide then how we are going to deal with this."

Durhan stands up and walks out of Frank's office without saying a word.

"This is just what we need," Frank sighs. "What are we supposed to do about this?"

He talks to Marion and Pet. They decide to bring in an experienced P&O

manager and to have them deal with the difficult situation.

"If everyone is going to start hitting each other on the head with pipes in the factory, there will be no end to this," Marion says.

No one has a response to this.

The next day, they manage to get a few verbal statements from co-workers from the relaxer department, but no one wants to put anything on paper. Frank suspects that everyone is afraid of Durhan. The P&O man recommends firing Durhan with immediate effect, to set an example for the others. Those two can't work together anymore anyway. On Friday afternoon, they get the necessary paperwork in order.

Frank uses that weekend to prepare the loan application for 2005. Things are not looking good.

10

SECOND REORGANIZATION

Spring has finally arrived; winter held on for a long time, but the time has now come. It's late March and an unseasonably warm 65°F, and everyone is heading out en masse into their gardens to rake the winter from their memories as fast as they can. At Unimeta, the phones have been ringing off the hook for weeks. Now that the weather has finally improved, it's like the consumers have all gone crazy at once. The mood swings 180 degrees from one day to the next, and everyone wants to get outside. They suddenly discover that their old patio furniture has been in need of replacement for a while, and the dealers are all contacting their suppliers with back orders. Unimeta's strength has always been its quick and flexible response in a situation like this. This is how they pull in extra sales.

However, in spite of the great weather, spirits at the company are low. The employees know that the delays in delivery from the production in China are coming at an extremely inconvenient time.

They are also aware that the management team is meeting regularly to discuss further cutbacks. Together with the company controller, Erwin, Frank is closely following the weekly sales and profit developments. Actually, Frank thinks, we should have made the move to China two years ago. But the world has changed so quickly, and this was hard to predict. They hardly have any room to manoeuvre with the existing cost structure and the many veteran employees. He has discussed the direction they have to take with the other members of the MT on a regular basis. They all agree that they have to switch from being a cumbersome production company to a slim "head-tail" business. This type of business means that the design and engineering activities are handled in the Netherlands, the production in low-wage countries, and then sales and marketing are brought back to the Netherlands again. This is easier said than done, however.

And then they have that man from Special Credits at the bank breathing down their neck every month. He literally wants to know everything, and asks them about every single detail. It has become nearly a part-time job for Erwin to make sure all the reporting is done perfectly, and Frank even spends one or two days a week to ensure all the communication goes smoothly. The pressure is clearly rising, and now and then Frank has to ask himself how long this will all continue to go well.

A couple weeks later, during an MT meeting, Frank drops the bombshell.

"I am sorry to say but the reorganization measures up to now are not going to cut it. We're going to have to make more cutbacks. We are heading towards a loss of over one million Euros, excluding the one-time reorganization costs."

Ruud and Pet are in shock. Erwin has known it for some time; after all, he's the one who did all the calculations.

"We will have to reorganize a second time, and will have to outsource our top brand, Preston, to China,' Frank says.

"But then we'll just be throwing ourselves to the wolves," Pet protests.

"That may very well be the case," Frank says, "but if we don't take action now, we will never get the financing approved. Either we really go for it and outsource all the production except the relaxers, or the bank will be closing the doors here soon. It's that clear-cut, in my opinion."

They look at each other. Outsourcing their flagship line Preston is not a very appealing idea. In doing so, they will truly be bringing all their technological knowledge to a Chinese production partner. No matter how iron-clad a contract is, it still doesn't feel right. This is a devil's dilemma for them, but at the same time, they don't really have a choice.

The new reorganization means that even more of their production personnel will have to be let go. They will have to make cuts in other departments all over again. From technical services to research and development, and from inside sales to human resources, they are all going to feel the pain. The technical heart of the R&D department, the lifeblood of the company, will also not escape this new wave of firings. Nothing and no one can be spared. It is a heavy blow when Frank realizes that Marion is also on the list.

It has also become impossible to retain Ellen, formerly known as Michel, at the company. She can no longer handle her original job as forklift driver and work on the assembly line for production. She is completely ignored by many of her co-workers who have the feeling that they are suffering because of a personal choice she made. Ellen started answering phones and working as a receptionist, but that isn't really working out either. Frank was originally happy with this solution as the problem had been eliminated, and it meant one less temporary worker. But every time the phone rings and she answers in her deep voice, "Good morning, Unimeta, Ellen speaking," the entire inside sales staff cringes.

One incident a week earlier was a complete embarrassment. The accountants were in Frank's office when they distinctly heard a woman wearing high heels walking in the door. Then when they heard a deep voice saying, "Gentlemen, here you go, your coffee," they all whipped around, shocked to find someone nearly six-foot-three standing behind them, in a short, shiny skirt, pantyhose and pumps. Ellen was heavily made up, and wearing bright red lipstick designed to draw attention away from her enormous Adam's apple. It took a great deal of effort on the men's part to keep a straight face, but their body language spoke volumes. Ellen will be one of the first people on the list; it's simply unavoidable.

Kuipers works out the plan further that spring to also outsource the production of the Preston line. They find a Chinese factory that specializes in the production of patio furniture for the higher segment. They also sign an extensive contract with this company to protect their intellectual property rights. Extra attention is paid to ensuring that all the specific know-how as well as the patents and model rights enjoy optimum protection. All the experience they had gained during the lawsuits in recent years and the partnership with Compex is definitely coming in handy now.

The engineers who are working on this don't yet realize that a few of them will soon be finding dismissal notices in their mailboxes. In essence, they are digging their own graves, which is particularly unsettling. Frank hasn't been sleeping well for weeks, but has no choice other than to keep going.

At the same time, he has to go through the entire procedure with the works council, the unions, and the UWV, the employee insurance organization. This is once again a frustrating and unending process, in which every single regulation has to be complied with. Even though being able to switch gears quickly is very necessary, the entire procedure will easily take a few months. In early June, Frank stands with a heavy heart for the second year in a row in the company cafeteria. He announces that they are once again being forced to reorganize. This time, 20 positions will be eliminated, and 16 jobs will be made redundant.

The hardest conversation is the one Frank has to have with Marion a few days later. He is really dreading it, but to his great relief and surprise, Marion quickly reassures him.

"I'm happy that I finally know what's going to happen," she says with tears in her eyes. "I was already afraid it would happen, and actually felt it coming. I guess you could call it female intuition. At least now I can start looking around for something else, and I'm happy that I have my HR diploma."

Frank thanks her for her understanding, and wishes her the best of luck in the future. She's going to have a hard enough time of it as it is. Marion already knows that she will be out of a job soon, yet she will still have to supervise the entire reorganization in the months to come. He has nothing but admiration for her practical attitude. He has lost over 10 pounds in the last two months, and knows that the worst is yet to come.

Just before the summer, Frank gets a letter at home from America, from the publisher of Journal of Product & Brand Management. He actually hadn't had very high hopes for the outcome, even though he had done his very best on the article. After all, he wasn't an experienced academic and had never published anything before. With slightly shaky hands, he opens the envelope. His eyes scan the text and in one fell swoop, his dark mood changes to absolute euphoria. He almost screams the news.

"They have accepted the article, and are going to publish it without me having to make one single change!"

His wife can only laugh at his sudden enthusiasm. Frank's eyes twinkle as he rereads the letter, but this time slowly and word for word.

"Yes, it's really there; I didn't imagine it," he says. "The article will be published next year, and they thank me for my contribution. Super. Finally something positive, after all the nightmares at the company."

He feels the adrenaline rushing through his veins, and is ready to take on the whole world again.

A few days later, the euphoria disappears again when an entirely different kind of letter arrives at Unimeta. Not from America this time, but from a law firm in Enschede. They represent Guslin, the Turkish employee who had hit his co-worker in the head with a metal pipe. Frank had actually completely forgotten about the incident; he thought the case was closed. They had arrived at a nice severance package arrangement with Guslin's lawyer, but now that silly Guslin had gone ahead and filed a lawsuit with the court anyway.

"And since he doesn't have two pennies to rub together, he gets a court-appointed attorney at the taxpayers' expense," Frank angrily tells Marion. "So we all end up paying for this, with our hard-earned money that we pay in taxes. And now we have to spend even more money, a lot of it, to pay an employment lawyer. There's no one I can send that bill to; we have to pay for it ourselves, even though we're penny pinching as it is here."

Frank is beside himself with anger about this kind of injustice.

"We actually have nothing to do with this. This guy hits Gorkan in the head with a pipe, and sues us at society's expense because he doesn't have anything left to lose. What kind of crazy country are we living in anyway?"

He doesn't have much time to worry about this anymore. He has to prepare for yet another meeting at the bank in Amsterdam.

Next week, it will be make-or-break time. Special Credits wants to know why Unimeta incurred a major loss again that year, in spite of the reorganization and outsourcing of production, and what management plans to do about it. Frank realizes that it is going to be an incredible struggle, and has been preparing his presentation for weeks, with the help of a few co-workers.

This is not just limited to the announcement that they're now going to start outsourcing Preston. He will also give a little sneak preview of a spectacular invention, one that they are counting on to rescue the company. Kuipers has kept his promise.

For over two years, the engineers have been working on the development of a new armrest for the relaxers for the English market. The result has been nothing short of revolutionary, and their research has shown that the invention is even patentable. The patent application process has been set in motion.

With this new armrest, Unimeta can increase sales in England by several million, and this is what Frank has to make clear to the managers in Amsterdam. He realizes that they will not survive with a new reorganization alone. They need heavier artillery to keep the company afloat.

On June 30, 2004, at exactly 10:00 in the morning, Frank arrives at the ABN Amro Bank headquarters in the Amsterdam southeast district. He takes a deep sigh, and looks at the external accountant, who has come with Frank to confirm the accuracy of the figures and to offer more clarity during the meeting about the financial consequences.

"Nervous?" the accountant asks.

"Not really nervous, mostly just a healthy level of stress," Frank answers. "I will fight to the damn end."

At that moment, the gentlemen of Special Credits walk in, shake hands with Frank and the accountant, and sit down at a large table. Frank carefully takes in his surroundings. It is a nice, neat room in an enormous building, but not excessively luxurious. The burgundy carpet looks thick, and would not have been his first choice. After coffee has been poured and the customary niceties have been exchanged, as the bank manager with authority here, Peter Groeleken begins.

"We have been very unpleasantly surprised by the results up to now at Unimeta, Mr. Krake."

Frank indicates that as far as that goes, he doesn't disagree with him. He asks if he may use 20 minutes of the time they have available to provide a more detailed explanation of the situation. "Might as well, while we're all sitting here," Groeleken says coolly, leaning back in his chair. Frank clears his throat and begins to present his argument. First, he explains that Unimeta targets three segments of the market. Preston is their high-end brand for the garden centers and patio furniture specialty stores. In this segment, Unimeta now has nearly 200 customers in the Netherlands, Belgium and Germany. Next, there's Sombrero for the middle segment, and these products are sold primarily to home-improvement stores and furniture chains throughout Europe. And lastly, there are the metal relaxers for the bottom segment of the market. This is Unimeta's bread-and-butter line, particularly with the home-improvement and supermarket channels in England.

"The production of the line for the middle segment, Sombrero, has now been outsourced to China," Frank explains. "We have had a four-month delay there because of the SARS outbreak, and all of the associated financial consequences. We have now worked out all the details of the plan to also have the production of the Preston collection outsourced to China. The entire production of the cushions will be handled in Poland. At the same time, we are undergoing a reorganization, which will bring the cost level way down, and this will have a positive effect on profitability. The margins will increase substantially as a result."

Groeleken frowns.

"And those dull old relaxers? I'm not hearing anything about these and you need financing for those, right?" he asks in a surly tone.

"We have developed a fantastic plan for that line," Frank says. He shows them a photo of the standard relaxer chair. "I'm familiar with that; that product has been around for 30 years," Groeleken says, disappointed.

"Exactly. And that is precisely the problem. This chair has reached the end of its product life cycle. The product is so hackneyed that no one is earning any money on it anymore. At the most, we recoup our material and wage costs with the sales of these, and that's it. We have to accept the orders for these ridiculous prices, since otherwise we wouldn't have any work for the permanent production staff and that would cost us even more. And now, our plan. With these standard chairs, you can adjust the chair back in seven different positions by lifting the armrest up about half an inch, and then using your weight to push the back downwards. At the same time, the footrest will come up, allowing you the comfort of lying nearly horizontally in the chair. This is why they love these chairs in England. We estimate the total market in the United Kingdom to easily be one million units. Unimeta supplies about one-fourth of this quantity each season. Our engineers have now discovered something that we expect to increase our sales to 350,000 to 400,000 units, and at better margins since we will be setting ourselves apart from the masses."

"That almost sounds too good to be true," Groeleken says.

"That was also my initial reaction. But according to all indications, this truly is accurate. We have shown a prototype to several customers after we naturally took care of all the legal aspects to protect the design first, since they immediately copy everything. The initial response has been overwhelming."

Frank pulls a prototype of the new armrest from his briefcase with a flourish.

"This is it; hot off the press."

Groeleken looks at him inquisitively, and even the accountant sitting next to Frank follows the scene with curious interest.

"I understand your confusion, but it really works," Frank says. "This is the new armrest. Instead of lifting the armrest up half an inch, two millimeters is enough to unlock the armrest and manoeuvre the back of the chair down. There, in the middle, are a bunch of miniscule partitions which enable you to adjust the chair in 28 positions instead of the standard seven."

"But no one will even use them all!" Groeleken barks, his voice resonating through the office.

"No," Frank answers, "but they don't have to. As long as it helps us sell the chairs. It's just like a bike with 21 speeds. You only use a couple of them, but consumers fall for it en masse. No one will ask for a partial refund because they only use four or five. That's how it will work with our chairs, too. And the positive effect on the financial results is tremendous. Here, have a look."

The accountant slides the forecast for 2005 across the table to the men from the bank. Groeleken's mouth falls open in surprise; obviously, he wasn't expecting this. The figures show that the loss of 1.5 million Euros for 2004 will be transformed into a profit of a few hundred thousand for the 2005 season.

"Well, okay," Groeleken says, "if you know how to live up to this promise, that changes everything, of course. We had already sort of given up hope here at the bank, but this offers good prospects. Do you really think that this new armrest will help you achieve a spectacular growth in sales?"

"Definitely," Frank answers. "In combination with the outsourcing of production and the downsizing in the factory, this will work. Everything indicates that we will also get new customers with this new feature."

"I am going to review it all here at the bank, and coordinate things further," Groeleken says. "But if we do decide to finance the 2005 season, then this will be subject to strict criteria. To start with, we will want to monitor the situation each month to make sure you are in fact achieving these higher sales you have forecast. It will also be very desirable for the company to acquire new capital. Your capital is negative right now. And that is highly undesirable. You will have to find a new shareholder who is willing to make a substantial cash injection to recapitalize the company. I suggest that you get the KPMG accountants involved in this, and that you, Mr. Krake, play a leading role in these efforts. And finally, if we decide to continue with you at all, then you will really have to adhere to this forecast in 2005. You have to make a profit, because if you don't, we will definitely not extend any new credit."

He looks around the conference room. A silence has fallen that no one seems willing to break. After a few seconds that seem more like minutes, Frank decides to speak.

"Your point of view is clear, Mr. Groeleken," he says formally. "I am going to make an appointment with KPMG immediately. It will probably be a project that lasts a few months, particularly now that the vacation period is upon us. When can I expect the confirmation of what we discussed here, and the proposed criteria?"

"This week," is the response from the other side of the table.

As Frank walks out of the conference room, he is already shifting gears in his head. It will have to be a real tour de force, one he will literally have to pull out all the stops to achieve. Lost deep in thought, he drives the hour and a half back to Twente.

11

LOOKING FOR MONEY

Groeleken's message hit hard, but came in loud and clear that morning. They have to recapitalize. In simple terms, this means they have to look for a new source of cash for the company. Frank has to find someone, a person or a company, who is interested in making a major investment in Unimeta, and they had already calculated that this figure had to be at least one million. Right before the vacation, he is sitting at a table at a specialized division of KPMG in Arnhem. These men know exactly what they have to do; it's their daily work, and they do it without emotion. Frank has no choice but to accept their sky-high hourly rates and posh way of speaking. This is all part of the world he has ended up in.

The men draw up an information memo designed to convince potential investors of the golden opportunities Unimeta can offer. After the vacation, a few interested parties come forward. Everyone must naturally be given the royal treatment when they visit the company. They are shown a presentation on the big screen, see the showroom and are given the grand tour of the entire factory. Each visit easily takes up a half day of Frank's time. During a few of these visits, when the guests are just oozing arrogance and pedantry, Frank can't help himself. This only gets worse when the men discuss what they view as inferior production employees in their stuck-up tone.

Frank decides to bring them to the professional coating set-up. He would love nothing more than to hang them up by their collars on a coating hook, whiz them through the blue powder lane, and then bake them in the oven at nearly 400°F. Of course he gives up on that primitive idea, but he does decide to test their knowledge. He tells them that the metal frames are epilated before they go into the first disinfecting tank, after which the powder coating is applied and that after being run through the oven, they are double-shebanged. The men nod in agreement, as if they completely understand what he's talking about. Frank winks at the manager of the coating department, who has trouble suppressing laughter.

There are also very serious visitors, who are genuinely interested in potentially investing in the company. They are pampered and spoiled by Frank and the men from KPMG. During these months, Frank regularly has lunch in establishments where he never would have had the time or money to go.

In the meantime, the bank is being increasingly more difficult about approving the payments that have to be made. Their credit line is limited, and the bills go unpaid for too long. The first worried suppliers have already called and are threatening to stop supplying them. Production has had to be stopped twice because they run out of steel tubes for the frames.

Unimeta has no choice but to submit an official notification of its inability to pay to the Tax and Customs Authority and the pension fund in September. It's all really touch and go at this point. Apparently the bank now first wants certainty that they will make good on their sales promises and find investors. By playing the game this way, they are shifting all the pressure to Unimeta, and the management team in particular.

The situation internally is explosive on some points, particularly now that the works council is getting involved. The employees want to know what is going on, and the last thing they need now is upheaval. Frank postpones a scheduled meeting; he wants to be absolutely sure of a few things himself first. He's just not so sure what he should tell them. If he explains that the situation is precarious and bankruptcy is not inconceivable, that won't do the general level of motivation any good. Not when there is finally a light at the end of the tunnel.

In early October, two private equity firms express their willingness to provide the necessary capital. One of them is from the area, and the other is from Amsterdam. The experts from KPMG have sent the investment proposals to Groeleken, who is considering the proposals. He is still waiting for the outcome of a special meeting that will be held in mid-October with a mysterious private investor. One of the KPMG managers, Justus, is responsible for this contact. The mystery man is adamant about coming by on a Saturday afternoon, and only wants to meet with Frank. Frank will do whatever he has to to save the company, and doesn't have a problem with this demand.

In addition to resolving the financial issues, they also have to introduce the new relaxer, particularly in England. Together with Hugh, Frank visits all the potential English customers during the fall. Every other week, he flies to England for yet another presentation, and it's going amazingly well. The results have surpassed expectations considerably. All Unimeta's existing customers are wholeheartedly on board, and are sending them great orders for 2005. Homebase, Unimeta's biggest customer, orders 120,000 relaxers for the upcoming season. Asda, a subsidiary of the American retail giant Walmart, wants around 100,000. Morrisons, Makro, the English chain Co-op and CWS also all send fantastic orders. The safety relaxer appears to be a resounding success, particularly since they are able to sell them at a higher price. For the first time in many years, Unimeta has achieved a healthy margin on every product it has sold.

Full of confidence, Frank goes to see the large retail chain Focus-DIA in England. He has never been able to supply one of the two companies that merged the year before. They weren't even willing to schedule a meeting with him, but when their buyer visited their booth in Cologne, he was so impressed that he invited Frank to come see him. After all, the advertising agency had created such a perfect presentation for the exhibition. The beautiful display really showed that there was no safer way to relax than in the Unimeta chairs.

To make this even clearer, the display featured a photo of a toddler in a chair, with her hand on the armrest. The armrest had a round silver sticker with the text "28 positions", surrounded by the words "safe relaxing system".

After Frank and Hugh receive a warm welcome, the people at Focus-DIA quickly get to the point. They had heard that the Trading Standards, the English consumer product inspection service, was tightening up the rules and that in the near future, chairs will have to satisfy the new European standard, EN-581-1 for outdoor furniture. This means eliminating any risk that people using these chairs will get their fingers pinched in the armrests.

Frank doesn't even dare look at Hugh. Their plan is working. Frank explains again that Unimeta's new relaxer is in full compliance with the new regulations since the armrest can only be raised two millimeters. This means people can never get their fingers caught in the armrest, not even small children. This is why it's such a fantastic concept, aside from the 28 positions in which the chair can be adjusted of course.

The men already know all this, but then the cat comes out of the bag. They are in the market for 100,000 relaxers, for delivery during the 2005 season. They are considering placing the order with Unimeta, but only if they can buy the chairs for the same price as they pay for the relaxers from Unimeta's biggest competitor, the Spanish company Tabervall, Focus' preferred supplier for many years. Their standard price is two pounds less than Unimeta's. Frank stands his ground, and bluffs.

"Sorry, but that's not realistic. Can you imagine how high the research and marketing costs are that go into a new product like this? And that's not even including all the investments and complicated dies. Besides, you can easily increase the recommended retail price in the stores, as long as you stay under the 20-pound mark."

The men from Focus-DIA do not seem cheered at all by this news, and an interminable discussion follows. After an hour and a half, Hugh and Frank finally leave the office, a contract worth millions in sales in their briefcases. They got the exact price they wanted.

Frank now realizes how comfortable his colleagues at the competition, Hartman, always must have felt when the market for plastic patio furniture was at its peak. It was a question of distribution back then, since production couldn't keep up with demand. This resulted in a considerable degree of arrogance at the company. Whereas Unimeta always had to slave away and had both feet firmly planted on the ground as a result, their neighbors over at Hartman were the market leader, and behaved accordingly. Frank makes up his mind that no matter how successful they may become with the new relaxers, he vows to never have this attitude.

Once in the car, Hugh blows off some steam, his face fire-engine red.

"I thought you had lost your mind. Risking losing an order like that because you don't want to lower the price. What a great bluff! And they've even agreed to pay it. Unbelievable."

"But Hugh," Frank replies, "we don't have a choice, do we? We would be crazy to give them their way in the negotiations. This is what the company has been working so hard for and aiming to achieve for years now. We have finally achieved our goal. For the first time, we have a unique selling point for this 30-year-old product that will help us beat everyone and everything. There isn't a competitor out there right now that can come close. The prototypes we sent to Trading Standards a couple months ago and the explanation you gave during those meetings are now paying off. Obviously a process has been set in motion that is working in our favor. That's why I didn't dare look at you when they brought it up."

Frank is proud of the results they've achieved. If he adds it all up, this means a growth in sales for next year from over 200,000 to nearly half a million relaxers, much more than he had promised Groeleken. This just has to mean the company's rescue. In the airplane, Frank drinks a beer to this success.

The following Saturday afternoon, Frank sets a thermos of coffee down in the company showroom. He looks out the window. His own car is the only one in the otherwise empty parking lot. He has prepared everything meticulously. The company presentation is ready to be projected via the beamer, and the Preston gems in particular are gleaming beautifully under the spotlights in the showroom.

The KPMG manager did not want to mention the name of his impending visitor. All he told Frank was when he should be ready, and that his guest would be coming from far away. Apparently, this was a man for whom an investment of a couple million was chicken feed, someone ranked high in the *Quote 500* list of the richest Dutch people.

Frank is still a bit nervous, and very curious about who it is he will be welcoming in a little while. If he shows up, that is; it's almost one o'clock. He calls the KPMG manager again.

"They're on their way," he informs Frank.

"They?" Frank asks. "I thought it was just one man who was coming?"

"That's true, but he's bringing his son and his son's fiancée. Just be patient; I'll speak to you later."

Frank hangs up and sighs deeply. What's with all the secretiveness?

When he looks out the showroom window again at around two o'clock, he sees a large Bentley drive up. He can tell from the license plate that the car's from Monaco. Someone gets out of the car, and with agonizingly slow motions, puts on a cap. The driver then opens the door on the passenger's side. A large, somewhat stocky man with gray hair gets out, dressed in a navy-blue suit and a white shirt with a red tie. The driver helps him put on his blazer. All the while, the man has his cell phone pressed to his ear.

A young man and young woman get out of the back seat, both fashionably dressed and no older than their early twenties.

The group starts making their way to the front door. Frank briefly doubts whether or not he should open the door. He doesn't know what to expect from all this, and isn't actually really in the mood for it anymore. His curiosity and the financial necessity ultimately win out over his emotions. He puts on the friendliest face he can, opens the door and welcomes them.

"Please come in. You've had a long drive. No problems on the road, I hope?"

Before anyone has the chance to answer, Frank introduces himself. The young man and woman only introduce themselves by their first names, Stef and Lietske. The older man is still on the phone, shakes Frank's hand, but doesn't say anything.

"Dad's otherwise occupied right now," Stef says.

Frank walks ahead of them, up the stairs and heads towards the showroom on the second floor. He hears the man citing figures in English, first 24 and then later 26 million dollars. From the sound of it, he's talking about a Falcon, but beyond that Frank is none the wiser. When he pours them all coffee a bit later, the older gentleman also sits down at the table. He asks Frank if he's from the area.

"Born and raised in this region, sir. And you? I could see from the license plate that you've come here all the way from Monaco."

"From Brasschaat, in Belgium, that's where I live, but I also have a pied-à-terre in Monaco, hence the license plate. We're a little later than planned because we went to Almelo first, close to where I was born. I practised as a GP there for years, and wanted to show the young people here a few of the historical and nostalgic spots from my younger years."

Now Frank is really confused. Although he didn't come away from the last few stressful years completely unscathed, he's pretty sure he didn't schedule a check-up with a GP. And he certainly didn't make an appointment with a doctor who lives in Belgium and drives around in a car from Monaco.

The man goes on to say he earned a lot of money with dollar options and investments, and that Justus was an old friend of his who gives him tips now and then when he comes across something interesting. That's why he had come to him about Unimeta, and the man's interest was piqued.

"Actually, these young people here are the ones who have to learn the business and ask the questions. I'll be listening in, but have to make a few calls about a plane I'm thinking about buying."

Now Frank gets it. This man is just negotiating about the purchase of a private jet. Frank realizes that he really has to pull out all the stops now. He can't let this big fish get away.

They spend the entire afternoon ploughing through the information memo that the accountant drew up. The two representatives of the younger generation ask a wide variety of questions. The young woman is an upstanding Belgian still studying economics, but is already being asked to help make decisions on a deal involving millions. That is unique, to say the least, Frank thinks, but he is not going to rack his brains any longer about the strange situation and focuses on presenting the company as the flavor of the month. He's really on a roll now. When he gets to the new safety relaxer and the confirmed orders for 500,000 chairs for 2005, he notices that the three people on the other side of the table visibly brighten up and also become enthusiastic. After all the questions have been answered, he gives them a tour of the factory.

By the time they get back to the showroom, it's almost seven in the evening. The older man asks if they can have ten minutes to confer among themselves. Frank leaves them behind in the showroom. He calls his wife to tell her not to ask any questions for now, and that he might be home late. When Frank is called back in a few moments later, the man tells him that he is very interested in investing, and that they are going to get to work on it first thing on Monday. Frank swallows a sigh of relief inaudible to his visitors.

"Would you like to be my guest for a meal," he asks, "before you make that long drive back to Belgium?"

They take him up on his offer, and are soon making their way to a good restaurant.

As Frank drives home at eleven that evening, he calls Justus, in spite of the late hour. It was actually very pleasant, and the three people from Brasschaat had gone on and on about their day-to-day business activities. Between the main course and dessert, the deal for the purchase of the Falcon was also settled; for a mere 26.5 million, the jet was his. The only thing is, Frank still doesn't know who "he" is. He comes right out and asks Justus.

"Who in heaven's name did you send to me? What kind of people are they? While they were at the office, the guy buys a private jet and they say they want to buy Unimeta. They will be sending an offer on Monday. A GP from Almelo with houses in Monaco and Belgium has a chauffeur to drive him around in a Bentley, and invests in patio furniture. I thought there was no such thing as fairytales."

Justus starts laughing.

"When you get home, go online. The man you just spent most of the day with is named Louis Reijtenbagh. His nickname is Baby Doc."

The following week is relatively calm. Much too calm for Frank's liking actually, since they need to have clarity very soon. Including the unusual visitor from the past weekend, the meter is currently at three interested parties, but Frank is not negotiating with them personally; the bank is the one running the show. While he waits for results, they are slowly getting up to their necks in trouble. In spite of all of Unimeta's promises, they are still unable to pay raw materials suppliers and transportation companies regularly, and these people are furious. On Friday, production is shut down temporarily. Once again, they have run out of tubes for the production of frames. Kuipers pulls out all the stops and manages to convince a Greek supplier to send a new shipment, but the truck won't be arriving until Monday. When it finally arrives, the entire company breathes a heavy sigh of relief. This will get them through another couple of days of production.

Frank is having difficulty with his role. On the one hand, he is struggling with the bank and is constantly feeling the uncertainty. On the other, he can't let this insecurity show when he walks through the factory and talks to the worried employees. The situation is becoming more serious every day, and Frank is becoming more and more doubtful. He can't help but wonder what on earth they're doing up there in Amsterdam. Each time he calls Groeleken, he tells him they're working on it. Probably working on Unimeta's demise instead of a rescue plan, Frank thinks.

The only sign of life he's getting is from some fool or other who has been foisted off on them. A youngster, no older than 25, comes from Amsterdam to Enschede to check the orders they've received. Frank has to show him all the orders they have received, and this guy makes copies of them at the office. Everything they have communicated proves to be accurate. They have even received an extra order worth a couple hundred thousand from Denmark, yet another one for the safety relaxers. The new product is a huge hit.

Frank still hasn't received word from the bank when it comes time to pay the salaries for the month. He's gone nearly completely crazy from the uncertainty, and the feeling of being so dependent is eating at him. After an intense discussion with an experienced lawyer he has hired, Frank arrives at an unusually rigorous decision. He will send Groeleken a letter by registered mail in which he announces that they are filing a petition with the court for a moratorium on payments. He doesn't know if he will actually go ahead with this if it comes down to it, but he can worry about that later. This way he will at least be able to send a message and dig in his heels when it comes to that black box over there in the capital city. He has to do it. If they can't pay the salaries on time, he may as well just shut the doors for good. The motivation of all these people who have had to endure so much lately will have dropped down below zero. And good luck trying to keep the ship afloat after that.

Whether it was his concise, to-the-point letter or there were other factors involved, Frank will never know, but two days later Groeleken finally calls him back, and he has good news.

"Mr. Krake, I know it's taken a while, but we've finally figured it out."

"It was about time, Peter. We are at the end of our rope here."

Frank intentionally uses the informal form of address again; it's the only way he can make it clear that he won't allow anyone to walk all over him.

"We're going to do it ourselves," Groeleken says.

"What do you mean, you're going to do it yourselves?" Frank asks. With all the stress, he's not immediately sure what exactly Groeleken means.

"Well, we have had a good look at the offers from the three parties, and have held a few meetings. We have come to realize that the story you told us here about the new armrest wasn't just some tall tale. We are surprised and extremely pleased at what a commercial success it has been. Our compliments to you. This is why we have worked out a plan where we will take on the financing for the coming season. This is naturally subject to strict conditions, since we are in essence providing your company with risk capital. One of these is that a consulting firm will be assisting you during the upcoming season. The projected profit must also be realized, and we will be requiring permanent monitoring of the collateral. This means that we will have all the property appraised and the accounts receivable will be managed via our colleagues in the factoring division."

Frank is only listening; he doesn't say anything else.

"Congratulations, Mr. Krake," Groeleken says cheerfully. "You can keep the business going. The payments will resume once all the paperwork has been signed. A courier is on his way to Enschede with all the documents."

Frank can't get manage more than "thanks and I'll speak to you soon" in response. He is dumbstruck, and gives himself a moment to let the latest developments really sink in. It has been a poker game, but he can live with the outcome. The cold sweats and the incredible mental pressure he has had to live with aren't important right now. They can pay everyone's salary, and that's all that matters. He breathes a tremendous sigh of relief, and calls the management team together to share the good news with them.

12

PANIC IN CHINA

It's December, and cold and bleak in Twente; the first snow of the year is on the ground. Indoors, the production employees are working up a sweat; production is running at full capacity.

The factory has never been this busy at this time of year. They are making a record number of relaxers, 500,000. It's going gangbusters; after all the problems they have been through, the employees are more motivated than ever. In the cafeteria, Frank has summarized the main points of the game he had to play with the bank, and the good outcome. This is met with loud cheers. For the first time in ages, everything seems to be going their way, and even the prices of fabric have gone down. This means they will finally have extra earnings on the purchasing side.

The outsourcing of Preston to China is on schedule. Naturally, they learned their lesson from all the problems they had had with the outsourcing of the Sombrero collection the year before. The specialized Chinese factory is accustomed to working at a higher level of quality. The engineers there are trained better, and that makes the entire process a lot easier.

The production of the Sombrero products in China got started on time, and Compex shipped the first containers in November, under the supervision of Unimeta's own quality control staff. This year, Compex has to produce just under five million dollars' worth of Sombrero products and rocking couches, but in spite of the fact that they started on time, they're still behind schedule. Shipments transporting half a million dollars' worth of products have been sent, but they should have contained double that figure.

Frank is in daily contact with his quality control staff there by phone and e-mail. Flora is also doing everything she can to ensure things run smoothly, and to apply pressure if necessary.

For the first time in a long time, the management team has the feeling that they have a firm grip on the situation. If this coming season continues to go according to plan, they will take a giant step forward in the transition from a cumbersome production company to a leaner "head-tail" business. It was a close call, but they're still here, even though Frank is having to contend with plenty of other problems.

In mid-December, the backlog in the delivery of the Sombrero collection has become unacceptably high. Each time they agree on a new shipping schedule, it is already moot before the ink on the documents has dried. They turn up the heat on Compex as high as they can. Patio furniture is shipped to Unimeta in fits and starts, but they never seem to manage to get any real momentum going. The staff works at full throttle between Christmas and New Year's to make sure that the massive flow of orders will be able to be filled as efficiently as possible, but the delays in delivery at Compex are only getting worse.

Since they can't afford to have any more slip-ups, Frank calls Ryan Tong, but he has no explanation about what's causing the extra delays. He won't come straight to the point, and this is not exactly reassuring for Frank. He finally makes a bold decision.

"I'm going to come see you, Ryan. And I'm not leaving until I have absolute clarity about what is going on, and the production is back on schedule. I'll bring my sleeping bag with me and sleep at the factory; make sure there's room for me."

Ryan tells him it's a bad idea for Frank, the director of one of their larger customers, to spend the night at the factory.

"I don't give a damn," Frank growls into the telephone. "They'll just have to get used to the idea."

On January 2, Frank is on the plane, headed for South China. After getting off his flight in Hong Kong, he arrives the next day in PingDi Town, the gray industrial city where the Compex factory is located. He walks into Ryan's office with a big smile on his face. The director of Compex stares at him, his eyes wide. Frank sets his rolled-up sleeping bag down on Ryan's desk with a flourish, and sits in the chair across from him.

"So, here I am, as promised, Ryan," he says. "And I'm staying here until our products come rolling off the assembly line according to plan. Did you arrange somewhere for me to sleep?"

Ryan tries again to convince him that he would be better off in a hotel, but he can see from the determination in Frank's eyes that the Dutchman is dead serious. He grabs his phone and starts making calls. Finally, after five minutes, he has news.

"It's taken care of. They're getting ready a room that is usually reserved for one of the production managers. Due to a death in the family, he's gone back home to Taiwan for two weeks. We're getting clean bedding for you, but don't expect too much."

Frank doesn't care. After his adventures in Newfoundland, he really doesn't mind where he spends the night, as long as he sleeps in a clean, dry bed. The rooms form a long row at the side of the factory, on the edge of the factory property. There are about 30 of them, with a makeshift cafeteria and small lounge in between. The entire management personnel at the factory is Taiwanese and lives there, just like the Unimeta employees who are staying at the factory on a long-term basis. The thousands of factory workers sleep in giant towers, apartments where four men share a small room. Frank is just happy that his plan has worked. He leaves his things in Ryan's office, and they walk through the factory together.

Together with the Unimeta team, Frank spends the next few days checking order after order to make sure they are sticking to the schedule. He notices that Flora is extremely well-informed. She starts flailing about wildly each time they try to pull the wool over her eyes, something that happens at least several times a day. There is an order for rocking couches on the production schedule that have to be loaded three days later. They go looking for the frames in the production department, but these haven't even been manufactured yet. Frank's experience has taught him that this is cutting it really close for manufacturing the products and loading them, but the production manager swears up and down that it's not a problem.

Frank has also learned a thing or two about promises like this. In China, when someone claims something isn't a problem, then all his senses go into full alert mode. Nine times out of ten, it turns out to be a major problem in fact, and that is also the case this time. Flora asks the production manager involved where the metal tubes are for these rocking couches. After searching for ten minutes in vain, the truth finally comes out; they haven't been delivered by the supplier yet. But then the manager acts as if he wasn't aware of this. This is how it goes every day, and it is exhausting.

After a little less than a week of hard work, they have finally nailed down a realistic schedule. An evaluation follows with Ryan who has given his full cooperation to creating clarity and achieving the production goals. However, Frank is still not entirely sure why everything requires such a monumental effort. He has the feeling he's still not getting to the bottom of the situation, but this may just be the way the Chinese think, and their general mentality. This wouldn't be the first time there is a major gap between Western and Eastern logic.

Nonetheless, Frank doesn't entirely trust it all, and on the last evening before his return to the Netherlands, he calls Flora, Raymond and GertJan together.

"Guys, we have to be ready for anything," he says, "taking our precarious financial situation in the Netherlands into account. Right now, we are at the complete mercy of Compex. We really have no alternative. It would still be a good idea to get prototypes of the most important products we have manufactured here out of the factory."

"But we can't do that!" the strictly religious GertJan shouts in response. "They check everything at the gate."

"I didn't say we should steal them," Frank replies. "Just make a list and write the name of a customer at the top. We will say that we are furnishing these samples to a customer, sending them from here, and that we will pay for the prototypes. We don't have anywhere near all the models in Enschede anymore, and it will take at least a month before we get them all over there."

GertJan's face lights up. Flora knows of a small warehouse just outside the city where they can rent space. Before Frank boards the flight to return home, he goes through everything once more in detail with his co-workers there. He is already looking forward to sleeping in his own bed again.

Unfortunately the schedule that they took great pains to put together is outdated again after only a week. After two weeks, Compex is already half a million dollars behind. It's enough to drive you crazy.

By late January, only half of the total package of orders worth five million has been shipped. Frank prepares for yet another trip to South China. The only thing he can do is continue to put the maximum amount of pressure on them to prevent the backlog from getting any worse. What makes it even more frustrating is the fact that Unimeta's own production is running at full capacity. They break one production record after the other, and the mood in the company hasn't been this good in a long time.

In early February, Frank returns to Compex, this time accompanied by Mike, an American who lives in Florida and who has been in charge of Unimeta's sales in the U.S. for around two years now.

Frank hasn't given up hope yet that things will turn around in America, and Mike has managed to build a nice foundation with the Preston products. Mike will now have the opportunity to see for himself that they are also capable of producing the right level of quality for the Sombrero products in China, so that he will be able to speak from experience in his attempts to convince customers in the U.S. Frank hopes this will be what they need to revive their past successes.

Slowly but surely, businesses in America are willing to start taking risks again, and are once again becoming more open to new products. At the last trade show, Frank succeeded in selling Sombrero products to Frontgate. Since Mike's wife was having a baby, he couldn't come to Europe to be there himself, and didn't initially believe it. When Frank e-mailed the orders to him a few weeks later, he was convinced. He was determined to sell these on a national scale.

Frank and Mike run into each other in the hotel in Chang An, half an hour's drive from Compex. They both check in, and then drink a beer in the hotel bar. After they have caught up, Mike asks Frank when they are finally going to ship the Sombrero products for Frontgate. Frank starts laughing.

"Are you that desperate for your commission, Mike?"

Now it's Mike's turn to smile.

"Is it that obvious? No, I just really want to move forward with Frontgate, and we should have shipped last month, that's why I ask."

"I know, Mike, and we're going to see it all with our own eyes tomorrow."

In good spirits, they walk into the Compex showroom the next day to see the new prototypes for the2006 season. They have only just sat down to a cup of coffee when Ryan Tong comes walking in. Cheerful as ever, he greets his guests.

"Have you seen my sleeping bag yet, Ryan? I would like to sleep in the same room again this time," Frank says.

Ryan's face clouds over, and he stammers that the room is occupied again by his colleague who has returned from Taiwan. Frank can't hold it in any longer and starts roaring with laughter. Ryan realizes that he's fallen for it hook, line and sinker, and laughs cheerfully along with him. He travels frequently to America and can take a joke. Frank would be better off not trying to pull a stunt like that with a true-blue Chinese; they tend to view jokes like this as a loss of face. Once they have finished laughing, Ryan grows serious.

"Frank, if your Dutch colleagues would be so kind as to show Mike the production area, you and I can catch up with my father-in-law, Steve."

Frank looks at Ryan and wonders if he's trying to pull his leg now. Ryan walks out ahead of him, and Frank tells Mike to enjoy the tour. They walk into the imposing office of Steve Lin, not only the owner of the factory, but also the father of four charming daughters, the oldest of whom, Jessica, is married to Ryan. This fact automatically means that he has an employment commitment at Compex. Jessica has decorated Steve's office tastefully by Taiwanese standards, but Steve doesn't really seem to be interested in this right now. When Frank walks in with Ryan, Steve is staring at a painting with a blank expression on his face. He turns towards Frank and looks at him with this vacant expression. Frank is taken aback, but tries not to let it show.

"We are in huge financial trouble, Frank," he says, starting the conversation. "Things were all pretty tight as it was, but in the last few months, the prices of steel have risen substantially. We hadn't counted on this happening. We failed to cover our steel requirements on the futures market. Now we have to pay top dollar, even though all our calculations take much lower prices into account. We have been to see a couple of large American customers like Walmart, Kmart and Target to see if we could raise our prices to them, but they don't have any sympathy for our situation. To make things worse, there's the loan we have to repay to the Bank of China this week. We don't have enough money to do that right now. I don't know if we'll be able to get the funds together in time either. I'm doing everything I can, but I can't predict the outcome. I'm so very sorry to have gotten you involved in this situation."

It's a good thing Frank is sitting in a solid chair. He feels the blood drain from his head, and has a sudden attack of dizziness. He can't seem to speak, and gives his left arm a hard pinch.

"But Steve," he finally manages, "you all have incredibly high sales and nearly all the major American brands are your customers, right?"

"That's actually the problem right now, Frank. That's why everything's happening so fast; the numbers involved are huge. If we have to sacrifice a couple of dollars on each chair, you have to multiply that by a couple hundred thousand units. Our sales are nearly 250 million dollars, but we barely earn a cent. And now we have to invest even more. Unimeta owes us half a million dollars for the shipments from the last few weeks. Will you please transfer that amount straight away? Every bit coming in now will help to reduce our debt at the bank, and increase our chances of getting a new loan."

Frank nods and says he'll take care of it. After all, Compex is entitled to this money.

All this time, Ryan has remained on the sidelines. He is so ashamed of the situation they have ended up in. Frank now realizes how dire it must be. Things have to get really bad before a Taiwanese or Chinese will come clean about something like this to an outsider. And not just any outsider, but a foreigner, a Westerner at that. It means a tremendous loss of face and in Asian culture, this is the worst thing that can happen to someone.

"We'll know more tomorrow," Steve says, walking to the door. Frank repeats that he will make sure the payment is made, and leaves the office alone. Ryan remains behind with his father-in-law, disillusioned.

Frank makes a mad dash for his co-workers in their own office behind the production warehouse. Seeing immediately that something's wrong, Flora makes him a cup of Chinese tea. Once GertJan and Raymond have been drummed up, Frank comes right to the point.

"I won't beat around the bush everyone. I have just found out why there were so many delays. I could just kick myself for not realizing it sooner. After all, we have just been through the same thing ourselves."

He sees three pairs of inquisitive eyes looking his way. They don't understand any of it.

"They have huge financial problems here at Compex," Frank explains. "If they don't make a deadline, this is quite simply because the parts haven't been delivered by a supplier, because Compex hasn't paid their bill. No one can say anything about the future of the company. Even Steve Lin doesn't know what will happen. He's wearing sackcloth and ashes."

Suddenly, he realizes something.

"Flora, what's going on with those prototypes of the most important products? The ones we were supposed to get out of the factory?"

"Half of them are in that space we rented. We're working hard on the rest."

Frank breathes a sigh of relief. And now for the rest of them. Flora grabs the list and shows them samples of all the products, of which more than 1000 are produced at Compex, that have been taken out of the company. They go through the list together, and Raymond points out a few that they still definitely have to get prototypes of. Flora and GertJan are aware of about eight products that are in production at this time. They agree that they will do everything they can the next morning to secure prototypes of as many products from the list as possible.

Frank impresses upon his co-workers the importance of not talking to anyone at the office in the Netherlands about the extremely difficult situation in China. This can only lead to panic. If anyone at the bank catches wind of this somehow, they're done for. Frank goes and sits down at a desk some distance from the group. His mind is spinning at top speed.

A million thoughts race through his mind, including all sorts of possible scenarios. All he can do is look at the ceiling and shake his head. This is just unbelievable. Now, of all times, when they think they have finally gotten back on track. This is the kind of thing you don't even see in movies, but it's really happening here. And he's part of it.

Frank has never heard of a company in China actually filing for bankruptcy before. Granted, they haven't reached that point yet, but he has no idea if this is even possible, and if so, what will happen next. The company is partly state-owned. The land the factories are built on can never fall into the hands of the factory owner; it will always belong to the state. That's all he knows. Everything else is one giant question mark for him, even though the consequences can be devastating. He can already see the blood draining from Groeleken's face if he has to give him this news in Amsterdam.

The next morning, he's got a clearer view of the situation. His co-workers are focusing on the missing samples, and he's reviewing the collection for 2006 with Mike. After all, this is something that must continue. Frank brought Mike up-to-date on the situation the evening before, and Mike could do nothing but sit there with his mouth open and listen, before finally wishing Frank the best of luck.

This morning, Frank asked Flora to schedule an appointment at Shin

Crest, another one of Unimeta's suppliers. They already outsource the production of patio furniture to this company, a couple hundred thousand worth of models that deviate slightly from their own. The company is located an hour away from Compex, in QingXi, and is also run by Taiwanese. Frank has been doing business with Shin Crest for about five years. The orders have never been in the millions since not all of their products are suitable for the European market. The design is too American for Europe.

Frank is able to get an appointment to meet with the CEO, Tony Liou, this same evening. Jack will also be there, an extremely experienced Taiwanese with roots in the Taiwanese patio furniture sector. Unimeta has been working with him for about 10 years, and in addition to his talent for building relationships, Jack is also a first-class entertainer. Customers who experience an evening of karaoke in China never forget him. Aside from having a great singing voice, he really knows how to set a fantastic mood, and speaks fluent English.

Together with Jack, Frank drives to QingXi in the early evening. Flora doesn't join them since a Chinese among all these Taiwanese would not be a good idea. They go through a huge gate to an incredibly large factory complex that could easily contain 20 football fields. The guard at the gate jumps to attention and salutes the visitors. Not long afterward, the car stops at an entrance framed by marble pillars. A female employee waits for them there, and Jack and Frank follow her to the elevator.

Frank notices that she presses the button for the sixth floor. He normally never goes higher than the fifth floor here, where their enormous showroom is. The sixth floor is the board of directors' wing.

Tony is waiting for them in his enormous office, not at his desk, but sitting on a huge, classic-looking, black leather sofa with mahogany accents. Tony shakes their hands cordially, and gestures for them to take a seat in the two large armchairs across from the sofa. He only speaks a few words of English. Jack had told Frank that Tony was completely up to speed on what was going on at Compex. After all, the Taiwanese community is a small one in that sense, Jack had explained with a meaningful grin. As the director of a competing factory, Tony may very well know more about the situation at Compex than Frank does.

A large metal platter filled with tiny holes stands on the coffee table in front of them, tiny teacups around the edge. A complex rack stands in the middle of the platter. Tony starts pouring water into a large metal pot. After a while, once the water has started boiling, he uses it to rinse the cups. He then pours water through a sieve filled with dried tea leaves. The entire process easily takes half an hour, but when it's over, Frank is slurping a small cup of real home-brewed Taiwanese tea, making just as much noise as his Taiwanese business partners.

Oddly enough, Tony doesn't say a word about the situation at Compex. After an hour of this, when the tea is practically coming out of Frank's ears, Tony finally leaves to go to the bathroom.

"Jack," Frank whispers, "shouldn't we explain what's going on and ask this head honcho here if he is willing and capable of manufacturing these 60 products for us, as quickly as possible?"

Jack looks at Frank with a sneer. "Is that what you want, Frank?"

"Definitely," Frank replies, "and for the long term, of course."

"In that case, I can give you one piece of advice," Jack says. "Just go along with his small talk and don't mention anything else, and you'll have the best shot at success."

Frank holds his tongue when Tony returns and continues with the tea ceremony. An hour later, he finally puts an end to the ritual. He pours boiling water over the used cups, and lays them next to the teapot with wooden tongs. Frank is almost dying from the anticipation, but sticks it out and follows Jack's advice. Tony stands up and shakes Frank's hand firmly. He's not very tall; the top of his head doesn't even come up to Frank's chin. He looks Frank right in the eyes and while still gripping his hand, says one thing, in his best English.

"I will help you. Everything will be fine."

They walk out the door and follow the employee back to the elevator. Before they have even gotten to the car, Frank can't help himself.

"What the heck is going on? This is driving me crazy. We sit around wasting our time, drinking tea."

Jack only laughs and mumbles the same thing Tony had said.

"Everything will be fine."

Jack's phone rings a little while later. It's Steve Lin; it's almost as if he sensed where they had just been. He asks them to come to his office. Frank takes a deep sigh, and wonders what kind of circus he has ended up in this time.

It's 10:30 in the evening by the time they drive onto the Compex factory parking lot.

"We have a rescue plan," Steve says. "Tomorrow afternoon at 2:00, we will have a big meeting with our creditors, in a hotel nearby. My son-in-law Ryan will run the meeting. We are going to submit a proposal to them all in which they would convert their debt into shares in the company. We can't pay anything right now. This way we'll be turning their debt into a small piece of ownership in the company. We will restore their trust, and we will be true partners trying to achieve the same goals."

Frank quickly looks at Jack, and can't decide if Steve is crazy or a genius. He just doesn't know what to think anymore. It definitely can't hurt; production is now at a standstill in various parts of the factory since the suppliers have refused to deliver until their bills are paid.

Steve now turns to Frank.

"We would very much appreciate it if you, an important customer, would put in a good word for us tomorrow."

Frank looks away and starts thinking at warp speed. It's actually not such a crazy idea, and they sure don't have very much left to lose. He will have to put a professional speech down on paper first. Jack will have to stand next to him to translate what he says since the majority of the suppliers don't speak English.

"I'll do what I can Steve, but you will have to speed things up now and manufacture our products. I have seen that the factory is full of raw materials and semi-finished products for us. These will have to be assembled and shipped tomorrow. Can I count on you to get your priorities straight to do that?"

Steve nods, barely visibly. They shake hands on it.

The next day, the lobby at the five-star hotel is jam-packed with people, and the noise is deafening. Numbering around one hundred, the suppliers invited to the meeting have all brought several employees and business partners with them. At five minutes to two, Ryan Tong appears and says something to them in Chinese. The chatter suddenly rises a few more decibels, but after a few minutes the noise stops.

"What did he say?" Frank asks.

"Only one person per company is allowed inside, otherwise there won't be enough room in there," Jack says. "They are now having huge arguments about which one of them gets to go in."

The door to the large room opens, and part of the mob makes their way inside. After a lot of pushing and shoving for the best spots, everyone has found a seat and Ryan speaks. He shows very few signs of his usual bravado, projecting shyness and speaking softly instead. He starts to explain the plan that they have put together at Compex. Jack is sitting next to Frank, and is translating what Ryan is saying into English in a barely audible whisper.

After half an hour, official-looking forms covered in seals are handed out to the audience. Frank recognizes the Compex logo in a seal on a document his neighbor is holding. A middle-aged man has now taken the floor. He is the only one of all those present wearing a suit. Frank recognizes him as Compex's corporate lawyer; he has seen him several times in Steve's office over the last few days. Oddly enough, Steve is not here, and Frank asks Jack if he knows why.

"It would be too emotional for him," Jack answers.

The speaker's exact words are not entirely clear to Frank since Jack's whispered translation is unintelligible. Emotions start running high, and a few suppliers are no longer speaking, but shouting. Chinese have the strange habit of turning as red as a lobster from so much excitement. Frank slouches down a bit in his chair and pays careful attention to what's going on around him. He really regrets not bringing his camera with him to the meeting. This scene is one you can't describe to anyone who wasn't there; you have to see it with your own eyes. One Chinese after the other blows their top. They seem furious. Everyone is shouting over everyone else, but amazingly enough, it doesn't come to blows or physical violence.

Ryan has now shrunk down behind the table, and drops of perspiration run down the sides of his face. Frank feels sorry for him. His father-in-law has left him in the lurch to take the full rap for this. Great, Frank thinks, you marry the oldest daughter of the CEO of a factory, and you get this misery for free.

In the meantime, Jack is telling him that all the excitement is being caused by the fact that the lawyer is telling the group that they actually only have two choices. Either everyone agrees to convert Compex's debt to share capital, according to a certain allocation clause, or no one will see another red cent from Compex and the company will go bankrupt. The suppliers are given three days to think about it. If even one supplier refuses to go along with it, the latter scenario will take effect.

"Talk about negotiations with the gloves off," Frank says to Jack.

Jack isn't listening, and instead grabs Frank by the arm and pushes him to the front of the room. Before he realizes what's happening, he's standing up in front of the group. This is a quite a different situation than addressing the Unimeta staff in the company cafeteria. He clears his throat and proceeds. Frank stops now and then after a few sentences to give Jack the chance to translate.

The crux of his speech is about how the factory is full of raw materials and semi-finished goods for Unimeta. These had been delivered over the past few weeks by the suppliers present in the room. If they would just give Compex the chance to actually produce all the outstanding orders and deliver them, then Unimeta would ultimately pay Compex for these, an amount in excess of one million dollars. After all, there are over 60 containers still to be shipped. This will in turn enable Compex to pay its suppliers. Frank then tells them that Unimeta transferred half a million dollars just yesterday, for the shipments the week before that. He does this to show that Unimeta is creditworthy enough, and is serious about continuing its business with Compex.

He quickly realizes he shouldn't have said that. Immediately after Jack translates this, the room erupts in uproar once again. The group's faces are getting so red that it looks like they might explode. The atmosphere is very tense and emotionally charged. In spite of the chaos, Frank doesn't feel as if he's in any danger at all. He only hopes that his story can contribute to helping Compex out of the trouble it's in.

It is now obvious that Compex has told its suppliers that the money is all gone and that no one can be paid. Half a million from Unimeta naturally doesn't correlate with this story, but he had no way of knowing this. Slowly but surely, things calm down in the room. His entire speech doesn't last longer than 20 minutes. Jack and Frank return to their seats and Ryan takes the floor again. After a few minutes, he stands up, a sign that the meeting is over.

"What did he say there at the end, Jack?" Frank asks.

"Ryan asked everyone to think carefully about the proposal, and said that the best results are always achieved when people work together as partners. He also made a reference to your story. He said that Compex has more loyal customers like you, and he firmly believes these are people they can rely on and whom they can't leave out in the cold. Finally, he wished everyone much wisdom in their decisions."

"Well, they'll definitely need it."

On Monday morning, Frank gets a call from Raymond at 8:00 as he's eating breakfast in his hotel. Today, he has an appointment to visit the other factory that makes the Preston products for Unimeta.

"Complete chaos and confusion here at Compex," Raymond tells him.

"And a good morning to you too," Frank says, in an attempt to be light-hearted, but Raymond is dead serious.

"Really Frank, you wouldn't believe your eyes. There is not a single Taiwanese left here. When we got to breakfast this morning, the Chinese cook had this really bewildered look on his face. The entire Taiwanese management has left. I looked in the sleeping quarters next to ours, and the suitcases are all gone; the chickens have flown the coop."

"What about Ryan and Steve? Where are they?"

"They're gone too. The rumor is that they all took off last night because they were afraid of the Chinese government's reaction when they find out that everything is about to go wrong here."

Frank realizes that Raymond could be right about this. After all, they are Taiwanese, and politically, that's a very precarious position here. If another large factory like this goes under and leaves the many Chinese suppliers with huge debts, he can imagine why they would have packed their bags.

In China, you can end up in prison for a long time for this type of thing.

He talks to Raymond and Flora, and says that they should pack all their personal belongings and get out of there quickly, leave the factory property and go to the hotel.

"There's nothing more I can do right now at Compex anyway," he says. "I'm going to go to my appointment now and I'll be back around 12:00. The outsourcing of Preston has to go on."

When they see one another again later that afternoon, it sounds like they just barely made it out of there on time.

"The police cordoned off the entire factory," Raymond tells him. "There are policemen guarding all the exits, and no one is allowed in or out anymore. We were able to grab our stuff and a few things out of our office. The guard at the gate told the policemen that we were foreign customers who had nothing to do with the bankruptcy. After a few phone calls, they finally let us through. I was able to sneak the new chair out, the one we worked on the development of for so long. It was still in the R&D department, but I just grabbed it and put it in the car. We were able to load 17 containers yesterday and get them to the port."

Frank compliments Raymond on being so alert and on top of everything, but is already a few steps ahead of this in his mind. He tries to foresee what the consequences of these events will be for Unimeta.

13

SOS CONTINGENCY PLAN

The next day, Frank is on the plane back to Amsterdam. Marion made the arrangements from the Netherlands to ensure he could get back as soon as possible. Frank uses the 12 hours he has on the flight to write up an emergency plan. Although he considers every possible scenario in the plan, he keeps coming to the same conclusion. Three main concepts will have to be worked out in further detail, running parallel to one another. It is obvious that the production at Shin Crest will have to be started up as soon as possible. They have to pull out all the stops and do whatever is necessary. At the same time, together with the relevant export managers, he will have to visit all the customers that have ordered products for which the delivery has been delayed. Last but not least, he can't get out of scheduling a meeting at Groeleken's office. He will have to find a way to make it clear to the ABN Amro managers that there have been developments they were powerless over, and which they must now respond to as quickly and flexibly as they can. These managers mustn't get the impression that he doesn't have the situation under control. He is at the helm, overseeing the playing field. This is an attitude he not only has to project, but also make good on.

Once back in the Netherlands, he quickly makes the phone call to the bank. Groeleken immediately sees the seriousness of the situation, and says that Frank can come see him two days later.

For the past few months, Frank has had to tolerate consultants looking over his shoulder. Fortunately these people are not annoying, and are more or less the eyes and ears of the bank at Unimeta. He is being forced to work with these men, and after a while, finds that he actually gets along well with them. They really are just doing their job, and can quickly see that the company really is doing everything it can to make sure they achieve the goals that have been forecast.

Max Epping, the CEO and owner of the consulting firm, is driving to the ABN Amro head office with Frank. He is in somewhat of a panic after hearing about everything that is going on in China. As far as this goes, Frank can't expect too much support. After all, this would be impossible; Max has never been to China.

The same goes for Groeleken.

"Hi Peter, I'm back. Just got back from China," Frank says after they have been escorted to the right office by an assistant. Groeleken is sitting at the conference table with a worried look on his face.

"Good morning, Frank. That sure must have been stressful."

Frank realizes that this is the first time Groeleken calls him by his first name. This galvanizes him in his intention to face the situation with the requisite amount of bluff and flair. They obviously are the ones who need him now, instead of the other way around. This may no longer be the case in a few months, but for now, Frank is the only one who can keep this ship afloat, and prevent the bank from suffering considerable damage.

He starts telling them about his adventures of the past week, a story which Groeleken and his co-workers listen to with bated breath. Max shifts nervously in his chair now and then, but stops when Frank shoots him a quick, piercing look. The story about the room full of Chinese creditors in particular is one that intrigues the men no end.

Frank slides the English translation of the letter containing Compex's proposal for its creditors to them across the table. When he then outlines his action plan to them, they only nod in response. Realizing he is in control now, he brings his story to a conclusion.

"In summary, what it boils down to is that we are going to meet our sales and profit targets, but with about a two-month delay. They are rushing to start production at Shin Crest right now. I will also be paying a visit to all the important customers in the next two weeks. I am sure that they won't have a problem with us delivering a bit later, given the unusual circumstances. And at the end of the season, we will simply achieve the forecast goal of a quarter of a million Euros' profit."

He tells this story with so much bravado that Groeleken nods in agreement and asks him if they, the bank, can do anything to help.

"Perhaps from one of our offices in China?"

"All you have to do is give us the time and opportunity to do our job, that's all," Frank replies.

He knows that it is a realistic scenario, but at the same time, an optimistic one. Particularly the part about the customers who won't have a problem with the late deliveries is pure bluff. Over the next two weeks, he will have to put on an incredible road show to manage it all, but he sees this as a challenge.

After getting the green light from Groeleken, the two engineers fly to China to supervise the start-up of production at Shin Crest. Flora calls him with good news.

"Over the last few days I've noticed that the way the Taiwanese here in China pass the ball to each other is actually not such a disadvantage for us. Compex had more than 20 suppliers for our products, the majority of which also supply Shin Crest. In other words, they were already doing business with each other, know each other and realize that the relationship with Compex is really over. Many of them were in the room when you gave that impressive but actually pretty hopeless speech. They did realize that as a customer, Unimeta really couldn't do anything about it. Now they can start supplying their products again via Shin Crest. This will help them earn back part of their investment in the molds for the various components. Over the past few days, GertJan and I have visited most of the suppliers and have obtained enough commitments from them. Luckily I was able to save all the binders and folders with technical drawings, lists of parts and purchasing information from our office in Compex. Shin Crest has all that information now, and has started to work on it all."

Frank breathes a sigh of relief. He can go on his travels with confidence now. His first trip is planned for right after the weekend. He's going to see three customers in England who will not be amused.

"Hugh, hey buddy, how are you?"

His reunion with Hugh on Monday morning is a very happy one; the two men get along famously. Thanks to the fantastic results they've seen with the new safety relaxer, Hugh is in very high spirits. He works primarily on a commission basis, and can already see his ship coming in. Not even the delay in the shipment of the Sombrero products from China is able to spoil his mood. Although it only represents a limited part of his sales, it is a growing segment and will be important in the future.

Together with Link Communication, an advertising agency in London that specializes in guerilla marketing, Frank works on a campaign to also draw consumers' attention to the safety relaxer. This morning, he, Hugh and two creative geniuses from the agency brainstorm about all sorts of amusing, eye-catching campaigns that aren't overly expensive.

Frank isn't able to fully concentrate; he's preoccupied with their appointment at Homebase this afternoon. He has to deliver the news that products representing a couple hundred thousand in sales will be delivered two months later than originally planned. They won't be very happy about this. For them it will mean postponing sales and profits from the first to the second quarter.

By the time the meeting with the advertising agency ends, they have pared down the dozens of ideas presented and have settled on two concrete campaigns. Given their limited budget, they have decided to market the product in the nine largest English cities. Frank had already come up with one idea for setting them apart from all the relaxers that can be hazardous for users' fingers: the front of every armrest will come standard with a silver recessed sticker. This sticker will be strategically placed so it catches shoppers' eyes when they stand in front of the chair in the store, and where their fingers rest when they sit in the chair. He has called this sticker "the silver bullet".

They design the campaign around the theme "Look for the Silver Bullet". In late March, exactly 100 silver bullets will be hidden somewhere in every one of these nine cities. To prevent them from getting lost or going unnoticed, they will be adhered to a card containing information. They will be everywhere and nowhere, in phone booths, doorways, on a table in the library and even on the sidewalk on a street in a busy shopping area. Anyone finding these cards can trade them in at the nearest Makro, Homebase or Focus-DIA store for an original safety relaxer. This will generate a huge wave of free publicity.

Students will handle the distribution, and will also play a starring role in the second campaign idea. In April, two attractive couples will take off their clothes in a prominent location in the middle of the city. Wearing nothing but swimwear, they will sit in one of the new safety relaxers, in front of a couple of large banners. This will naturally attract a lot of attention in the middle of a city. Professional photographers will shoot this amusing campaign. Accompanied by an appealing text, the photos will be sent to over 2000 newspapers, free local papers, and magazines.

Frank is really enthusiastic, and his mood only gets better when he receives nothing but sympathetic, positive reactions from his biggest English customers in the days that follow. Even the publicly traded company Homebase agrees to give him a two-month grace period. The subsequent reactions from customers in Denmark, Germany and Switzerland are no different. It is only the smaller customers, the specialty stores and garden centers, that don't show as much sympathy and start cancelling a few small orders left and right. Although this is a pity, it's not an outright catastrophe.

Things don't go quite as well with Frontgate. The furniture is already in the catalog, but won't be delivered for another two months. This is of course hard to explain. With dread in the pit of his stomach, Frank gets in a taxi at the Cincinnati airport. The taxi drives him to a hotel where he experiences déjà vu. Mike comes walking towards him in the lobby, only this time he's clearly less enthusiastic than he was the last time. It was only two weeks ago that they met each other like this in the hotel lobby in China, even though it seems like months ago.

Mike has arranged for them to have dinner that evening with Ron Solstein. After a refreshing shower, they drive to the crab restaurant where they have reservations. Frank actually can't even think about food, since the possible reaction from Frontgate is sitting in his stomach like a rock. It wouldn't surprise him if they cancelled their orders.

"What are these crazy stories I'm hearing about China?" Ron asks after a hearty handshake. In adding, "Did you personally shut that factory down in China?" he breaks the ice. Frank is able to laugh hard at this, and jumps right in. He describes the events of the last few weeks in living color. Ron shakes his head a few times, and at others, bursts out laughing.

"Don't you worry, Frank," he says during dinner. "We're going to come up with a solution. We are going to send every customer ordering a chaise lounge from us a letter, telling them that the delivery might take longer because the product has been such an overwhelming success. They will all receive a hurricane light as our gift and to make the wait more pleasant. These lights will only cost us two dollars if we buy them in China, and customers always respond so well to free stuff. When they hear that the product they have ordered is such a big seller, this will be confirmation for them that they have made the right choice. Believe me, they won't mind waiting a little while." Frank listens intently to this explanation, and breathes an inaudible sigh of relief. This was a much more positive reaction than he ever would have imagined.

Ron won't be joining them the next day as he has been promoted again and now has "Commercial Director" printed on his Frontgate business cards. This comes with all sorts of other obligations which mean he has to take even more distance from purchasing activities.

"Mary will be doing the honors. I'll be sure to whisper the right information in her ear."

The next day, Mike and Frank even walk out the door of the Frontgate headquarters with an additional order worth no less than a hundred thousand dollars in their hands. Ron did an excellent job on the preliminary work. The woman in purchasing is super sweet and completely understands the situation. Frank is determined to never get so nervous and worried again about things he has no control over.

When Mike asks him how things are going in China, Frank tells him that they are still having a few problems.

"Production is getting started. Shin Crest is being really helpful, and we are right on schedule. That's not the problem. It's the containers from Compex that have already been shipped that are causing all the problems. During the weekend they went bankrupt, we were able to load another 17 containers, but it took a major effort. Still, it was a little less than four hundred thousand in business. These containers were all stopped by the Chinese customs authorities in the port of Yantian.

They are being held under embargo there because the Chinese authorities know the value these containers represent. They want to see money from us because Compex still owes them a lot of money. Kuipers is negotiating with them now, but it's taking forever. We don't mind paying for the containers because we need these products and our customers are waiting for them. We would have had to pay Compex otherwise. We can't get an iron-clad guarantee that the goods will be released after we have paid, and that is a criterion."

"Sure, of course," Mike says.

"Have you heard what happened with that director you met there Mike, Steve Lin?"

"No, tell me."

"He took off to California. He apparently has a U.S. passport, in case of emergency. Well, this was an emergency. Remember he wasn't there that Saturday with those hundred or so angry Chinese? That's because he was already on the plane, headed for America."

Mike stares at him, his eyes wide.

"With that half million you transferred, I'm assuming."

"That could have been the case, but he wasn't such a bad person. He transferred that money to a friend of his, a textile supplier in the area, instructing him to pay back wages to the thousands of Compex employees. This supplier contacted the employees the next day, and every single one of them got what they were entitled to."

"What a story, Frank," Mike sighs. "It's a snake pit, I tell you, that's what it is."

After nearly three weeks of constant travelling and visiting customers, Frank sits down to take stock of everything. Luckily he discovers that the damage isn't nearly as bad as he thought. Almost everyone understands the situation, and hardly anyone cancels their orders. They are still on schedule at Shin Crest. Tony has made good on all his promises. It looks like Unimeta is on its way back up.

14

STORM CLOUDS

It's chilly and rainy, and much too cold for the time of year. It's already the end of March, and the temperature stubbornly refuses to rise. Frank immerses himself in the report that the consulting firm has written on the bank's instructions. Although he had helped them prepare it, he's still surprised by the positive tone of the report. There had been times that he believed that the bank would only be using the consulting firm as the messenger, the bearer of bad news. Nothing could be farther from the truth. In fact, their recommendation is to give him time to work out all the plans. This will help make Unimeta profitable once again, a hurdle they have taken.

Groeleken has thawed somewhat, and comes to the factory personally to discuss the report. He has a pile of paperwork with him, and announces that ABN Amro will be making a credit limit of 20 million available to them. A record high in Unimeta's history, this credit is made up of different components, including a new mortgage on the company buildings. An absolute criterion is that they must ultimately earn a profit. This is their very last chance.

"We will ask the NTAB to draw up an appraisal," Groeleken adds hurriedly.

"The NTA who, Peter?" Frank asks.

"The NTAB, the Dutch appraisal and consultancy organization. It's standard in these types of cases. When we extend a credit line of this size, as a bank, we want to know the exact type of securities we can fall back on. We have to know precisely what the company buildings are worth. The same

153

applies to the machines and equipment. We also take a really good look at the inventory. Mind you, we don't do this ourselves, as the bank; we hire licensed appraisers for this. That's why."

"So we'll be having even more strangers walking around here," Frank tries. "We already have those people from the consulting firm here, and they literally give me the third degree all day long. They want to know everything."

"Then at least we know they're doing their job well, just the way I asked them to."

Frank will have to be satisfied with that for now.

"Finally," Groeleken says, "I have the surety contract with me, in duplicate. You have to sign it and so does your wife."

Frank looks at the official document and starts to laugh.

"A surety of 100,000? 100,000 Euros? For what? As the bank, you're the ones who can control whether or not you continue to provide financing, and you're hanging a 100,000-Euro millstone around my neck, without me having any way of influencing the decision? I don't think so, Mr. Groeleken."

Groeleken can see that Frank is serious.

"No surety, no credit," he says, bouncing the ball back over the net. He is obviously an old hand at this game.

"As the bank, we have to be sure that the CEO and manager are fully cooperating at all times in order to do the most they can for the company."

"For the company? For you, the bank, you must mean."

The mood changes dramatically.

"Mr. Krake, listen very carefully," Groeleken says. "In addition to CEO, you are also a 30% shareholder in this company. This comes with obligations, including to us as the financier. By providing financing, we are taking the risk this year, but we want a maximum commitment from the CEO in return. This is completely normal."

"The decision to continue financing was your own choice. After a great deal of effort, I was able to find three parties who were willing to take over the financing. And now you put me on the spot like this? I'll go over the documents with my legal advisor and let you know."

"No problem," Groeleken says, "but remember that we will not approve any payments until the underlying paperwork is in order. That's why it would be better for you to just sign them."

This feels like pure blackmail to Frank. As tempted as he is to pull

Groeleken over the table by his necktie right now, he also knows that this won't help the company any. He swallows a couple times and asks Erwin to answer the remaining questions about balance sheet items and depreciation.

As Groeleken is once again on his merry way back to his tower in Amsterdam, Frank calls Ronald van Gurp, the lawyer who had supervised the reorganizations at Unimeta. He gives Frank the name of a colleague, Wim Haafkes, who specializes in this area and has experience as a bankruptcy trustee, which means he's very familiar with this game, but from the other side of the table. They make an appointment for later that week.

In the meantime, the Chinese authorities have taken back out of the port all the containers that Compex shipped during the days leading up to the bankruptcy. The container shipping companies want their big steel boxes back. They need to be filled with goods that will be sailing back and forth on ships travelling to Europe and back, not just sitting there in the port. They are unloaded at the closed factory building at Compex. Kuipers has gone back to China and wants to make another attempt, with Raymond and Flora's help, to sort out the saleable products and buy them back from the Chinese authorities. After all, they have no use for them.

Once back at the sealed factory, the chaos is complete. In addition to the 17 containers destined for Unimeta, there are another 40 or so destined for other customers that have also been unloaded there. "Unloaded" is putting it nicely. "Dumped" would be a better description of what Kuipers finds in the forwarding warehouse. It's an incredible mess. Everything has just been tossed onto one big pile, and the products are all jumbled together. Packaging has been damaged, and metal parts are protruding from the boxes. It will be a major task to pick out the products that are still usable from this mess.

After a lot of deliberation and discussions with customers who want their products as soon as possible, they make an offer, 60% of the original value. Kuipers and Flora have to drive to a government building near the closed factory. Once again, the Chinese want Unimeta to pay first before they will allow products to be transported. They still don't get a guarantee that they will get the right documents and forms that will enable them to export the products. This means that they will run the risk of being out nearly 200,000 dollars, and may not even be able to get the containers out of the country.

"Unacceptable," Frank announces, when he gets the news over the phone.

"We don't have any other choice; the customers will have to wait until the new production is ready at Shin Crest. It's a shame, but that's the way it is."

And with that, the Compex case is finally closed.

It is now early April, and it's still cold and bleak outside. The mercury hasn't even risen above 50°F, and the spring seems farther away than ever. Oddly enough, these weather conditions actually offer good prospects for the success of the second campaign for the safety relaxers in England. The first one was a huge hit. In all nine cities, hiding the hundred cards with the silver bullet attracted a great deal of attention in the media, in newspapers and on a few local television stations. Hundreds of consumers in each city are able to share their experiences with everyone about the new relaxer they received for free.

Since it's still so cold, the new campaign with the scantily clad students will attract even more attention. Attractive models in swimming trunks and bikinis on a new relaxer in all the major downtown areas in England! The advertising agency updates Hugh and Frank each day on the campaign's progress. The response has been overwhelming. Articles appear repeatedly in all the local newspapers, and even the nationally distributed Sun prints a large photo of the four models sitting on safety relaxers in downtown Manchester. The campaigns from that week alone generate a media value of around 300,000 British pounds, and they've managed this with a budget of only 20,000.

It is a resounding success, but Frank has other things on his mind. During his first meeting with Haafkes, he makes no secret of his disgust with the deceitful contract that the bank wants him to sign.

"This just can't be true, Wim. If I don't sign, they'll cut us off. They've already started doing this as it is. I'm hardly able to get any payments out. We're heading in the same direction as last year, suppliers complaining that if we don't watch out, they won't supply us anymore. That would be disastrous for the factory; all the trust we have built up will be gone. My wife almost had a heart attack when she saw the amount."

"I can imagine, but this is how these things work. You really don't have much choice. On the other hand, if you just cooperate and do your job the best you can each day, then the bank really won't be that bad. I see this on a regular basis, and as long as you do your thing in a constructive manner, no bank will call in your surety. The amounts tied up in receivables, inventory and good progress are many times higher. What they care about is that you protect these interests the best you can; that 100,000 is peanuts to them."

Frank realizes that he is out of options, and will have to sign the surety contract. Holding in his anger, he signs the document. Three young children, a substantial mortgage, and now this millstone.

The ship transporting the first 15 containers from China is rapidly approaching Rotterdam. This represents the first wave of production from the Shin Crest factory. The company has worked miracles, and Tony Liou is the great miracle worker. He has turned out to be a man of few words but great deeds. Granted, he has had the help of all the Unimeta employees in China, but still. Within a mere two months of Compex's bankruptcy, he had managed to get the first products shipped. This would normally require six months of preparation, but it is only early May, and they are already working on the production for the last containers in China, shipments that will arrive a month later in Europe.

It is still cold outside; spring just doesn't seem to want to spring. They even get sleet on Easter weekend, which later turns to rain from a completely overcast sky, and the sun is nowhere to be found. Customers are complaining left and right about the slow sales. Consumers seem to be staying away from patio furniture stores in droves.

Jasper is responsible for all the logistics in the inside sales department. He books the containers on the ships, and processes all the documents. As the ship gets close to the port of Rotterdam, he makes agreements with the customers about delivery schedules. They had initially hired him via a temporary employment agency, but Frank was happy to give him a permanent contract two years ago. This same Jasper now walks into Frank's office with a dismayed look on his face.

"They don't want them," he says.

"They don't want what?" Frank acts, unsuspecting.

"The containers that are now arriving."

"What do you mean? We have agreements with them about that, don't we? The customers know that the products will be arriving later."

"Yes, but now I'm not getting approval to deliver the shipments. They want me to call back next week."

A week later, it is still cold. The next wave of 20 containers is about to arrive at the port in Rotterdam. Frank holds an emergency meeting at

Unimeta. There are six of them sitting in his office, and in addition to Jasper and three salesmen, Erwin is also in attendance. Jasper tells them that his latest round of calls hasn't produced results. Even the customers who have placed the orders that are in the new shipment of containers are holding off. He's dejected.

Frank discusses it with the salesmen, deciding which of them will approach which customers, and the strategy they will take. He has had enough commitments, but in practice, this doesn't appear to be worth much. With a list in their hands, the salesmen get to work.

"This is the final blow, Frank," Erwin says when they've left. "This will cost us the business. We have nearly one million in sales in those containers, orders that we really have to invoice in order to stay on the right side of the bottom line. In addition to these containers from China, we also have dozens of containers for CWS in England sitting in the port. They don't want these shipped until the weather has improved for a longer period of time. There are at least another 200,000 sitting in those containers. To make matters worse, we're selling hardly anything to the garden centers in the Netherlands. The starting inventory for the Preston collection was shipped to our customers in February and March, but with this crappy weather, no one has placed any new orders. Production keeps making Preston chairs and tables. The warehouse is packed to the rafters here."

"Time for Plan B," Frank says.

At the end of the month, the salesmen have been to see all their customers, and Frank has even gone with them on the visits to the six largest of these. Unfortunately, it didn't do much good; the same old story everywhere they went. No room, the warehouse is full, the weather is terrible, the bank account is empty, no customers in the store. It's driving them crazy. After all, no matter what they do or how hard they work, there's nothing they can do about the weather.

Spring has still not really gotten started. The sky is gloomy and gray. The managers from the consulting firm are in a total panic. Erwin and Frank urge them to calm down. They tell them it won't be long before the sun is shining again and the patio chairs are selling like hotcakes, but they are doing it more and more against their better judgment. When by June the temperature still hasn't broken the 70 degree mark, the season is over. It's too late; it's hopeless. None of the customers will accept the containers now. Next season, they'll be the first to order, they say. This doesn't do Unimeta any good right now.

The people from the NTAB have been able to do their job without interruptions all this time. They have examined every machine and desk chair, but mostly all the products in inventory, in meticulous detail and estimated the value. The building has also been reappraised. Over five million Euros, the report said, two million more than the book value. Hopefully that will give them some breathing room. The CEO of the NTAB, Pieter de Wit, is definitely not an annoying person, but it is his job to take up a lot of their time, particularly Frank and Erwin's time. At the same time as all this is going on, they are still hard at work on Plan B. There are also meetings with the various credit insurance companies almost every week. They want to know how things are going at Unimeta so that they can determine whether or not the suppliers will be able to get credit. Up until now, that has all gone well. After Frank's wife also signed the surety contract, which took a great deal of effort, the bank starts paying the bills again, and reasonably on time. It all still involves some jostling, but at least things are still moving.

Several months before that, Erwin, Frank and the men from the consulting firm had had a meeting, during which they were completely open with the credit insurance companies. This really worked in their favor, and they were given all the necessary credit limits without a problem. However, now these organizations also want monthly updates and to see figures. This comes at a particularly bad time given the poor sales performance. They are walking a very thin tightrope, in every sense. Every movement in the wrong direction can be punished mercilessly.

During these months, Frank is completely exhausted when he comes home in the evening. His three children barely notice. The youngest is now four and is often asleep by the time Frank gets home. With a little luck, he still sees the two oldest, albeit briefly. It is hard to muster the energy he needs to horse around with them, and tease them like he loves to do.

Luckily, his wife is incredibly understanding about the situation. She just keeps in mind that it's all only temporary. Besides, they've grown accustomed to not being able to spend a lot of time together. Still, it gnaws at him.

15

END GAME

The letter slides through Frank's fingers. This does not bode well. In the letter, Groeleken says that he wants to call an emergency meeting on July 4th, and that the situation is extremely worrisome. Frank could have told him that himself. They are about two million Euros behind on the forecast sales, and 500,000 behind on the planned financial results; a 200,000 loss instead of a 300,000 profit. Now Groeleken wants to hold a meeting, together with the consulting firm and the external auditor, at the head office in Amsterdam. He also says that he wants to review the plans for the future. Frank recharges one more time and gives his all to save the company. Together with Max Epping, he hammers out a long-term plan which provides for a decent profit for the next few years. It is a decent scenario that you don't even have to be an optimist to believe, more like a realist.

Within an hour, they're standing outside again. It may be Independence Day in America today, but Frank feels incredibly dependent. Dependent on what the managers at Special Credits will decide about his company. The meeting didn't go badly; Max even fully supported the plans and ultimately, it was his firm that the bank had hired to supervise Unimeta. Frank expects that if anything, they'll listen to Max for this very reason.

Groeleken promises to give them his decision within a couple weeks. They hold their breath the entire time, and plug away some more at Plan B, just in case. One of Groeleken's co-workers finally calls, and confirms their fears. The bank will not be renewing the credit agreement, and is going to start the procedure to collect on the surety as soon as possible. A company bankruptcy has become nearly unavoidable unless they find another financier.

This is precisely the crux of the matter. After all the reorganizations and changes in direction in Unimeta's strategy and structure, the company is as good as ready for the future. All they need is one good spring season, and then all the inventory can be sold and they will earn a really good profit. Frank is convinced that there has to be an investor who will be interested given this situation, but he needs more time. Time he doesn't have.

He decides to play his last trump card and calls Groeleken. After his call is transferred twice, Frank finally gets him on the line.

"Hi Peter, it's Frank; is this a good time?"

"Hello Frank, what's on your mind? And if it was a bad time, I wouldn't have taken the call."

"I'm sure I don't have to explain how disappointed I am and how unfair I think your decision was. Is there anything I can do that will help change your mind?"

"No, I'm afraid there isn't. Our decision is final."

"And if I can see to it that you get more than one million in extra cash?"

"Although it sounds interesting, it seems highly unlikely."

"No, Peter, that's where you're wrong. We have been doing some calculations here. You just have to give us a couple more months. Then our customers will pay our outstanding bills and we can bring in at least one million in extra sales this summer. This will only be better for you, and we will have the time to come up with other solutions for the financing for next season. We have come so far and are so close now. Surely you can't take this away from us?"

Frank can almost hear Groeleken thinking on the other end of the line.

"Can Max back up these calculations?" Groeleken asks.

"Completely. Why don't I just put him on the phone?"

Frank hands the phone over to Max, and gives him the "thumbs-up" sign. After a few minutes, Max hangs up.

"They are giving us another chance," he says. "I have to go to Amsterdam the day after tomorrow with a complete report, including all the calculations worked out down to the last detail. I think it will work."

"In that case, I would like for you to write up the proposal for attracting new financiers."

At the end of that month, the official letter from the bank arrives, by registered mail. It contains words Frank is not familiar with, so he calls Max to discuss it.

"Listen to this Max: '...because the future plans are not propitious for the bank...'".

"That just means that they don't like the amount of profit projected for the next few years."

"But later on they say that we will have until the end of September no matter what, as long as we can stick to the forecasts."

"Well, that's definitely positive news in these circumstances. That means we have another month or two. I'm going to get right to work on it."

The weeks that follow are filled with talking, talking, and more talking. They have meetings with the local branch of the Rabobank, the ING Bank, various holding companies and informal investors. Everyone listens with a great deal of interest, but none of them ever makes a firm commitment. ING seems to be the most serious candidate so far in terms of taking over the ABN Amro credit, under very strict conditions of course. Before taking any steps, Frank consults Haafkes first so that he can be sure that everything is by the book. The last thing he wants is to get into trouble as a result of carelessness now that he is bending over backwards to save the company.

In August, production stops for the entire month, the way it does every year. This way the foreign employees can travel back to their country of birth and visit their families. The seasonal production starts winding down in mid-July. One morning, sitting at home, Frank opens the newspaper. A huge headline screams to him from the front page.

Patio furniture manufacturer Hartman bankrupt.

He can't believe his eyes, and takes a second look. It's really there; Hartman is bankrupt. Frank doesn't know what to think of this. He knows that they also do their banking at the ABN Amro.

It almost seems like the bank is doing a major sweep of all of its patio furniture customers, but losing a competitor can also work in Unimeta's favor.

Max is not quite as enthusiastic, and unfortunately, a week later, his suspicions prove to be right. ING pulls out, giving the argument that if even the market leader can't make it, then it will be a very difficult road ahead for Unimeta. That evening Frank comes home extremely disillusioned.

This is a really unexpected twist," his wife says.

"I didn't expect this for a second either, let alone that it would have such a negative effect on our situation. If we had been a financially sound company, we would have been able to really take advantage of the fact that such a major player is dropping out of the market. But okay, that is only if... Hartman is one step ahead of us, once again."

Over the last few weeks, a plan has taken shape in Frank's head. The chance it will work is minimal, but he must and will cling to every lifeline he can. He calls Jack in Taiwan and explains the situation in broad terms. Jack is quite shocked at the news. Frank knows he's taking a huge risk. There is a risk that Shin Crest will also wash its hands of Unimeta, but at this point, he really has nothing to lose. He will ask Tony Liou if he is interested in investing in Unimeta so that in addition to a factory in China, the Taiwanese will also have a factory and distribution channel in Europe.

Jack calls him back a few days later and says that there isn't much interest on Shin Crest's part. They are, however, willing to listen to Frank's story and help him come up with other solutions. This is probably just the Chinese way of saying "no," but it is still a chance and he seizes it with both hands. It's already the end of August; he doesn't have much time. He is supposed to be in Cologne again next week, where they are presenting their new collection at the world's largest patio furniture trade show. He puts together a very tight itinerary; fly there on Monday, arrive in Hong Kong the next day, and then by car straight on through to China. They have a meeting scheduled with the highest level of management at Shin Crest for Wednesday, and on Thursday he will fly back, so that he'll be back in the Netherlands again by Friday. Just in time to prepare for the trade show.

It is exactly 24 hours from his front door to the factory in QingXi. Frank knows the way all too well; he makes this trip two to three times a year, but has never gone for a period as short as this. This may definitely be called a lightning visit, but the situation calls for it. On the plane, Frank works on a summary of the long-term plan in English. He will be able to print this out and distribute it to the Taiwanese members of the management team at the factory in China.

His wife is completely understanding about the fact that he has to go to China for the umpteenth time, and even on this occasion, at the drop of a hat. As often as he is away from home, she always manages to keep the family with three young children running like a fine-tuned machine. These days though, it is particularly difficult now that his father-in-law has been diagnosed as terminally ill. Although he has had surgery, it will be a bonus if they have him around a little longer. These are the types of thoughts that run through Frank's head as he types texts under the sales charts. He has just finished the presentation as they start their descent to the Hong Kong airport. He quickly puts away his laptop and fastens his seatbelt.

He thinks back nostalgically to the landings he experienced at the old airport, Kai Tak, which is no longer in use. Now that was truly spectacular. The planes would make a sharp turn just before the landing strip, squeezing between the mountains. The last part in particular was phenomenal. Flying as close as possible to the skyscrapers on both sides of the plane, you could practically see the food on the plates of the residents sitting inside.

But that was then. The old airport was replaced by an ultramodern one with every facility, built on an artificial island off the coast of Hong Kong. Dutch dredging companies had earned tens of millions on the development and construction of the airport.

As the wheels softly touch down and the plane taxies to the gate, Frank turns his cell phone back on. Within a few minutes, the phone starts beeping and Frank sees that he has six missed calls and four voice mail messages.

He calls his voice mail right before the plane arrives at the gate. It's Edith, his wife. Between the sobs, he hears that her father has passed away very unexpectedly, while he was sitting on the plane, out of reach. The other messages are also from his wife, who is now easier to understand, and from several other family members.

He quickly makes a decision. Lifeline or not, the home front comes first. He walks down the aisle towards the door of the plane and signals a flight attendant. The other passengers get off the plane, but he actually has to take the same plane back home. He explains the situation to the flight attendant, and she understands immediately what has to be done. She asks the pilot to contact KLM's ground personnel in Hong Kong. A bit later, a woman from a special service department meets him at the entrance to the plane, and asks Frank to come with her. He realizes that they don't have very much time. The plane will be departing again for the Netherlands in two hours. The new crew is already standing at the gate, waiting for the cleaning staff to finish up in the plane.

The woman quickly guides him everywhere he needs to go. He has to first go through customs and then officially enter the country. Next, he has to retrieve his suitcase from the belt in baggage claim. This fortunately is quicker than the usual delays he's accustomed to at Schiphol. Then they walk to the desk where the KLM ground crew are already packing up their things. He's lucky; there is still one seat available. After they have gone through security and Frank's passport is stamped, he has officially left the country again, 45 minutes after entering it. As he arrives at the gate after a ride on the underground train, the last passengers are just boarding the plane. He gets behind them in line and thanks the woman from the special service department. Sweat is beading on his forehead.

In the meantime, he has been able to reach his wife and hear the sad news from her personally. His father-in-law had probably gone into cardiac arrest, on the street in front of the local Rabobank. What a tragedy, Frank thinks. The fact that he is flying straight back home reassures her a little.

Back on the plane, the realization of what has happened back home slowly dawns on him, and how much sorrow this brings, for the family but also for himself. He adored Edith's father, and it is a great loss, particularly for his mother-in-law. For thirty years, they shared life's joys and sorrows.

As the plane is being prepared for take-off, Frank quickly calls the office in Enschede to explain the situation. His final phone calls are to Flora and Jack. Frank explains to them in detail what has happened, and why he has to turn right back around and go home. Jack understands completely, and in spite of Frank's absence, will present the investment story to Shin Crest for him. While he was waiting for his boarding pass, Frank had quickly e-mailed the presentation to him. Not long after this, they are airborne, and on their way back to the Netherlands.

Exactly 40 hours after he left home, Frank opens the front door to his house with unusually sad days ahead of him.

The funeral home is packed to the rafters. Gerard was a well-loved and socially involved man, that much is clear. Among the sea of flowers, there is one arrangement with a red ribbon. In graceful gold letters, the message reads *Blessings from Tony Liou.*

In late August, the first group of Unimeta employees are back at work after the summer vacation. They still have various irons in the fire for saving the company. The preparations are in full swing, and with the commercial team, they work their fingers to the bone to finish the collection. It's rock solid, and beautiful. Commercially viable products have been developed for every segment. Innovation is stamped on everyone's forehead in capital letters.

The trade show is going to be a resounding success. The Unimeta booth is jam-packed full of customers, and even the most critical patio furniture store reps embrace the new collection. Euphoria dominates the mood for three days. Unimeta has the reputation of being a company with pioneering designs. Their ability to consistently stay this course is really paying off at this trade show.

The sales of the safety relaxers are also going well, but Unimeta is not out of the woods yet. They still haven't found a new financier. They held frantic meetings in the days before the trade show, often until late in the evening, but nothing has been finalized. It's driving Frank crazy. They've finally been able to turn the tide at the company, after all the setbacks and difficult times, and are having the best trade show in years, but they can't get the financing they need.

Right after the show, they get the news that the Rabobank in Enschede is also pulling out. It feels like being hit with a sledgehammer, and immediately erases the great feeling they had during the show. This situation isn't doing Frank's sleeping habits any good either.

A week later, Max walks into his office, hesitating and with a blank look on his face. He is holding a letter. Frank has developed a real aversion to people walking into his office with a letter in their hands. It is almost never a sign of anything good. This time is no exception.

"I wanted to give you this letter in person," Max starts. "We have to return the order to find investors for you; we weren't able to find any. Everyone pulled out. The only ones left are a couple of vultures circling over the company, but they're no good to us. I'm so sorry that I don't have better news for you."

Frank curses loudly and his voice starts shaking.

"Is there absolutely no one who still believes in us? We just had the goddamn best trade show in our history! Our customers are incredibly enthusiastic. We will sell the inventory that we still have in stock next year because of the bad season this year, and at the full price. And now the company bank is cancelling our credit? This is a terrible world, Max. What a goddamn mess."

The next day he's at his lawyer's office. They're going over the situation and Wim points out Frank's rights, but mostly his obligations.

"It's now obvious that you can't save the company anymore, and that it is heading for bankruptcy. This means that you can't take on any new obligations. Other than that, I don't foresee any legal problems. You've stuck to all the rules."

"But what about that surety of 100,000 then? How can I get out of that? My wife hasn't slept well in weeks because of it."

"You won't be able to get out of that for the time being, Frank. All you can do is wait it out and keep giving them your full cooperation. If you do, hopefully the damage won't be too bad."

Yet another left hook to Frank, but he takes it like a man, and doesn't let his feelings show.

"We'll see," he mumbles.

It is almost time to pay the salaries, but that will never happen. Frank is sitting in his office staring off into space, and decides to make one last attempt. He dials Groeleken's number. A woman answers the phone, and tells him that Groeleken is on vacation and won't be back until mid-October. She can, however, put him through to a colleague. Frank swallows, and waits until he gets the other bank employee on the line. He doesn't get anywhere with him either.

"The decision is final, and we won't be making any more payments," the man says, in a way that does not leave any room for doubt.

"But that means I have to apply for bankruptcy now, even though the prospects are so good."

"That is your decision, sir. I have my instructions. The people from the NTAB will contact you about making further preparations."

Resigned, Frank hangs up. That same afternoon he calls his lawyer to get the necessary documents ready to file for bankruptcy. They have to act fast now. It's Monday, and once a week, every Wednesday morning, the district court in Almelo, the district Enschede falls under, handles bankruptcy applications. A trustee will be assigned the same day. This means that the application for filing must be made legally valid on Tuesday and all the relevant documents signed. These must be filed together with the minutes from a special general meeting of shareholders, which must submit in writing the decision to take this step.

The next morning, Pieter de Wit from the NTAB walks into Frank's office. He is holding a letter.

"I have some documents from the bank that have to be signed. I understand you spoke with one of Groeleken's colleagues about this yesterday."

"Yes, I did speak with the bank. They warned me that you would be coming here, but they didn't say anything about signing documents. What kind of documents are they?"

"Oh, just the usual red tape that is part of preparations for completing a bankruptcy procedure. We do this every day in my line of work."

Frank looks over the paperwork and sees documents he has never seen before.

"What does this mean, Pieter, a rental/leaseback contract for real estate and a statement of transfer of property held as security?"

"After these documents are signed, we put padlocks on certain parts of the company premises and the bank will then have access to everything they are holding as security. Buildings, machinery and the inventory. This is to prevent the trustee from selling off these things independently, and the bank from coming up empty-handed, even though they're the ones that provided the security."

"Is that how it works? But the bankruptcy filing papers have to be sent out tomorrow. If the documents aren't signed, what happens then, Pieter?"

"I just told you that, didn't I? That's why I'm here with these contracts. To prevent the trustee from getting a hold of them. This will save the bank millions."

Frank has to make a real effort to suppress a triumphant feeling.

"Pieter, you tell those jerks in Amsterdam that they can take a long walk off a short pier. I'm not signing anything. *Niente, nada!*"

Pieter looks at Frank in surprise. "You won't sign?"

"I just told you that, didn't I?"

De Wit is taken aback for a moment. Frank elaborates.

"I will think about signing the paperwork if I receive a signed statement from the bank that they will waive their right to collect my surety."
Frank hasn't had the chance to check with his lawyer to see if what he's saying is all even legal and ethical; he's acting purely on instinct now. His gut feeling tells him that he has to play this trump card.

In the meantime, De Wit is starting to bear a resemblance to all those excited, red-faced Chinese men in the room during the Compex bankruptcy.

"I will pass it on to my client," he says gruffly, and hurries out of the office. Once De Wit has closed the door of Frank's office behind him, Frank calls his lawyer and tells him what just happened.

"I've never seen anything like this before, Frank. The two are completely unrelated."

"So?" Frank answers.

"Actually, you're not doing anything you're not allowed to do, and if you ask me, it's pretty creative. You can assume that De Wit will be back later, after he has spoken to the bank. I'll come right over now, so I can take a look at the documents to see if they're legal."

Half an hour later, Pieter de Wit and Wim Haafkes walk into Frank's office at almost the same time. De Wit has clearly cooled off, and has regained his normal color. Frank pours a cup of coffee for the men, and waits.

De Wit opens the discussion.

"The people at the bank are absolutely not amused, Frank, and that is putting it mildly. You are confusing two issues that have nothing to do with one another. It would be better all-around if you just signed both documents, then you'll be rid of your troubles, and we can start our work."

"You mean that my troubles will only be starting. I'll be100,000 poorer and the bank will be millions richer. I don't think so."

At that point, Wim joins the conversation, backing Frank up.

"My client's position is completely legitimate, and this is why I have advised him to adhere to this course of action. First, the surety needs to be off the table, and I have already drawn up an agreement."

Haafkes pulls a letter from his briefcase with a flourish.

"After that, my client will sign the documents in question," he says, "and you can start doing what you have to do."

"I'll never get this approved in Amsterdam," De Wit says.

"I have already prepared the bankruptcy petition. Here it is," Haafkes says. "This is going to the court tomorrow, no matter what. With or without the signed agreements. My client has no other choice, given his liability as a director, given the salary payments that the bank is not approving for payment tomorrow. The bank has left us no other choice. Why don't you give the people in Amsterdam a call? Here is the letter about withdrawing the surety."

De Wit has no choice but to take the letter from Haafkes. He excuses himself and walks out of the office.

"This is going to be okay," Haafkes reassures Frank.

"I think so too, but let's not start celebrating yet."

When De Wit returns a little while later, there is a visible hint of relief on his face.

"The bank has accepted your proposal. They have never experienced this before and it took them a while to get used to the idea, but they've given me the green light. They are now getting the second signature they need and then the letter will be faxed to this number. If you would just sign the two agreements now, Frank."

Frank bursts out laughing from all the stress.

"You just don't give up, do you Pieter? We're waiting for the fax, and once that's in, then I'll sign."

Two minutes later, the letter rolls off the fax machine, with two signatures and a few ABN Amro stamps.

Nearly six years after his baptism of fire as general director, Frank once again stands in the cafeteria, ready to speak to the company employees. He insists on giving them this bad news in person. It is unusually difficult for him, but he's not alone. The other members of the management team and the works council are also incredibly shaken. After all, they know what he's about to say. A company with a 38-year history is meeting an inglorious end.

It's a huge blow. Some of the employees don't want to believe the news. There are also a few trade union officials in attendance to provide any necessary support. A few employees burst into tears. Frank also gets a lump in his throat a few times during his speech.

In one fell swoop, everyone is unemployed. They are all given a form they can use to apply for unemployment, except for Frank. As a majority shareholder, he's not entitled to benefits, in spite of everything he has done for the company. That's just the way it works in the Netherlands. He feels like something inside of him is about to explode, but he gathers his courage, straightens his back, and explains the situation to every employee who asks.

16

JOB SEEKER WITHOUT UNEMPLOYMENT BENEFITS

The next afternoon, Rob Wilderink, the appointed trustee, comes to see Frank. At first glance, he doesn't seem like a bad guy. He's wearing jeans and a trendy blazer. Frank figures he's in his mid-fifties, but he has a boyish appearance. Rob gives Wim a friendly handshake in the executive office. It turns out these two already know each other; Wim works as a trustee on a regular basis, and Wilderink ends up sitting on the other side of the table from him now and then. After Wim has explained what his role has been the last few months, he picks up his briefcase and leaves the office.

Frank is now alone with the trustee. He didn't get a wink of sleep last night, and is pretty nervous. He has no idea what to expect. Wilderink takes the initiative and starts.

"So, Mr. Krake, why don't you tell me how you ended up in this situation?"

Frank starts with the story about the fireworks disaster, and the loss of sales that they are still struggling to make up for to this day, more than five years later. He also covers the events of 9/11, the copycats, the SARS drama and the adventures in China. He tries to make the financial consequences of all these events clear to Wilderink, who listens attentively. After Frank has also explained what has been going on the past few months, Wilderink takes a deep sigh.

"Well, that is quite a story. I don't see this that often in my work. I think that no matter what, we need to keep the key people involved here. Everything in the bookkeeping department also has to continue. Can I get an estimate from you of what it will cost to keep things running here for another week or two? I'm not talking about production, but the staff departments that support it. I would also like to walk through the factory to take a good look at the production line and the shipping warehouse."

"You'll have to talk to Pieter de Wit about that," Frank answers. "He and his accomplices replaced all the locks last night. I can't even get in there anymore. Look, they made me sign this."

He hands over the statements about the lease and property held in security. The trustee doesn't say anything, just reads the documents in silence. The silence continues for another 10 seconds or so. Finally, Wilderink speaks.

"I understand. This changes things. It looks like the bank has taken charge now, more or less, so I will contact them."

He doesn't look very happy, and hurries out of the office. After half an hour, he returns. "I have spoken with the bank, and also De Wit. I have two keys here, one for me and one for you. This will at least allow us to do what we need to do in the near future."

They walk through the factory together. It is eerily quiet now, with no-one around and all the machines turned off. Frank gives him a step-by-step explanation of how the production works. Wilderink listens, shaking his head, and then finally speaks.

"It's incredible that you all held on as long as you did. I still have to look at all the numbers, but my first impression is pretty clear. My background is actually in business economics. When I see this, I realize you all really are one of the last few Mohicans. You can't keep producing this way in Western Europe these days. Mass production of consumer products this labor-intensive has to go either to Eastern Europe or the Far East. It's just not possible here anymore."

"We did manage it, just barely."

"Yes, this year. We won't even talk about the future. I need to plough through the figures first, but I can already tell you that this is not going to be a full restructuring. Sometimes, production just has to be taken out of the market. When you earn margins as low as you did on these chairs, then that line simply has to disappear from the market."

"But they also restructured at Hartman, didn't they?"

"Yes, but that was a completely different story. There, the machines did most of the work, and production was far from being as labor-intensive as what you had here. I know the company well, and the problem there was that the market for plastic patio furniture had collapsed. The factory has now been sold separately to a group that specializes in the production of plastic products: baskets, watering cans, garbage cans, plastic containers and so forth. This new company will also be producing plastic chairs for Hartman, as long as there is still demand for these products. The new Hartman has become a pure head-tail business, without the millstone of the factory hanging around their neck."

For the first time, Frank realizes that they really were beating a dead horse, or at least a very sick one, for a very long time.

Back in the office, Frank hands the trustee all the reports from the past year. It's quite a stack of paper, written by the accountants and consulting firms.

"What are your plans, actually?" Wilderink suddenly asks.

"We're working on a Plan B right now," Frank says, and gives him some background. "But first we have to see about getting the financing for it, so I'm going to be really busy with that in the near future."

A little less than two weeks go by. Frank doesn't have time to think, reflect, or take a serious look in the mirror. The train rages on. The trustee contacts him with questions on a frequent basis. Wim has made it clear to Frank that it would be better to lend his full cooperation to these requests, in the interest of his liabilities as a director. He holds long meetings with interested parties and competitors, from Germany and also in their own backyard. The newly formed Hartman is interested, and the trustee gives them the opportunity to inspect the books.

Once again, Frank has got a lot of plates spinning in the air. He is working on Plan B with the management team, and staying in touch with salesmen and customers, so that they can hold onto as many sales as possible. Frank's dozens of meetings with investors, banks and holding companies in recent years are definitely coming in handy now. He knows the ritual and speaks their language.

Within two weeks, Plan B is finalized and they have got the funding. They can keep 18 employees on the payroll. The essence of the plan is that the relaxer frames will now also be made in China, and then shipped directly to England, just like the cushion covers from Poland. At a central location in Birmingham, the cushions are filled with stuffing and packed together with the frames, and then shipped all over England. This system offers a very cost-efficient way to ensure that nearly 500,000 relaxers make it into stores. They are able to hold onto nearly the entire sales figure of 20 million Euros, without needing 150 employees to do so. They also continue to procure the Preston and Sombrero products from China.

An extremely professional holding company from Zeist, Nimbus, is interested in investing 1.2 million in the restructuring. All they're waiting for now is a response from the trustee. After a few days, Frank corners Wilderink to get information on the status of the offer they have received. Wilderink says that he has told the ABN Amro about the offer, and is waiting for their reaction.

Another week goes by, and still no news from the bank. During that week, they are all talking a blue streak to their customers to reassure them. After all, they are getting restless. This is understandable, of course. In January and February, the new collections have to be delivered and in the stores. Production still hasn't gotten started in China. It is now mid-October, and if they don't restructure fast, they can forget about it altogether. The buyers at Unimeta's larger customers' companies are fully aware of this too. They realize that their jobs are also at risk if this doesn't work out, and push as hard as they can. Frank's entire body is tensed up, and he has been walking around with a headache for days. It shouldn't all be this hard, he thinks.

As the icing on the cake, a fax comes in on Wednesday from one of Unimeta's biggest customers, complete with ultimatum. If they don't get a firm answer by Friday at 5:00 in the afternoon about restructuring the company, they will go to Unimeta's competition to ensure they can stock their stores. Frank can't really blame them. He would have done the very same thing during his years at Wehkamp. In fact, he thinks they have been given an unusually long grace period. You really can't ask your customers for any more than that.

He regroups, picks up the fax, and walks into the office where Wilderink has taken up temporary residence.

"Look at this, man. This is what we get from all this dilly-dallying. What are we still waiting for? If we don't get this show on the road, all the customers will bail on us, and we will be left here with nothing."

Wilderink looks up in surprise, and grabs the fax from Frank's hands. After he has read it, he gives Frank a serious look.

"I realize that they're pressuring you, but we have to stay calm. I will let the bank know and keep you posted."

"That's not enough," says Frank. "You have to go see them in person. I'll go with you. We have to convince them how serious this is, and force them into making a decision. It's now or never. Waiting any longer will be fatal. Besides, by the time they've even looked at this fax, it will be Christmas. And by then, it will be too late."

"I understand how important it is, of course that's clear to me, but we can't force anything. Believe me, they're working on it."

Frank walks out of the office with an unsatisfied, uneasy feeling. He is amazed at how calm and resigned Wilderink is able to remain. He probably does this all the time, but it's still remarkable. Five minutes later, he dials Groeleken's number. The banker's assistant shields him with professional expertise; the men are meeting about this topic again this afternoon and this is all she has been authorized to say. Frank takes a deep breath and explains how crucial timing is right now.

He bites the bullet and makes another call, this time to Pre-scan in Hengelo. He has decided to have himself checked out from head to toe, and makes arrangements to have a full body scan done. Frank has been burning the candle at both ends the last few years, and he feels like he has been running on fumes particularly these last few months. He feels completely worn out, and wants to be sure there is no damage. This much stress, tension and pressure just can't be healthy. A clinic in Germany has an opening for him the very next week, so he makes an appointment, restructuring or no restructuring.

The customer's Friday 5:00 deadline is rapidly approaching, and it is painfully quiet. No trustee, no bank; no one is contacting them. The hours tick by agonizingly slowly. As Frank makes a pot of coffee, he waves away the first fruit flies from the machine in the small kitchen. It's amazing how quickly deterioration and decay set in. Not even four weeks ago, this was a lively factory full of people and energy, employees who did everything possible to do the best job they could, and to save the company. Now it's nothing more than a dead building, where the bugs are slowly but surely taking over, starting with the trash cans. The entire kitchen is next, but they have already gotten into most of the offices. This is what it must have been like for the entire textile industry in the 1970s and 1980s. Factory after factory shut down, as more and more production was outsourced to low-wage countries. Every now and then, one of them would restructure in a downsized form, but even those companies eventually went under. These failed companies were the reason they were able to rent their storage space in the Bamshoeve back then for so little. One man's loss and all that.

Suddenly, it's five o'clock. As if on cue, the fax machine jangles and the long-dreaded letter comes rolling off the machine. Not from the bank or trustee, giving them the news that the offer has been accepted. No, it's from the customer, cancelling the order worth millions. Frank is momentarily incapable of comprehending what has just happened. He is completely empty. He tosses the fax into his briefcase, locks up, and goes home. He turns off his cell phone; there is only one thing he needs right now, and that's peace and quiet.

Once home, he takes a cold shower. He then takes a long, hard look at himself in the mirror, and realizes that he has done everything, absolutely everything, he could have possibly done. He flops down on the couch and gives in to the feeling of resignation. No tears, no anger, no frustration. Obviously, this is what was meant to be. He can hardly believe it himself, let alone explain it to someone else. It is, however, reality.

The next day, Frank knows exactly what he has to do. He has slept like a rock, relieved from all the tension, and starts making phone calls. His first call is to the manager at Nimbus. He was aware of the deadline, and is very disappointed that it has now passed, with all the associated consequences. He will hold a meeting at the company and take action. Next, Frank calls the other members of the management team and tells them that it is truly all over now. The responses on the other end of the line are impassioned, even though they had all seen it coming. Frank's final calls are to the salesmen who were to be involved in the restructuring. He asks them if they are willing to do everything in their power to hold onto the sales a little longer. Who knows? There may be an unexpected twist he tells them, against his better judgment.

Finally, his own phone rings. Nimbus has retracted the offer with the trustee. Sales can no longer be guaranteed, and this makes the entire financial scenario a different story. Frank completely understands their position; it's entirely logical. As he hangs up the phone that Saturday morning, he is officially a job seeker without unemployment benefits.

He has his regularly scheduled meeting Monday morning with the trustee. It takes all the energy Frank can muster to force himself to go. Not even five minutes into the meeting, after laying his grievances out on the table, Wilderink's cell phone rings. He looks at the display and answers the call. He listens, without saying anything. Barely a minute later, he lays the phone back on the table.

"That was the bank," he says. "Hartman has just decided that they won't be putting in an offer on Unimeta."

"Hartman?" Frank mumbles. It all becomes clear to him now, and he can't suppress a faint smile.

17

BUKATCHI

An unusually strange week goes by. The trustee contacts him with questions on a frequent basis. Now that the restructuring is off, he tries to sell off parts of the company property at the highest possible price. A German competitor is interested in all the machinery and the corresponding dies and molds so that it can produce its own relaxers at a location in Poland or the Ukraine. In strategic terms, this doesn't even sound like a bad idea to Frank; it's a good way to avoid the relatively high costs of labor in Western Europe. It doesn't do him any good of course since they don't need him to do this. They have already been in touch with Hugh; they need him, but not Frank.

Initially, his head is mostly just empty, aside from the disappointment, that is. He mostly needs these first few days after the silent death of the restructuring plan to process the blow, but he quickly starts to get the itch again to get back on the horse. Frank can't let go of the idea that continuing as a head-tail company offers opportunities. Developing patio furniture in the Netherlands, producing it in China, and then marketing and selling it in Europe. Keeping it as simple as possible, no more than four or five employees, with Jasper in inside sales as the focal point. Just one or two salespeople on the road, and Flora and Leo in China to supervise things there. Frank can be the one to manage the company. This is really all they need to get started.

It does mean he would have to start a new company. He would have to set up a limited liability company and find an office and a showroom, but the most important thing is still money. In order to pre-finance the production in China, they need hundreds of thousands, possibly even more. He also wonders which products they would be able to sell. Preston is difficult since the high retail prices are hard to justify if production will be taking place in China. Sombrero would be a better alternative in this case, but the intellectual property rights, the model rights and the trademark rights are all still vested in the old limited liability company. He would have to talk to the trustee about the idea, but he will certainly want to charge top dollar for these rights.

A thousand and one questions race through Frank's mind, but at least there are ideas bubbling and buzzing away and he slowly feels the energy flowing back. The one thing that does continue to bother him is the simple fact that he is now the one with final responsibility for a bankruptcy. It doesn't even matter whether or not there was anything he could have done to prevent it. He had even heard afterwards that they had managed to hold on a few years longer than most trade union officials ever would have thought possible.

This doesn't do Frank any good right now either. The fact is he was ultimately unable to save the company, and this is now stamped on his forehead. At least, this is how it feels. He feels like a loser. Frank can still remember his first speech in the cafeteria as though it were only yesterday. He had started out brimming with ambition, without the slightest notion of what he would encounter along the way. This deep-rooted drive to create something successful is still there, but his self-esteem has taken a major hit. He does know that he has it in him.

He realizes that if he wants to make something of this, he has to act fast, now, while the momentum is still there. They know all the customers, know what they want. He has contacts in China that go back ten or twelve years, to the time he worked for Wehkamp. Frank calls Flora and Jack and tosses out there his ideas and plans about the future to gauge their reaction. They promise to check a few things with the factories in China.

Saturday evening, exactly one week after Unimeta's demise, Frank is at a party celebrating the birth of the child of one of his old college friends. He and his wife have had a baby girl, and are celebrating this in a reception room with family and friends. The atmosphere at the party is great, and the occasion gives Frank and his wife a reason to get out and spend time together alone. Still, he can't switch off entirely from all the thoughts running through his head. One of his old friends from his study program, Rodie, asks him how he's doing. Frank tells him the entire story in a nutshell. An independent financial advisor, Rodie listens attentively to Frank's story.

"Could you put together some kind of financial plan for me, Rodie?" Frank asks. "Just really basic, a couple sheets of paper?"

"My schedule is completely full for the coming week, but I could free up a couple of hours tomorrow."

"We could get together tomorrow, if you don't mind doing this on a Sunday."

That Sunday evening, they put together a business plan for the new company. On paper, it is profitable from the very first day, but then again, Frank will have to be quick and reel in the orders that are still floating around the market immediately. And in order to do this, an awful lot of things will have to be taken care of first.

After one more sleepless night, Frank has made a decision. He's going to go for it. He is going to give it his all too, first of all to prove to himself that he can, no matter what the world thinks. On October 21, 2005, he registers the new company with the Chamber of Commerce in Enschede, as a limited liability company in formation, with one employee for now.

It didn't take him long to come up with a name. He had heard the word so often during his dozens of trips to China, that the decision was easy. It has to be Bukatchi, with the emphasis on "kat" instead of the last syllable, so that it sounds more European. Bukatchi means "you're welcome" in Chinese. It's a great name for a company. It has a chic ring to it, and is similar to the name of an exclusive Italian car brand. When he types it into Google, he doesn't find a single hit. The word simply doesn't exist outside of China. It's perfect for his new company. He can't wait to be back in China so he can see his suppliers' faces when they hear the name. They're going to love it. It is much more distinctive and unique than the names of all the other patio furniture companies. They usually use the words "garden" or "sun" in their names. Bukatchi is going to be a huge success, Frank is absolutely sure of it.

The weeks that follow really put him to the test. He tries to strike a balance between keeping the trustee happy, and focusing on the start-up of his new company. This results in about four hours of sleep each night, but at least it gives him the opportunity to use Unimeta's office, computers and phone lines. The salesmen are sitting at home now, out of a job, yet still trying to keep the customers interested until the company is fully operational. They can't afford to lose the orders that are still in the pipeline to the competition. Up to now, this seems to be successful.

He also gets some good news. The body scan he had done didn't show anything to be worried about. The human body can obviously handle a lot.

The reports coming from China are also positive. The most important suppliers have said they will start delivering again if Frank starts a new company. And they are even willing to do this without payment upfront. He won't have to pay the bill until the goods are shipped. This gives him some breathing room. Frank and Rodie crunch numbers until they are blue in the face to arrive at an acceptable analysis that they can show the bank. This is Frank's greatest challenge, getting the financing.

During his time at Unimeta, he developed a good relationship with Banque Artesia, a small bank that is trying to gain a foothold in the Netherlands. They have a branch in Enschede and have experience with trade financing. He works out a financing plan with them and manages to get a preliminary commitment.

By early November, Frank has rounded up the most important ingredients: orders from customers, production facilities from suppliers, and bank finance that he needs to actually get started. All that's left are the rights to the Sombrero collection that are under the trustee's control, or actually, ABN Amro's. They want hundreds of thousands for them. And there are other candidates waiting to jump at the chance to the rights; after all, Sombrero is well-known. Frank scrapes together all his savings and uses the equity in his house as collateral to arrive at the amount he needs. He then makes an appointment for a meeting to be held at the Unimeta office. In addition to the trustee, Groeleken and Pieter de Wit will also be there. After negotiating for two hours, they reach an agreement.

Bukatchi is now the new owner of all the model and trademark rights to Sombrero. It may be a huge noose around Frank's neck, but this won't prevent him from doing it. Finally, they can get started.

Bukatchi is born.

A few days later, Frank's phone rings. It's Wilfred Goedhart, the director of the OPM, a local venture capital firm.

Frank knows Wilfred well. They had sat down together a few times to discuss the rescue of Unimeta, but OPM's supervisory board had put a stop to that.

"I've read in the paper," Wilfred says, "that the only brand Hartman bought from Unimeta was Preston."

"That's right," Frank says. "Rumor has it that it was a defensive purchase. They bought it to prevent the competition from running with it. Hartman is apparently not going to do anything with it. They're welcome to it as far as I'm concerned. We're very happy with Sombrero, and it offers a lot more opportunities commercially."

"Okay, got it. Have you ever heard of Support Plus, by the way? Known as SP? We've talked about them before."

"Yes, I've heard of them. Successful group, right?"

"Extremely successful. It's one of our most profitable and fastest growing ventures. We are one of the largest shareholders and have just closed on a 55 million Euro credit facility with ABN Amro."

"Wow, that's some facility!"

"Well, they are growing fast. This year their sales will increase from 100 to 150 million Euros, and the end is far from being in sight. Last month, SP won the China Trader Award from Cathay Pacific for companies that do successful business with China."

"Congratulations. As long as they don't grow too fast. That's when you lose control."

"No worries, we're on top of it. It's a rolling train that's gaining momentum and heading in the right direction. They pick up every new product in the electronics market and sell them through customers like Kruidvat, Action, Aldi, Lidl and you name it, all the big chains. MP3 players, docking stations, portable CD players, but also vacuum cleaners and fitness equipment. They are going to open a sales office in Austria soon. They now have their own offices in almost every European country, and America is next. So I was thinking, we're looking for something to supplement sales, particularly during the first half of the year. You are in the patio furniture business, and also get your products from China. Do you think there's a way for us to work together?"

"I just set up my own company, Wilfred. I want to run a business, not be absorbed by some giant conglomerate."

"I realize that, but just go talk to them, you never know. The one doesn't necessarily have to exclude the other. On December 1, they're moving into a new building in Enschede. Over 1000 square meters of office space and a couple of enormous storage warehouses. You could move right in. Just talk to their founder and director, Diederick van Buiten."

Ten days and five meetings later, Frank has a difficult decision to make. Should he remain completely independent and therefore keep his decision-making authority? If he is successful, he doesn't have to share the rewards for the huge financial risks that he is taking, but the low economies of scale also make the company very vulnerable. Or should he take the offer of Support Plus, an organization that is willing to pump extra capital into the company, and is offering Bukatchi every facility a start-up could ever need? This means from people manning the phones to computer systems, and from a bookkeeper to laptops. And in a beautiful new office building to boot. They are serving it all up to him on a silver platter.

Bukatchi could also take advantage of SP's extensive and successful sales network. This means access to a lot of new customers, all at once. When it comes to purchasing, he will be able to benefit from good container rates because of the thousands of containers that SP already ships. Frank is really struggling with the decision. The offer is unusually appealing, particularly during Bukatchi's shaky start-up phase, a time when they are far from having everything arranged.

During the negotiations, he makes sure to demand a permanent form of independence within this giant group. They have it set out in writing by a notary that Bukatchi will continue to function as a separate limited liability company, with its own bookkeeping and independently financed. He will keep all the decision-making authority. Frank wants to be able to manage and control the company himself, without outside intervention.

What finally tips the scales is the incredible hesitation he is picking up on the part of the German customers in particular about doing business with the new Bukatchi. After all, Unimeta didn't go bankrupt all that long ago, and Bukatchi is in fact a sort of phoenix rising from the ashes of the bankrupt inventory. Although it is not a true restructuring, the customers are still hesitant. In Germany, you are considered to be tainted after a bankruptcy, and it would be better for them to shake that negative stigma all at once.

Two weeks after he started Bukatchi, Frank is sitting at the notary's office to make official the transfer of two-thirds of the shares to Support Plus. Although it gives him an uneasy feeling, the protective umbrella will also offer safety and security. They are no longer on their own.

After he has finished with all the necessary ceremony, he drives to the

Unimeta factory. The enormous complex is a dreary sight to behold. As Frank turns the key in the lock, he vacillates from one emotion to the other. This is where he worked for eleven years, sometimes day and night, particularly over the last few years. It has become a part of his life, a part that is now definitely over. And it is never coming back. For him, it is akin to a death; in the vernacular, it's called being bankrupt. There's nothing left here now, apart from the annoying fruit flies that seem to be multiplying exponentially every day.

At the same time, he's happy about this new opportunity, even though this baby has only just been born, and the neighbors are already doing the babysitting; at least this is how it feels. He takes comfort in the fact that he's involved too, and clear agreements have been made about how the baby will be raised. Frank isn't worried.

He sits down at his old desk, and starts making calls. The first call is to Jasper; Frank is making good on his promise that if a new company was started up, Jasper would be the inside sales guy. Next, he calls Adri, the experienced export manager who is supposed to handle the Dutch market too. Then Carsten, the still young salesman for the German market, who is German and lives in the border region. His charm works particularly well with the female buyers. Frank's last call is to Ruud Kuipers, to ask him if he wants to become a part-time advisor.

The next morning, this group of four meets in Frank's office.

"I am happy and relieved to finally be able to offer you all a job, officially," Frank says. "As you all know, I started Bukatchi last month, and registered it with the Chamber of Commerce. Since that time, things have moved very quickly. We are going to go to Support Plus in a little while, our new parent company."

Half an hour later, they are walking through the enormous office building where they too will be working from now on. Diederick van Buiten gives them a hearty welcome. He says he hopes their partnership will be a productive and enjoyable one. After this surprising introduction, Frank's co-workers head homewards, a bit bewildered. Frank calls Flora in China to give her the good news. After that, he drives home, with a proud, satisfied feeling.

One month later, he signs a new credit agreement on Bukatchi's behalf with Banque Artesia for 2.4 million Euros. They can put the pedal to the metal now. The future is smiling upon Frank once again.

18

CUSTOM-MADE ITALIAN SUITS AND EXPENSIVE SPORTS CARS

From hell to heaven, that's how the Unimeta men feel in their new life. Within a few weeks, Frank has his own office on the fourth floor. His co-workers are one door down, three of them working from a slightly larger office. Everything works; the phones ring, the computers are running, the printers are purring away. An enormous buzz is tangible in the new company.

Frank is still forced to play chess on two different boards every day. The completion of the Unimeta bankruptcy procedure is still placing huge demands on him, and the start-up of Bukatchi also comes with extra concerns. In spite of it all, he sails right on through it all. The inspiring environment at Support Plus gives him new energy, each and every day. It is only now becoming clear to him what the repercussions were of the financial problems on the atmosphere and culture at Unimeta. Everything is different here. Finally, they don't have to pinch every penny, twice. Frank keeps a careful eye on the money, but at least there are funds now if they need to make a purchase.

SP is also a truly international company; the official company language is English. This is necessary, given all their offices throughout Europe. Seventy people work at the office in Shanghai alone. The subsidiaries in Europe are in charge of local sales, but the most important employees visit the headquarters in Enschede on a regular basis. One minute there might be Danes walking down the hallway, and the next, French, but mostly an awful lot of Germans. A substantial part of the sales are generated from Germany. The foreign employees all come to Enschede at the same time for sales meetings. They evaluate the latest gadgets and features in the electronics market, and devise their sales plans for the further roll-out of these products throughout Europe. Frank enjoys this dynamic, one that may not be compared with the traditional and conservative patio furniture sector.

He talks about this regularly with Jasper, Adri and Carsten. They pinch themselves and realize that it all really is true, and wonder what they have been doing wrong all these years. They feel like true patio furniture hicks in this world of fast deals and even faster cars. Frank can't help but be amazed at this now and then. Sometimes there are so many of these shiny cars in the parking lot out front that it looks like the showroom at the local Porsche dealership.

Everything is going so fast, including the addition of new employees. A week doesn't go by when yet another new employee is introducing themselves. It really takes an effort to remember all the new names. Knowing exactly what everyone does isn't always very clear either. Oh well, Frank thinks, if your sales are so high, you need people to supervise and organize everything.

A few times, Frank is even there when the telephone rings and yet another huge deal is made, usually by the commercial director. One afternoon, he even negotiates a deal with Media Markt in Italy worth ten million dollars. These are sales they can only dream about at Bukatchi. When Frank asks what they earn on a deal like that, he often doesn't get a clear answer.

Support Plus's guarantees and its good name help Bukatchi get off to a running start. The German customers, initially hesitant to do business with a company where the employees had just been through a bankruptcy, change their tune faster than a radio. Frank and his co-workers manage to round up a few respectable customers with great sales that first year.

He goes to see the men at Special Credits two more times. This time, it's not to ask for a credit line, but instead to buy back some of Unimeta's inventory. The bank asks the NTAB to take care of everything, and this is how Pieter de Wit comes back into Frank's life a couple more times. Their contact is a bit more pleasant this time, now that they need Frank and his co-workers to help them get rid of the inventory.

In the winter of 2006, Frank flies to China to place the new orders. He visits several of the suppliers he knows, and is welcomed with open arms wherever he goes. The welcome is even extra warm at Shin Crest. And of course, the tea ceremony with Tony and Jack is on the schedule once again.

Carsten and Adri have a few meetings with the SP sales staff, but are not really very enthusiastic about the results. There is a cultural gap between the world of electronics and the patio furniture sector. Different people, different products and mostly, a different mentality. The people from Unimeta have always been used to doing what they promise, and to even surpass expectations when possible. The people at SP obviously have different ideas. They proclaim so much, but very little actually comes of it in the end. Everything moves fast, and is extremely unreliable. What is black today is white tomorrow. It's not the style they are accustomed to or what their customers want. So they make their own plans and leave the synergy for what it is.

For the time being, Frank does as much as he can himself. This is why he also waits before making a commitment when it comes to China. SP has a professional office in Shanghai with every possible facility, and Flora and Leo can move in any time they like. Apart from the geographical distance between Eastern and Southern China, it doesn't sound like an appealing idea to Frank. They'll take care of their own business for now.

One thing he doesn't understand is that no one in the bookkeeping department at SP seems to be worried about accounts receivable management. No one is involved in getting outstanding bills paid. This was something that took absolute priority at Unimeta, but at SP, it is an area frequently neglected. Obviously it's not necessary here, Frank thinks, and he was always on top of anything involving money, for the simple reason that there was too little of it. Then again, if you have just been approved for a credit line of 25 million, it's a lot easier to be blasé about these things.

The thing that really rubs him the wrong way is how the commercial director does business. When possible, Frank avoids him like the plague. He does this inside the building as it is, since the hallway leading to his office is always thick with cigarette smoke. What really ticks Frank off however, is that he has his BMW X5 cleaned by Wilma, the cleaning woman who works at SP. He parks his sports car right in front of the main entrance, and not long afterwards, we always see Wilma heading that way, carrying a vacuum cleaner and bucket with suds.

In June 2006, a wave of excitement rolls through the building. Support Plus is about to close a mega-deal worth tens of millions for a completely new product, the Wunderbar. This is a brand-new home tap system for kegs of beer. Heineken has its Beertender, and Grolsch and Dommelsch their own Perfect Draft. Support Plus is going to launch an attack on the competition. The Wunderbar can be used with every brand and type of keg, whether it's filled with beer made by Heineken, Grolsch or another brand. Eureka! The product has been developed in Hong Kong and Support Plus appears to have gotten hold of the sales license for Europe. This is contingent on an enormous minimum purchase quantity of course. The rumors are flying all over the place, with numbers of up to 100,000 being tossed around. Frank wonders if they have thought carefully about the risks, but he assumes they are professional and experienced enough for that.

On Friday morning, the sales managers from SP subsidiaries fly in from all over the world to meet in Enschede. Because of the distance, many of them come in on Thursday. All that chatter in a variety of languages makes for a lively atmosphere at the office. The wildest stores are told, and the men from Bukatchi listen enraptured to these tales. The thing is, they don't know what they should really believe.

Manuel Stass, one of the five owners of SP, runs the sales meeting on Friday. Manuel is the sales director for Germany and is the stereotype of a smooth operator. Well-groomed, blond hair smoothed back and held in place with gel, fire-engine red tie under his smart blue suit and of course the most beautiful Porsche in the whole parking lot.

The meeting starts at 10:00, and with a theatrical gesture, he pulls the sheet off the prototype of the Wunderbar. The ensuing ohs and ahs are genuine. In his best English with a heavy German accent, Manuel talks about "dze killer". In an impassioned speech, he talks about all the things this gadget is capable of. Next thing you know, he'll be telling us it also has an automatic ironing function, the Bukatchi men snigger among themselves. It's all very giggle-inducing, this American-style sales show, and Manuel is like someone right out of a home-shopping channel commercial.

Then comes the serious part of the meeting. One by one, the sales managers all have to give a number for the quantity of products they think they will be able to sell in their market. Stass gets them all riled them up and quantities of ten thousand and higher fly around the room. None of them wants to be outdone by the others, and Manuel sets the stakes high with 70,000 units for Germany. France has to match this, naturally, and they love their beer in England, don't they? After Stass has written down all the quantities, he realizes he is still 60,000 short. He looks around the conference room, and asks who's willing to raise their forecast. He sets a good example, and raises his number from 70,000 to 80,000. Some of the others follow his lead.

Once everyone is finished, he looks at the flip chart with satisfaction. Over the next year, they will sell half a million Wunderbars in Europe, with a total cost price of dozens of millions of Euros. Frank keeps quiet; he doesn't believe a word of this. He is used to dividing the forecast sales numbers by two. He then orders half, and sets aside the other half as an option.

Diederick van Buiten is visibly pleased in his role as the general director of Support Plus, and is not afraid to show it. He drives his own Porsche, but if he takes his BMW 7, he prefers to be driven by his personal assistant. He's not the only one with a big fat BMW 7 either. Lately, another one of these huge boats of a car has been parked in the company parking lot on a regular basis. A middle-aged man Frank doesn't know gets out of this car, and always gives a polite greeting. SP management spends entire days with this man.

And he's not the only one. Heavy hitters in suits are coming to SP from all over the country, with increasing frequency lately. When Frank leaves to go home at six or seven in the evening, they are often still at the office. It is obvious something important is going on. Rumors of a sale are circulating. Wild speculations may be heard around the coffee machine about who these people are, but one thing is certain, some of them are bankers and investment managers. Wilfred Goedhart from OPM is also regularly in attendance. Every now and then he stops to chat with Frank, but doesn't give anything away about what is going on behind closed doors.

One Thursday morning in the spring of 2006, it appears the die has been cast. Bouquets of flowers are delivered for the five owners of Support Plus, complete with a card. The truth has finally been revealed; the deal has been closed. Support Plus is being acquired by Commodore. The renowned computer brand from the 1980s has been revitalized by a Dutchman, and is now listed on the NASDAQ stock exchange. This group views SP as the ideal distribution partner for the European market. The five owners of the venture capital company are really to be commended on this count, Frank thinks. In one fell swoop, they are set up for life, and they can fly the flag, literally and figuratively. Last night they were in negotiations at the notary's office until the sun came up. An internal memo is circulated with an explanation, and almost everyone gets swept up in the euphoria of it all.

Except for Frank. He congratulates everyone politely and sincerely, but mostly wonders what all this means for Bukatchi. Besides, Frank has been witness to too many things he can't find a logical explanation for, and which don't really make sense for a normally functioning company.

Even after the big day, the men in suits continue to show up at the white office building in Enschede. They hardly see any customers anymore; it is mostly accountants and bankers who are taking up all of management's time. The deal is interesting for many parties in the financial world, and the newspapers are full of stories on it, from the local *TC Tubantia* to the national *Financieele Dagblad*. Support Plus is hot.

At Bukatchi, they slog away at developing the new collection for 2007. In spite of their limited resources, they still manage to put together a commercially attractive line of patio furniture. Frank also plans to publish a real catalog again for the first time since the bankruptcy, to draw the attention of as many customers as possible to the collection. The prospects are bright, and the mood within the little group of patio furniture guys is excellent.

They see the management of Support Plus less and less; these men are still hard at work on the take-over. One Wednesday afternoon, Frank suddenly sees the men rushing in one by one. He wonders what could possibly be going on now. From the window of his office, he has a good view of the parking lot. There is a big black van parked in the middle of all the Porsches and BMWs, with tinted windows and an Italian license plate. It's almost as if the Mafia has moved all the way up to Enschede.

He soon hears what is actually going on. The commercial director was in Italy a few weeks ago, and made all the arrangements. It's a professional Italian tailor who is measuring all the men for a custom-made suit. He has a selection of fabrics with him and the SP owners take turns going into the van. Every member of the board orders four or five suits. The VIP van stays parked in the parking lot all afternoon.

During the summer of 2006, stress clearly dominates in the building. Once again, it is not clear what exactly is going on, but one thing is for sure and that is that things aren't quite going as planned at SP. Frank puts out his feelers and goes to see the executive secretary a few times. The pieces of the puzzle are slowly falling into place. After speaking with a real estate friend of his, who confides in Frank that Diederick van Buiten has called off the purchase of an enormous mansion, he is sure; the sale of SP to Commodore is off. He would be willing to bet a bottle of wine on it. Since no one else is talking about it within the walls of the big building, he really just makes the bet with himself.

A few weeks later, the headline of the regional newspaper reads *Commodore can't afford Support Plus*. Frank can't imagine how this is possible. It goes contrary to everything he's seen, heard and sensed. The mudslinging between the two marital partners has begun, and more and more juicy details are exposed. Slowly but surely, Frank hears what has actually happened. All in all, the acquisition procedure has taken up a little less than a year. The board and management invested an incredible amount of time, attention and energy in the take-over. So much in fact that the focus was no longer on daily operations and managing the extreme growth, and this had gone on for months. In the fast-paced world of consumer electronics, trends follow one another in rapid succession, and this can be fatal.

This appears now to be the case here too. The investigation of the accounts showed that sales had spiraled downward as if in a vortex. All sorts of skeletons came out of the closet. The managers that were pushing for the acquisition by Commodore were apparently shocked out of their skulls. They certainly hadn't counted on this. The investment bankers, the dealmakers and all the other parties from the financial world that were involved switched all the signals to red.

It is a catastrophic situation for the company and the employees wonder in desperation what will happen now.

The SP board tries to play down the entire situation through reassuring memos, but Frank knows better. Fortunately, the sales of patio chairs for the 2007 season are on schedule. This is what they focus on.

One fine day in the fall of 2006, as Frank walks down the hall to the bathroom, he gets the fright of his life and gasps. He sees a man walking towards him from the end of the hallway. A man he was forced to work with at Unimeta for six months. It's Pieter de Wit from the NTAB. In a matter of seconds, the past year and a half flashes before his eyes. The hallway is so

195

narrow that Frank can't exactly act as if he doesn't see Pieter. They hold out their hands to each other at the same time. Pieter couldn't be friendlier.

"Frank, how nice to see you again! Everything okay?" he says.

"Yeah, sure Pieter, things are going great. And with you?"

"Fine, fine. Busier than I've ever been."

"Great; we all gotta pay the bills, right? What are you doing here at Support Plus anyway? You can't be here looking for me."

"We've been doing some consulting work lately," Pieter says without moving a muscle.

"Consulting work? Probably consulting on where to dig the hole you mean."

"No, we help companies when they have to reorganize and so on."

"Yeah, sure," Frank says knowingly. "Well, good luck with it all and I'll see you around."

They shake hands again, and go their separate ways. Frank has the feeling his face is as red as a lobster. Checking himself in the bathroom mirror, he sees it's not that bad. He splashes his face with cold water anyway to help get over the shock of seeing Pieter. Pieter de Wit was the last person Frank had hoped to run into here. He knows all too well what this means.

19

TOTAL CHAOS

Weeks go by. Things remain relatively calm, but Frank realizes it has to be the calm before the storm. Things can't continue to go well for long though, now that the NTAB has become involved. And this appears to be the case pretty soon. From out of nowhere, a new general director is hired at Support Plus. He comes from the well-known consultancy firm, Boer & Croon. Apparently, a top-level executive meeting was held to discuss this.

ABN Amro and the investors arrived at the conclusion that there was not enough trust to allow them to continue with company management in its current form; external management and supervision was necessary. They needed someone to get the company's house in order, and take a critical look at whether or not the right things are being done the right way. He will naturally also act as the eyes and ears of the bank, which wants to see its money again.

Diederick van Buiten is sidetracked, assigned to some unclear position or other, and the power falls into the hands of Jos Zwieper of Boer & Croon. Together with the bank, he blocks all the payments. Jos has to personally approve every payment, and then route it through the bank for the final transfer. It is all starting to sound damned familiar to Frank.

That fall, the Wunderbars arrive. Finally. Everyone has been looking forward to this moment, first and foremost for their own benefit, of course. Nearly every employee at SP has ordered one of these magical tap systems at a major discount, including the guys at Bukatchi. It is truly an amazing machine. Hooking it up is a little tricky, and now and then beer sprays out of it, but once it's set up, the thing does its name justice.

Containers full of the product roll into the warehouse. This is also fortunate for all the customers who have been waiting for them since they are delivered later than planned. It is incredibly busy in the warehouse. On one side, containers are being unloaded, and on the other, full pallets are being driven into the trucks for delivery all over Europe. Dozens of containers are unloaded and trucks emptied and filled again.

"*Dze Killer is dze best*," Manuel constantly calls out through the hallway.

After a week or two, the shipments out of the warehouse stop, even though the containers keep coming. In no time, the warehouse is packed to capacity with Wunderbars. When Frank and his co-workers go to take a look, they see racks full of the machines, stacked all the way up to the warehouse ceiling. Row after row after row of them. There must be tens of thousands of them, and there isn't room for one more. The building next to the existing warehouse is also rented. With this additional 3,000 square meters of space, the problem should be solved, but nothing is farther from the truth. The containers keep on rolling in. Jos Zwieper's face is getting gloomier by the day. Two weeks later, another 3000 square meter warehouse is added for storage.

Frank carefully asks Jos about the background of this story. It turns out that they had to order 500,000 Wunderbars in order to get the license for Europe. The problem, however, is that they've only sold 150,000 units. They're trying to hawk the rest. They have to get rid of them as fast as possible; there are dozens more containers on their way and the production is continuing. Jos asks Frank if he knows anyone who would be interested. The Wunderbar does in fact appear to be "dze Killer", of the company, that is.

This goes on and on, each story wilder than the last, but the gist of all of them is the same. A lot of products are shipped back, and this costs SP mountains of money. The 50 trucks filled with fitness equipment from Italy, for example. The director in charge of the sports division didn't even know these products had been ordered. The commercial director did this behind his back, for shipment to a major Italian customer, including the right of return, of course. The products were barely in the store when this customer took advantage of his right to return them, as stipulated in the contract. Everything that isn't sold goes back to SP. Judging from the packaging, the products never even made it into the store. Truck after truck drives past the Bukatchi employees who are sitting out on the street, watching it all. Additional warehouse space is rented, again. An email is sent to all the employees, asking if any of them need an exercise bike or weight-lifting bench. They are fighting a losing battle.

SP's financial situation only gets direr. Suppliers are no longer getting paid, and bills lie around untouched. ABN Amro blocks and freezes everything. Fortunately, none of this affects Bukatchi. Frank is so unbelievably happy that he had insisted on separate financing from Banque Artesia. The situation only gets awkward on one occasion. SP owes the container transport company hundreds of thousands, which then refuses to keep delivering containers. This also affects Bukatchi since their containers are on the same ship. Frank has to move heaven and earth to get them out of the port, while SP's products are held there.

The connection to SP is now starting to work against Bukatchi. More and more customers are starting to ask what is going on. It's a difficult question to answer, since they can't reveal too much and discredit their parent company. Frank has an urgent meeting with Banque Artesia to figure out how they can get out of this complete chaos. The bank has other things on its mind, however. Right when Frank needs them the most, they are working on a strategic reorientation at the bank. They are considering closing several branches, including the one in Enschede. Just what they need.

Frank decides to contact his local Rabobank branch in Oldenzaal where he has been doing his personal banking for 15 years. He knows the account manager well and explains the situation to him, supported by figures. The Rabobank's response is positive. He will have to buy up Bukatchi's shares in Support Plus so that he has full control of all his shares again. This will return full ownership to Frank, but he needs to find out what Bukatchi's value is and what Support Plus wants for the shares. The company hasn't even existed for a full year, and is only making a small profit, so it can't be a huge amount.

When he discusses it with Jos Zwieper, he pulls a report from his desk drawer. Coincidence or not, they had just calculated a value for Bukatchi. Frank can't believe his eyes. He blinks a couple of times, and then looks again.

"Isn't this one zero too many, Jos?" Frank asks, just to be sure.

"No, Frank, that's really the amount. I can tell you that the venture capital firm and the bank are really pleased with this."

"I can imagine they are, but this isn't accurate."

"But it is accurate Frank; a few people have looked at this and agree."

Frank swallows and mutters to himself.

"Seven million Euros. Seven million. For a company that isn't even one year old, and has made a small profit because Unimeta's old inventory was sold via a one-time deal."

He gets angry and struggles to keep his temper.

"You are all totally out of your minds, Jos. All I can say is good luck with that; sell it to another fool. You people are stark raving mad."

In spite of the report in his hand, Frank leaves Zwieper's office, figuratively empty-handed. He calls Rodie from his own office and tells him all the gory details of what just happened. Rodie is flabbergasted. Together they conclude that the only point in discussing it further is if they start all over again, and the people with decision-making authority are present. Jos is just a pawn in the entire chess game for the proverbial silverware. ABN Amro just wants to recover as much of its investment as possible.

"But I refuse to be trampled on in the process," Frank tells Rodie, determined. "I refuse to go through that nightmare again."

A subtle game begins. If Frank exerts too much pressure, and acts too hungry, he will definitely pay the price. If he waits too long, time will not be on his side, and he might unintentionally get caught up in the bad situation. In the meantime, he is also talking to Rabobank, and the development and production of the patio furniture is continuing. If he didn't know any better, he could almost forget what his core task is. Frank has the feeling he has to keep ten plates spinning at the same time.

The chaos at SP only gets worse. Now there are also universal remote controls that have been returned by a customer. Lidl bought 650,000 of them. SP's colleagues in China forgot to check if the products came with a manual in German. As it turns out, they didn't. All the remote controls are being recalled from all the Lidl stores and repackaged with a German manual. Trucks full of them come to Enschede. A small amount of space has been freed up in the second warehouse when some of the Wunderbars are sold. This is where they unload the shipments of remote controls. They contract all the sheltered workshops in the region to help add the manuals to the packaging. Trucks with blister packs come and go on a frequent basis.

The Bukatchi employees can't believe their eyes. What a catastrophe!

A few weeks later, Frank finally gets a call from Jos. A shareholders' meeting is planned for later that week, and the men from Special Credits will also be there.

The sale of Bukatchi has been put on the agenda, and Frank will be given 15 minutes to give a presentation. He can't stop worrying about what he has to do to get the offer of seven million off the table. The best he can do is make it immediately clear how ridiculous that amount is.

At one o'clock in the afternoon, it will be his turn to speak. He has brought Rodie with him; the two of them form a stronger, united front. They have been sitting in Frank's office waiting since 12:30. It takes almost another two hours before the phone rings, giving them the sign they can go into the meeting. Frank puts on his jacket and straightens his tie.

They walk into the large conference room and remain standing to take in what they see. At least 10 men are already sitting at the table. Jos Zwieper, Diederick van Buiten, Wilfred and his right-hand man from the venture capital company, two accountants, Pieter de Wit from the NTAB, and two men from Special Credits whom Frank has never seen before.

A delegation of heavyweights, and this is exactly what Frank needs. He shakes everyone's hand, giving them his business card. They look at the card, then up at Frank, then back down at the card. Frank can see the wheels in their heads turning. He's won the first battle; he now has their complete and undivided attention.

As chairman, Jos speaks, welcoming Frank and his financial aide-de-camp. He immediately asks about the meaning of the strange card. Frank waits a bit, allowing the anticipation to build before he speaks.

"What you have before you is the card for my new company, HKMK BV."

The company name is printed in green letters on the card, next to a simple line drawing depicting a man's head, with curly hair and glasses.

"The illustration is meant to represent me. My new profession is also mentioned on the card, 'magician'. After all, gentlemen, let's be honest, shall we? Imagine that you start up a new company and invest a couple hundred thousand in it. You buy back some old inventory for, let's say 100, and sell it again for 110. A little less than one year later, this same company is worth an amazing seven million! No normal person is capable of doing this.

I don't believe in wizardry, but at the very least, you have to be a magician to manage this. Apart from the absurdity of the calculations, I can only get financing for a fraction of that amount. Our current bank, Artesia, can't even play a role in this. So why don't you tell me what the realistic value is?"

Jos whispers with the bankers to his left. They then confer among themselves, making furious notes on paper. The realization of the absurdity of the amount they've quoted slowly starts dawning on them.

"Frank, we will get back to you on this," Jos says, and closes the cover of the report. Frank understands that this means the conversation is over, so he stands up and walks to the door with Rodie. Before he can put his hand on the door handle however, one of the bankers addresses him.

"Mr. Krake, before you leave the meeting, I have one more question for you. What do the letters 'HKMK' actually stand for?"

Frank turns around and with a cold stare, answers his question.

"*Hans Kazan Met Krullen*, a famous Dutch magician, but with curly hair." Pieter de Wit almost chokes on the sip of coffee he has just taken. One of the bankers bursts out laughing, while Jos stares at the business card, his mouth open in disbelief. Frank stoically walks out of the room and closes the door behind him. Once in the hallway, Rodie is no longer able to contain himself.

"Who's the idiot here now, man? How could you do such a thing? The big-wigs involved with the financial aspects of Support Plus are sitting in there, and you pull a stunt like this?"

"Mission accomplished," is all Frank says, with a huge grin on his face.

Frank's stunt doesn't have any other consequences for the office atmosphere and the relationships between the people in the SP building. The people there are too consumed with their own problems to worry about Bukatchi and its employees. And this is actually the crux of the matter; there's a very real danger that everything will just stay the way it is. Frank wants to go forward, but is completely dependent on other people, even though he's not exactly sure on whom. There may have been ten people sitting at that table that Friday afternoon, but if all they did was sit there and stare at each other, then nothing will happen.

In the spring of 2007, the chaos within the walls of the big white building only gets worse. No one knows who does what and who is responsible for what anymore. There's even talk that Jos Zwieper is going to buy into the company. He supposedly wants to invest one million Euros, as long as the venture capital company also invests, and ABN Amro normalizes the relationship.

Frank listens to it all and has his own opinions. He actually wants to get out of the mess called Support Plus as fast as possible. Customers don't really trust it anymore. Their history at Unimeta naturally doesn't help matters much. They are now really getting to a breaking point.

He decides not to wait for Special Credits any longer, and calls Groeleken to schedule an appointment. He also makes preparations to move Bukatchi to its own building.

They have already rented a small showroom in a multi-functional business center, barely 500 yards from SP. They are also going to rent office space there.

Groeleken gives Rodie and Frank a really friendly welcome.

"I thought I had gotten rid of you, Frank," he says with a grin. "Now here you are again, in Amsterdam. At some point, it has to stop. What on earth are you doing to end up back here every time?"

"As if you didn't know. Your minions have undoubtedly told you about the background of my visit and the conversation we had in Enschede."

"Conversation? You're obviously referring to that stunt you pulled with that new company of yours, and the amazing trick with the magician? Oh man, we had such a good laugh about that. I actually shouldn't be telling you this, but we passed your business card around. My two co-workers who were there told anyone who was willing to listen about all the gory details of that meeting. They had never experienced anything like it before, and nor had I. But your message was received loud and clear. However, we need to see some money in order to sell you the shares to your little enterprise. Bukatchi is making a profit, the prospects are good, and SP has ensured you got off to a flying start. That comes at a price."

"Peter, I'm not saying I don't want to pay anything for my shares, just that it has to be reasonable. The first accounting year was heavily affected by the one-time inventory deal with you. All the synergy with SP will be gone, we will have to rent an expensive building, and we will have to see if we keep any customers after all the chaos we're in the middle of right now. Banque Artesia is pulling out of the Dutch market, and has cancelled the credit line. I can't get more than a limited amount in acquisition financing from my local Rabobank branch. Actually, the company isn't worth all that much, in other words."

They go back and forth for a while, and Rodie shows calculations that offer a more realistic picture. After an hour and a half of arguing and a few short breaks to discuss it among themselves, they finally arrive at a figure they can all live with. They shake on it.

"And be careful Frank," Groeleken says with a sly look. "I don't ever want to see you here again."

"The feeling is absolutely mutual, Peter," Frank says.

The Friday after Ascension Day in 2007 is also a day off for the employees at Support Plus. Many of them take advantage of the extra days to go away for a long weekend, a brief respite from all the problems and fuss, and away from everything that has to do with SP. An ideal day to move, Frank has decided. Actually, it's really strange to just leave, of course. They are officially still part of SP. At the time of the start-up, they had only made an official agreement about the amount of compensation for office space at SP. Frank carefully checked the contract on this. However, there was nothing in the document about actually moving into and occupying this space. Bukatchi is free to set up its offices elsewhere.

The four Bukatchi employees can do their thing in peace; there's no one else at the office anyway. All the desks and cabinets are lugged down three flights of stairs since there is no elevator. In a rented van, they bring all the furniture and files to the multi-functional building a little ways away. They set up everything there the best they can. Over the past few weeks, the telephone lines and computer network have been installed and tested. By the afternoon, Bukatchi is up and running, but now, for all intents and purposes, completely free from Support Plus. The connection now only exists on paper. On the Monday, a letter goes out to all the customers that Bukatchi is going to be continuing independently, in order to create a bit of calm in the market. They don't mention the fact that the financial connection has still not officially been cut.

Frank is curious how SP management will react. After all, they did leave rather suddenly. This move may just not go down very well at all.

As it turns out, there is no reaction whatsoever. Resignation, that's really the best way to describe the situation at SP. Frank even negotiates with Jos about the value of the office furniture. He approaches him and boldly offers him a couple thousand Euros for the whole lot. They reach an agreement within five minutes.

On July 17, 2007, Frank goes to the notary's office to make the acquisition official. The notary checks to make sure Rabobank has transferred the acquisition price to the escrow account. Frank is amazed that Diederick hasn't arrived yet. The notary makes a few calls, including one to Pieter de Wit at the NTAB. Only then do the wheels seem to be set in motion. A bit later, Diederick also shows up at the office, and in Amsterdam, they unleash a herd of lawyers on the case, who seem to have waited until this moment to start looking at the contracts. They consult with one another over the phone.

Frank just sits there and watches the show. They probably waited all this time because they just assumed he wouldn't be able to get the money together for the acquisition. They sure were dead wrong about that. They only now start making a move, now that the amount has actually been deposited to the escrow account. It seems to take an eternity. Frank is starving, but has sworn that he won't set a foot outside the notary's office until he has all the right signatures on all the documents.

At 8:30 in the evening, five and a half hours after he walked into the office, Frank finally walks outside again, with all the signed contracts and deeds in his hands. He has taken on the greatest financial obligation of his life, but he finally feels free. Free as a bird. Delivered from the Support Plus millstone.

20

ON THE RIGHT TRACK

Support Plus is ultimately dismantled by the bank a year and a half later, going bankrupt after two years, but at Bukatchi, they can finally focus on what they're good at, designing and selling patio furniture. Frank hires Bas who has just obtained his degree in product development, and has shown them some great examples of his design work. He asks Bart to help out part-time to help improve the quality in China. After the Unimeta debacle, Bart has worked on several other projects, and is interested in what Frank has to offer. The Chinese are full of goodwill, but if you don't supervise them closely, you never get the exact results you expect, and for Bukatchi, good quality is a basic criterion. Frank hires his former Unimeta co-worker, Laurens, to handle the bookkeeping.

Of the new customers they pull in, Aldi is the most prestigious. They get a first order of over one million Euros for three different products, with order quantities of at least 10,000 units each. It's a real dream order. These quantities do not come without risks, however. They have to deliver all these products on pallets to six depots spread throughout the country on a single day in April. If the trucks are even one hour late, they can head straight back to the warehouse, and Bukatchi will be the lucky owner of thousands of patio chairs or chaise lounges. And to make matters even worse, Aldi will send them a big fat invoice, with a penalty of tens of thousands of Euros or more. An order like this therefore demands meticulous preparation and military precision, but thankfully it all goes well.

Frank has noticed that their larger customers are travelling to China more frequently. They want to see the patio furniture factories for themselves, and if possible, even buy directly from them, in spite of all the problems this usually causes. The Bukatchi showroom in Enschede doesn't get that many visitors. Bukatchi should actually follow its customers to China. They already have the contacts with the factories there, and the salesmen fly there a couple of times a year to help develop new products. The logical next step would be to open a showroom somewhere in China, and then the customers can combine their buying tour there with a visit to Bukatchi. Flora looks for available space since the office they are renting there now is not suitable at all for this purpose. They find a few potential locations, and Frank flies to China to see them.

One of the buildings seems perfect for the goal he has in mind. It has over 600 square meters of showroom space on a single floor, but the whole place is in need of renovation. The bright fluorescent lighting hanging from the ceiling and the shiny beige tiles on the floor have a distinctly Chinese look, and make a cheap, cold impression. They also have to have sleeping quarters for three people and a kitchen built into the facility since it's normal in China for an employer to offer his personnel a job including room and board. They also include an office in the sketches. There is only one little problem. After the renovations, the showroom will have to look European, and there aren't many Chinese people who are capable of pulling this off.

Flora suggests a company that builds booths for Nokia, Sony and Nike for the trade show in Canton. They at least understand that you have to work with spotlights and warm colors, and not with huge neon signs, white walls and shiny tiles. Bart is appointed as the "construction priest", and in the fall of 2007, they start the renovations. Every day, Bart gives the team in the Netherlands updates by telephone on the progress, and sometimes he'll send a photo. He's usually unrecognizable in the picture because of all the dust.

Bart discovers that the Chinese sometimes have a different approach to things than they do in the Netherlands. Once the old interior has been knocked out, he gets curious about where they are taking all the rubble. Wheelbarrow after wheelbarrow with debris is rolled out of the building, but they haven't rented a dumpster.

"I just walked out with them to see," he tells Frank. "They have built a jetty, right above the river that runs past the building here.

"A jetty? What do they need that for?" Frank asks.

"They wheel the debris down the jetty until they can't go any further, and then tip the wheelbarrow over, dumping it right into the river. No one gives a damn about this at all. I had Flora ask the foreman about this, what the deal is exactly, but he just shrugs. No one asks any questions here."

It reminds Frank of the story of the market vendor from Twente. He used to buy up broken relaxers and Unica bike frames from Unimeta. He would make one functioning chair from two frames, and sell them at his stall. He would dump the frames he couldn't use in a pond outside of town. Dozens of years later, when that area became a new residential development, the rusty frames came to the surface.

"We were no better here in the West," Frank says. "It's a matter of time before they also start realizing in China that they are fouling their own nest. The working conditions have already improved a lot. That's where it starts. I experienced it myself, back in the early 1990s, when I was still a buyer for Wehkamp and was given a tour of a new factory in Xiamen. None of the dozens of welders there wore goggles. I confronted the director about it."

"Just look outside," the director had said.

I saw crowds of people standing outside the factory gates.

"They're all looking for work. If the welders here in the factory can't see anything anymore, they can take a hike. Their successors are raring to go and ready to take their jobs."

"That was the mentality back then. Fortunately, things are a lot better now."

After only two months, the showroom is ready. There is even a coffee pod machine in the new office, so that they can offer their customers decent coffee instead of the usual Chinese dishwater. Frank brought the machine with him in his own carry-on bag.

The showroom has turned out beautifully. The ceiling has been painted charcoal gray, and the light-gray reflective curtains look great next to this color. A path of charcoal-gray carpeting has been laid down in the aisle. The presentation platforms have been covered with tan, burgundy and silver laminate flooring. All of this is illuminated using dozens of spotlights, giving it a very chic European look. And this was precisely their intention. Frank absolutely loves it, but when he asks Leo and Flora what they think, they answer in unison.

"Awful! It looks like a mausoleum!"

The European customers think it's perfect, and come to visit the showroom more and more often when they are in China. It's easy for them to combine this with a visit to Shin Crest, ten minutes away, where Frank gives them a tour of the factory. If he allows the metallic smell and the sounds of the machines to penetrate his senses, he can almost imagine he's gone back in time and is walking through the Unimeta factory again. The big difference now is that he no longer has to worry about all the people who work here, and whether or not the order portfolio will be as full as it should be next month.

In the new head-tail structure, he is a lot more flexible. If necessary, they can quickly shift gears, for example when wicker latticework suddenly becomes popular in Europe. A few years ago, Frank had stood looking at this material in America, shaking his head, and now everyone wants it. Not only can you make tall chairs from this material, you can also use it to make entire couches for outdoors, like wicker lounge sets. This is a very special field of expertise, and Shin Crest can't manufacture these products in their factory using a semi-automated production process. They find two production partners who can translate the design team's wishes into latticework products. It's all made by hand. Craftsmen braid or weave a complete chair onto a welded aluminum frame. It takes them one day to make a chair they only earn a couple dollars on.

They regularly add new materials and new designs to the collection. The only segment they don't serve is the top segment; after all, Hartman bought the Preston brand from the bankrupt company's assets. Since Unimeta had five million in annual sales from this line back then, Frank really wants to add the high-end segment to the range. They need an extra salesman to do this, to promote the products to the specialty stores.

He plans a trip to Indonesia with Carsten and Adri. They have a long-standing tradition of superior craftsmanship when it comes to perfect weaving work in this part of the world. Back in the 1960s, they made furniture using materials such as bamboo and cane, and these items made their way to living rooms in the Netherlands. They have now also mastered the art of attaching plaited synthetic strands to aluminum frames, making the pieces suitable for outdoor use.

With a connection of theirs, they spend two weeks criss-crossing the immense island kingdom in the spring of 2008. In Cirebon, on the north coast of Java, they find many suitable factories that can supply smaller series of high-quality products. This place is the cradle of the weaving profession. Out of a population of one million, 100,000 of these people are weavers. On every street corner, they see people sitting down, weaving or trying to sell their woven merchandise.

Not everything they see is suitable. The commercial team is able to separate the wheat from the chaff. They make unique products by changing the colors of the plaited strands, or by modifying the shape slightly. They put together a container full of prototypes that will allow them to promote these products to the top segment of the market for 2009.

During the trip, they meet Bambang, a friendly and skilled Indonesian manager. He acts as driver, interpreter, engineer, quality control supervisor, coordinator and fixer. They have a lot of arrangements to make; nothing happens by itself here, and you have to chase down everything. During Frank's years at Wehkamp, everything always took an incredible amount of time. It seems little has changed in the ten years since then. Whether they are dealing with production times or the document workflow, everything takes longer than they are accustomed to. They tolerate this though because the quality of the weaving is still high; fortunately, this hasn't changed either. It is a lot prettier and more neatly woven than the rushed work being produced in China, but this quality comes at a price. By Dutch standards, it is not expensive, but compared with the level of prices in China, they charge top dollar in Indonesia.

When one of Bukatchi's biggest customers comes to visit them in Indonesia in the spring of 2009, they open a showroom there too. With 75 stores, Hellweg is one of the larger German home-improvement chains. They come to visit with a three-man buying committee. For Frank, this is reason enough to rent a gorgeous colonial building, with a sign bearing the words "Bukatchi Indonesia" on the façade.

Proud as a peacock, Frank poses with Bambang in front of the latest addition to the company. To Frank's great relief, the visit is a huge success because now they can spread their risks. Indonesia is a wonderful country, with its tropical climate and very friendly, hospitable people. It makes the many trips he has to take to the Far East that much more pleasant and varied.

Now that Bukatchi is getting more and more customers who aren't only interested in importing containers directly, they have to make it possible for these customers to order smaller quantities from a local warehouse. Frank signs a distribution agreement with a German trading partner for this purpose. This will give Bukatchi access to a huge warehouse just across the border near Münster. From this location, they can deliver within 48 hours throughout the Netherlands, Belgium and Germany. This way they will have everything they need, ready and in position for an "attack" on the specialized retail stores. All that's left now is the showroom in the Netherlands; the building in Enschede has become too small for their needs.

In its first three years, Bukatchi has grown 15 to 20% each year, and in spite of the financial crisis, the prospects are still good. All the lights are green for a financing application with the local Rabobank branch where Frank is still doing his banking, to his full satisfaction. In no time, the financing for the new building has been arranged, and they even manage this at a time when the financial world has been turned upside down, with banks that have to be bailed out and countless companies going bankrupt.

Even at a time like this, Frank wants to keep pressing ahead and take a giant step forward. The competition definitely isn't. In his view, this means that they can get a headstart right now, or at least start catching up. The contractors are standing in line, the price of steel has dropped, and all the construction materials have gotten cheaper. It's the perfect time to drive the first stake into the ground, at a location along the A1 highway, easily accessible from the Netherlands and Germany.

Frank handles the supervision of the construction himself so that the team can focus on their work and not get distracted. He puts up with the fact that for nearly one year, he has spent every evening and most of every weekend dealing with the construction. Building on the future demands sacrifices. "Focus" is the magic word. Focus on the company and focus on patio furniture, and on nothing else that can distract him from either. No acting like a big shot in all sorts of clubs and business networks, just good, honest hard work. And he has the results to show for it. The building is finished in a couple of months, exactly on schedule and precisely within budget.

Since cutting a ribbon is so common on such an occasion, Frank has Bas design a special wicker patio chair, in the same style and with the same features as the building. When the mayor reveals the chair during the big opening celebration, everyone is impressed.

The growth continues on steadily in the Netherlands and Asia, so much so in fact that they have to hire new people from time to time. Flora and Bambang each get help from a quality control inspector. The whole affair with the remote controls without manuals is still fresh in Frank's memory. He does everything he can to prevent a disaster like that from happening at Bukatchi.

All the activities mean increasing pressure on Frank. At least six times a year, he is in China or Indonesia for about ten days. This really takes a toll, on him and his family. In spite of the incredible support from the home front, it is getting harder and harder for him. He has been to China almost 100 times in total, and has never had the time to see the Great Wall with his own eyes.

The week before he leaves, he prepares for all the meetings. He doesn't get the chance to do this during the day, so he works on into the wee hours. Jetlag and the huge temperature difference place incredible demands on his stamina. He doesn't have time to recharge and recover; his schedule is completely full. When Frank arrives in his hotel room at around 11:00 at night and opens his email, he dives right in, going through and answering all the incoming messages. After eight or nine days, he flies back. Once home, he continues, full speed ahead, so that jetlag doesn't get the chance to slow him down. A huge pile of work is waiting for him at the office, but his wife and children also deserve the necessary attention. After a few days, he has finally taken care of some of the backlog, and is rummaging around in his yard on a Saturday, when his neighbor unwittingly asks him a very naive question.

"Hey, neighbor! How was your vacation?"

Eighteen families are dependent on Bukatchi's achievements, and for Frank, this only adds to the stress. After the many dismissals at Unimeta, he had sworn that he would never fire anyone ever again, or at any rate, not for financial reasons.

Every year, the sales counter starts over again at zero during the summer months. That's when the big battle for orders begins. Frank always refers to this time of year as catching balloons. There is only a period of a few weeks that the balloons float through the air. The trick is to catch as many as you can before the competition does. If you're not fast and sharp enough, they'll blow away. This is how they pull in sales every year. Fortunately, they always manage to grab a few extra balloons, so that sales continue to grow, but having to start from scratch all over again every year and be dependent on factors they don't always have control over starts eating away at Frank.

More and more orders also means that the pre-financing amount they need grows along with them, which in turn means an increase in risks. The accountant has warned him about this a few times. The Rabobank is more accommodating, but still, it feels like a heavy burden. Frank also prefers to keep the organization as flat as possible. No more layers of management with bosses and supervisors; he saw too many adverse effects of this structure at Unimeta. The result is that he has to manage 18 employees himself, and this is getting increasingly difficult. Having already gone bankrupt once means that he wants to maintain absolute control over the entire process. This is also adding to the stress.

But the train keeps chugging along, and the conductor keeps pushing the pedal to the metal. In April 2010, his next trip to China has been scheduled, and Carsten will be joining him. Yet another major German customer is coming to see them, and they pull out all the stops to leave an indelible impression. The growing product range no longer fits in the existing showroom. They rent extra space every year from February to May. For two solid days, Carsten and Frank work hard with their Chinese colleagues to make sure everything is in place and decorated nicely, down to the very last detail.

The visit goes really well, so all their efforts aren't wasted. The response is incredibly positive. Carsten and Frank raise their cups of European coffee to toast their success. Their Chinese colleagues keep the used coffee pods, and Frank knows they will use them again after he is gone. In spite of this, the result of a second round, re-using the pods, is still better than the local coffee they are used to drinking. The Dutch people joke among themselves, wondering what they do with toilet paper.

Frank and Carsten are packing their bags to leave when Flora comes in and asks if they have already heard the news.

"What news?" Frank asks.

"About a volcano in Iceland. It erupted yesterday, and I just heard on the radio that the ash cloud is affecting all the flights from China to Europe."

"You're pulling our leg," Frank says, thinking it's a joke. "You just want us to help you clean up the showroom. All that dismantling and packing up is a hellish job. We've been here almost a week now. I'm going home tomorrow."

Carsten is less sure. He goes online to find news about volcanoes in Iceland.

Some of the news sites and all of the sites showing videos are censored, but he still manages to find one report on possible delays in air traffic.

All Frank can really do is laugh.

"A volcano erupts in Iceland, and of course I'm in China and can't get home. How unbelievable is that? Just my luck, again!"

One phone call to the travel agency confirms all the speculations. A volcano with the unpronounceable name Eyjafjallajökull has spewed a huge ash cloud out over the world. This cloud is so large and expansive that air traffic between China and Europe is in danger of being brought to a standstill. The women at the travel agency have no idea what is going to happen now.

Carsten decides to just fly to Shanghai the next morning and get on the flight to Düsseldorf from there, if it hasn't been cancelled, that is. Frank has to go to Hong Kong early, to get on a direct flight to Amsterdam from there. He decides not to take any chances. The risk that he will end up stuck at the airport in Hong Kong is too high.

In the morning, it becomes clear that all the flights to Europe have been cancelled. Carsten is stuck in Shanghai and won't be able to leave for the time being. The travel agent tells him that it could be a week before any flights will be leaving again. Frank is feeling relaxed. He has been in worse predicaments. Besides, this is beyond anyone's control. He calls his wife and lets her know that it's going to take a bit longer before he can fly home. Next, he calls Bambang. He knows that Frank is in China, and has heard about the ash cloud. Frank asks if he has time for an impromptu trip to see a few Javanese business partners. This is no trouble at all for Bambang.

"I'll just make time for that."

When Frank takes the first flight back to Europe a little less than a week later, he can look back on a fantastic time in Indonesia. He visited around 20 factories with Bambang, and combined this with great meals and a relaxing massage every now and then. Carsten went back a day before, after spending four days in Shanghai and with a two-day layover in Dubai.

21

SHIRT SPONSOR

Frank continues to innovate and look for ways to expand growth. Investing in his own stores is not an option, but the Internet offers possibilities for supplying consumers directly.

This is how the idea for his own online store is born. He designs a plan of attack, the goal of which is to become the first large, independent online store for patio furniture, one that is not affiliated with the large chain stores in the Netherlands such as Blokker, Leen Bakker or Kwantum.

Frank realizes that it's a pretty big leap of faith, but anything is better than sitting still and not doing anything, and besides, once he has started, he can always make adjustments. The train has started down the tracks at any rate, and they break out of the iron cage of being only an importer and wholesaler.

On May 1, 2011, the online store goes live, and the major tests begin. They're still operating under the radar for now to give them time to remove every possible glitch. It appears considerably more difficult to deliver a pallet with more than 225 pounds to a consumer's back yard than just handing over a box of shoes at the front door. However, after a few weeks, they've ironed out all the bugs and they even manage to deliver an order to a fourth-floor apartment three days later.

The great thing is that Bukatchi can handle this new venture with its current staff. A special phone line has been installed that allows incoming calls to come into Bukatchi's inside sales department. This line has a special ringtone so when a call comes in, the staff member knows to respond to the caller in the right way. There is already an entire lot of patio furniture in stock in Bukatchi's warehouse in Münster, to handle back-orders and re-orders to various foreign customers. They can draw from this stock to avoid every inventory risk. They develop all the furniture themselves, and have them made directly at the source in China and Indonesia. All the ingredients they need are there to start, and at relatively low costs.

Frank has had the name for this new business in his head for months, TiTaTuinmeubelen.nl. When Frank mentioned the name to his advertising agency for the first time, they all turned a bright shade of red. They asked him if he thought an unusual name like that was a good idea.

"That's exactly what it is," Frank answered. "There are already so many names that are all so similar: the *Tuinmeubelstunter, Tuinmeubelvoordeelhal, Tuinmeubelgigant* and so on and so forth. These are dime-a-dozen names; this is not how you stand out in the crowd. We have to be different, unique. This name will put a smile on the face of anyone hearing it. It's pleasant yet gets your attention. It sticks with you. *TiTaTuinmeubelen.nl, tuinmeubelen tegen toverprijzen*, not only is there a reference to magic, but also to an old television show that will appeal to people's sentimentality. You only need to hear it once. And all those t's; the alliteration makes it catchy. Mark my words gentlemen; this name is part of what will make this new company such a big success."

Frank has plans to take a vacation with his family in early August. They're going to Greece. They have booked a great apartment at a huge complex with an enormous water amusement park. The children are really looking forward to it. For weeks, they have been trying to decide which wild water slide they are going to whizz down first.

Frank will be leaving for Greece with mixed feelings. Since the beginning of the year, he has already been to China and Indonesia three times, and has just returned from a trip to America. As far as that goes, he is happy to be able to relax, but he actually barely allows himself the time to do so. He has been wracking his brain trying to find the right way to put the new online store on the national map as the Netherlands' largest online patio furniture store. This is in addition to all the stress of the online marketing efforts, which will also be necessary of course.

A few weeks ago, Frank had discreetly looked into what a series of advertisements would cost in the national newspapers. His idea was to introduce the new company in a full-page ad, and then run repeat advertisements during the patio furniture season, to really drill the name into people's minds. Unfortunately, he was shocked by what a campaign like this would cost. A couple hundred thousand is apparently chicken feed to some advertisers. And then an ad like this is naturally gone the next day, and in all likelihood, forgotten.

It has been clear to Frank for a long time that this is going to cost a lot of money, but it has to be done the right way. This campaign has to have a huge impact, and remain visible for a longer period of time. The topics from his brand management days run through his head. This was a similar problem. He only had 150,000 Euros to spend, 200,000 tops, to launch the new online store on the market. Normally, a good market introduction for a new brand in the Netherlands costs millions. Money he doesn't have. He lies there on his sun lounger, all these questions running around in his head. This is a really fantastic resort, the kids are having the time of their lives and that means Frank and his wife can relax and enjoy their vacation too. Time to catch up and read a few books and magazines. Their first day in Greece goes the way a first day of vacation should go, nice and relaxed. Frank feels the tension slowly leaving his body. He knows he places excessive demands on himself. Bukatchi is everything to him, but it is also all-consuming.

Before they left, Frank tossed a stack of *Voetbal International* issues, the Dutch soccer magazine, in his suitcase. It's his favorite magazine, but he's hardly had time to read any of them in the last few months. He grabs the most recent issue to start with. It looks like the soccer train has dropped Ronald Koeman off at Rotterdam Central Station this time. He's featured on the cover, larger than life, as the new trainer for Rotterdam's team, Feyenoord. Surprising. Leafing through the magazine, Frank gets up to date on all the transfer gossip and news from the world of soccer. He also reads an article about the three clubs in the Dutch province of Gelderland: Vitesse, De Graafschap and NEC. The one thing they all have in common is that none of them has a new jersey sponsor for the coming season. Crisis in Gelderland!

Looks like they had better hurry up, Frank thinks. It's Tuesday today, and the league competition starts this coming weekend. He flicks through some more and reads a few more articles about famous soccer players. The day goes on like this, and they're enjoying their vacation to the fullest. In the evening, an enormous buffet is set up for the resort guests, and they savor the Greek specialties. A couple of cold beers make the ultimate vacation feeling complete, but somewhere in the back of Frank's mind, a fire smolders that just won't go out.

The next morning, Frank has no idea how many hours he had lain awake turning it over and over in his mind, but he has figured it out. He's got it. This is what he has been looking for for a while; TiTaTuinmeubelen.nl as the jersey sponsor for a professional soccer team in the Premier League. That would be one heck of a feat, but it would help him achieve what he has in mind, namely a fantastic introduction with tons of national publicity and a high frequency of repetition during the entire season. He can't stop thinking about it, and Wednesday is turning out to be the ideal second day of their vacation. It is the type of day on which his wife and children adjust to the languid situation and the slow pace at which life passes them by. Half of the time, Frank is also present in this world, but the other half he spends working out plans, and all sorts of ideas race through his mind.

He has now figured out that De Graafschap is the only serious option. For a full-blooded and fanatic Twente supporter such as Frank, Vitesse is out for obvious reasons, and NEC is a bit boring. De Graafschap is much more of a team after his own heart, the underdog of the Premier League.

It is a team that is made of the right stuff, that has a reputation for being trustworthy and arouses sympathy in everyone. Besides, Doetinchem, where the team is based, is easy to get to from Hengelo. With his limited budget, Frank thinks he has the best chance with the blue-and-white zebra striped team.

In May, Frank had been to a fun evening for businessmen put on by the team Heracles, from Almelo. This team has always held a special place in his heart. As a boy of 12, he would ride his bike to the stadium on the Bornsestraat, and crawl under the fence with a friend of his. He had watched Hans Polko play, and saw Hendrie Krüzen shoot nutmegs against Feyenoord as a 16-year-old prodigy. But that was 30 years ago. These days, Heracles is a proud Premier League team with a professional organization and trainer, Peter Bosz.

During that networking evening, this same Peter Bosz made a few revelations about the team's structure. One of these revelations was about the opportunities for sponsoring. He told them that as the main sponsor, Ten Cate paid around 800,000 to get their name on the Heracles' jerseys. This didn't include what they paid for the artificial turf field. In terms of publicity value, Heracles is reasonably comparable to De Graafschap. But 800,000 - no way, not in 800 years. Two hundred thousand, that's all he has to spend.

"Papa, catch!"

A big ball comes flying at top speed in his direction. Frank catches it just in time, and brings it back over to the swimming pool. The entertainment crew has set out the goals for a game of water polo, and his children want him to play on their team. For half an hour, he's focused on swimming, throwing and catching the ball, holding others down under water and having a whole lot of fun. Exhausted, Frank limps back to his lounge chair, and his wife laughs at him.

"Hey old man, couldn't beat them?" Frank barely hears her. In his mind, he has already returned to the Vijverberg, De Graafschap's stadium.

This coming Sunday is the opening match of the league competition. De Graafschap will play last season's champion, the team from Amsterdam, Ajax. This is about as good as it gets. It means the maximum amount of media attention. He'll wait until Friday. If De Graafschap doesn't have a main sponsor by then, he might have a shot.

After all, everything flows under pressure. Frank can remember how Centric quit as the main sponsor a few months ago, followed by the usual arguments, and that the team has been looking for a new sponsor ever since. The economic malaise is hard on everyone.

He will offer to become main sponsor, but not for the entire season. They won't like it, but he has no choice. If he has any hope of doing this with only 200,000, then this is the way he has to do it. He will have to be creative about it. An online patio furniture store on the jerseys of a Premier League team in January, when the snow has just been cleared off the field, won't get him very far. This won't draw any traffic to the website. It would be pointless and a waste of money. The best option would be to feature on the jerseys for half of a season, in August and September, and then to resume in mid-March when patio furniture season starts back up. But this is hardly something they will be interested in at team headquarters over in Doetinchem.

On Thursday, Frank drafts a plan on two sheets of paper. It's not really all that difficult. He knows what he wants, and he knows what his goal is. Frank can hardly wait; he's incredibly excited about this.

After fuelling up with a big breakfast, he takes the plunge and calls De Graafschap.

"Hello, this is Frank Krake from TiTaTuinmeubelen.nl calling. I'm interested in becoming your main sponsor. Pardon? Did you say the connection is bad? That's possible. I'm calling you from Corfu. No, not Nkufo. Corfu."

Frank is put through to two other people before he finally gets commercial manager Martin Koenink on the line. He tells his story once again.

"Yes, that's right, TiTaTuinmeubelen.nl... Corfu...no, not the sign sponsor, the main sponsor."

Frank can almost hear the doubt on the other end of the line. He almost expects them to ask if they are on Candid Camera or something. They obviously have the feeling someone is playing a joke on them. Frank can understand their confusion; 48 hours before the start of the league competition, someone they've never heard of calls them from Corfu on behalf of TiTaTuinmeubelen.nl saying they want to be main sponsor. And for only 200,000, and then for only half of a season. It's logical that it would raise some questions, but Frank sticks to his story and makes it clear that he's serious. The commercial manager slowly comes around. Martin has to get used to the entire idea and particularly the part about only half of a season.

"That's actually impossible, of course."

"Do you already have a main sponsor then? You're playing Ajax the day after tomorrow, aren't you?"

Nothing but silence on the other end of the line.

"Why don't you take some time and let it sink in, Martin," Frank says. "Discuss it with the CEO and coordinate things internally. We can talk again right after lunch and see where we stand."

With a broad grin on his face, he walks back to the swimming pool, and allows time to do its thing.

At exactly one o'clock, his phone rings.

"This is Martin Koenink, from De Graafschap. We have thought about the plans and could arrive at an agreement, with a few adjustments."

This is music to Frank's ears. During the next half hour, they negotiate about all the terms and conditions of the sponsorship. The result is that TiTaTuinmeubelen.nl will be seen on the torsos of the players for 16 league competition matches, and in many other team communications. Frank also succeeds in getting the National Cup tournament and any play-offs included in the deal.

There's only one problem. The contract has to be signed with an official signature, and they can't do this by email, and there isn't a fax machine to be found in the somewhat ramshackle reception area at the resort. Frank makes a fuss about it at the reception desk. Suddenly, an older woman remembers that there should be a machine somewhere in the filing room. The fax machine is retrieved and dusted off. Wonder of wonders, ten minutes later, the document with Frank's signature rolls through the machine.

The next phone call is to Rabobank in Oldenzaal. Frank briefly explains what is going on. An hour later, 200,000 has been transferred to De Graafschap's bank account. The marketing machine may now officially run, and with barely 46 hours before kick-off.

All this time, Frank has been updating his wife on the gist of his plans. As he comes towards her, she asks if she should congratulate him or offer her condolences.

"I guess the latter," Frank answers.

"Why is that?"

"Well, I'm afraid I have to fly to Doetinchem and back."

"Doetinchem? But we're here in Corfu."

"Yes, and that's actually the problem. Sunday before the match, there will be a big introduction for the press and the general public. They are organizing a professional press conference and I have to be there, of course. It's a golden opportunity to put TiTaTuinmeubelen.nl on the map in the Netherlands, in one fell swoop."

"If you ask me, you actually have to be here. We're finally on vacation, the five of us. The kids are having a wonderful time. No way are you going back to the Netherlands."

The message is clear. Frank has already called the travel agency to find out if there is even a way for him to get off the island. This isn't that easy. He will check his email later; this is not the time. Not long afterwards, the kids come running over to him, enthusiastic. They have just been down the tallest giant slide, and are full of stories about their adventures. When Frank tells them about his adventure, they don't believe him at first. The oldest two are true soccer lovers and can reel off the selection list for the "Superboeren", as De Graafschap is affectionately known.

Esmee, his 12-year-old daughter, is the first to plead his case.

"Mama, sweetest mother in the world."

"Yes, what is it? Whenever you do this, I know you want something. You've already had an ice cream, and you're not getting another one."

"I don't want an ice cream, Mama. But I think that Papa should go back to the Netherlands."

Edith looks up in shock.

"Papa has to go to the Netherlands? Papa doesn't have to do any such thing. He's staying here. There'll be another match next weekend."

Then his oldest son Sven gets involved.

"But this match is against Ajax! Papa will never get a chance like this again."

Peep, the youngest of the group, senses the tension and wisely keeps silent. Edith gets in the pool to get away from all the whining. The kids jump in after her.

The next day, Saturday afternoon, Frank is on a plane to Zurich. It's the only connection he could find that will get him back to the Netherlands for Sunday morning. He arrives in Amsterdam at one in the morning, nothing but his carry-on with him. Half an hour after landing, he's driving back to Twente. He listens to all his voice mail messages in the car; his phone has been ringing off the hook since Friday evening. Friends, acquaintances and business contacts come out of the woodwork to congratulate him by phone or email on the sponsorship. Even people he doesn't know try to contact him.

While Frank was enjoying his vacation, a hilarious scene was playing out on the program Voetbal International, or VI, on RTL7 that Friday night. The host, Wilfred Genee, wanted to announce the new jersey sponsor, but couldn't get the name right. This was of course grist for the mill of the co-host, Johan Derksen, and when the name was finally revealed, the other co-host, René van der Gijp couldn't resist joining in the fun. While the three men were getting their jollies from the announcement, the name TiTaTuinmeubelen.nl was mentioned an amazing total of eight times. Live on television, for an audience of millions. Johan Derksen had suggested that Wilfred was just dropping hints so he would get a free new set of patio furniture. Frank couldn't have come up with better publicity himself.

After a few hours of sleep, on Sunday morning, he puts on his best suit and heads to Doetinchem. From the car, he calls Take, the most brazen salesman at Bukatchi. He asks him to deliver a complete patio furniture set to the studio, on Monday afternoon a few hours before the next edition of VI.

"And don't let the security guard outbluff you, Take. I want you to bring that set all the way into the studio. And bring a couple of large sheets of paper with our color logo printed on them. Let's just see what happens."

Once at Vijverberg stadium, Frank is allowed to drive all the way up to the main entrance. He's feeling a little awkward, and has no idea what's in store for him. First, there's a round of introductions to the members of the board and the people from the commercial department. Martin Koenink also introduces himself.

"So you're that TiTa magician from Corfu? Ha-ha, that was such an unusual phone call. At first I thought someone was playing a trick on me. I'm glad you could make it. I understand it was a major ordeal getting here. We'll be going to the press room in a minute, and our general director will officially present the jersey to you during the press conference. You'll also be expected to say a word or two to the press."

Frank sits down at the large table, next to the press officer and the general director of De Graafschap. He looks into the room. It's full of familiar faces, the top Dutch sports reporters and commentators such as Theo Reitsma, Eddy Poelman and Humberto Tan. The marketing department at De Graafschap has really gone all out. All the advertising materials now bear the TiTa logo. Proud as a peacock, he accepts the new jersey, and tells the story of his company and the how and why to the press gathered in the room.

After the press conference, Frank is also interviewed by various camera crews, and then it's time to go onto the field. The teams of Ajax and De Graafschap are already in the middle of their warming-up. Frank poses with the jersey on the sidelines.

On Monday morning at 9:00, Frank knocks softly at the door of the apartment. Frank was somewhat emotional after they lost the match yesterday, and even though the defeat by Ajax wasn't unexpected, it was still hard. Frank is glued to his phone in the days that follow. Literally every media outlet wants a chance to speak to the jersey sponsor; they all want to hear the story behind it. It starts with RTV Oost and TC Tubantia. This local television station and newspaper are soon followed by the national newspaper outlets *De Telegraaf* and the *Algemeen Dagblad*, and the popular television network, SBS 6. The patio set, including the logo, is in full view during the VI broadcast. Take did it again; nothing can stop this guy. Once again, the company name is mentioned several times. This is going really fast, Frank thinks. He has gotten his 200,000 worth, twice over in fact.

Using Google Analytics, at the Bukatchi office, they can see with exact precision how many hits they are getting and the orders that are being placed. It is even immediately visible whenever De Graafschap plays at home. During these matches, they score double the hits and sales. It seems that the signs with the logo that are visible behind the players when they are giving an interview have a huge impact. The signs along the walls bordering the field also play a role. During away games however, both are lacking.

Thanks to the sponsorship, the recognition of the name is increasing by leaps and bounds, and everyone seems to find the company. Sometimes this isn't exactly desirable. Various bingo clubs, billiard teams and community centers contact them looking for sponsorship, but to no avail. Frank immediately draws a very clear line. Sponsorship is limited to De Graafschap, and no one else, if anything, to prevent him from having even more work than he already has.

The only exception he makes, and it is a small one, is for the local soccer team, FC Twente. They want to meet with him, and he can't nor will he refuse. Only Frank isn't entirely sure what they want to talk to him about. FC Twente already has a sponsor, TUI/Arke, the travel organization, and the 200,000 he has already paid won't even get him a spot on the inside of the team's shorts. There's not much point in talking, he thinks.

As it turns out, they're looking for a new main sponsor for their women's team. When he hears this, Frank bursts out laughing.

"I don't think it would be a great idea to have these women walking around with 'TiTa' emblazoned on their chests. That just wouldn't be a good idea."

The manager of the women's team doesn't seem bothered by this. "I think we can get away with it. We were recently in touch with Melkunie, the dairy company, and no one in the organization had a problem with that either. The captain even mentioned last week that as long as we don't end up with jerseys featuring 'The Twente Central Box Depot', it's not a problem."

Although Frank appreciates her openness and snappy answers, he still decides not to make any commitments for the time being. He wants to first wait and see how things go with De Graafschap.

In December, about one-third of the way through the contract, he receives the latest figures from the Premier League limited partnership.

An independent research firm calculated the value of all the advertising messages that have been visible in the media. When they add up all the values up to now, they arrive at a figure of over one million. This means that, if they extrapolate this, they will have created a total media value of three million by the end of the sponsorship. Not too shabby for an investment of 200,000, Frank thinks. Equally as important in his view is that they have started the ball rolling now. Bukatchi has broken free from its wholesaler straitjacket. The consumer market is calling, and all sorts of new commercial opportunities are arising.

22

CLOSING DINNER

Six months before his vacation in Corfu, Frank had had a remarkable phone call. A company, Marktlink, had called to ask if they could come speak to him about Bukatchi. They had a potential acquisition candidate, and wanted to come exchange ideas with him about this. Frank gets calls like this fairly often, from companies he's never heard of who want to talk about Bukatchi and his future. He had always kept them at a distance, pleading a lack of time and that he had other priorities, but he knew that Marktlink was an extremely serious and professional organization, one of the biggest players when it comes to acquisitions of small-to-medium-sized businesses. This time, he decided that talking to a specialist couldn't hurt.

So a few weeks later, in the early spring of 2011, there he sat, at a meeting with two other men. His feeling told him that it had been a good meeting, even though Frank didn't think the potential buyer was really a good fit for Bukatchi. He closed the door on the deal, and otherwise, it was just business as usual.

In spite of this, their conversation still lingered in the back of his mind. Although Frank wasn't really eager to sell his company, he kept running into obstacles. Managing consists primarily of setting priorities, and if there was one thing he had made a sacred vow to himself to do after the bankruptcy, it was to never allow anything that he had an aversion to at Unimeta happen at Bukatchi. They have as few meetings as possible at Bukatchi; for Frank, this is only inefficient nonsense and a waste of time.

They also don't hold performance evaluations for employees. If someone does a good job of something, they immediately get a pat on the back, and if something isn't right, they also let the employee know. In Frank's view, you don't have to wait to do either until the end of the year. Keeping track of working hours and vacation days was something they didn't do right from the start at Bukatchi, and they still don't do this today. Flexibility takes priority. You take a day off when you can, and work when the company needs you. It doesn't matter if this is in the evening, on the weekend or in the middle of the night. The company motto is the local version of "you're there when you're needed". This corporate culture is what got Bukatchi where it is today; they have just passed the milestone of 11 million euros in sales. Keeping to the basic agreements from the time the company started is proving to be more difficult as the business grows. This is something Frank struggles with.

He actually hasn't had any time for two years now. He runs around all day like a madman just to maintain the status quo. He knows he only has himself to blame, and he also knows why it happens. After all the nightmares at Unimeta, he only has one chance to do things better.

Frank had scraped together all his savings, took out a higher mortgage, and borrowed money just to make the new company a success.

This pressure ensures that he keeps a tight rein on everything. He handles the most important purchasing negotiations in the Far East himself. He personally checks the documents for accuracy. Bukatchi doesn't pay a single invoice without his initials at the bottom. He insists on seeing all the returns on sales for the important orders, and signs off on them himself. The same applies to credit notes. He hates these as it is, since of course it's never the customer's fault if something is wrong with a table or chair. Bukatchi always gets the short end of the stick and pays the costs. In cases like this, Frank always wants to know exactly what's going on.

This is one way he tries to maintain control over the organization, but this is becoming more and more stressful. He is hard at work from early in the morning until late in the evening. Eighty hours a week is his standard working week, and extremes of 100 hours are no exception. Fortunately he has the complete sympathy and cooperation of his wife, Edith, but Frank knows this is not healthy. He does realize that the more sales Bukatchi makes, the more hours he will have to work. He feels that he has reached his limit in terms of what his body can still physically handle. Everything will be fine until I end up driving my car into a tree, he sometimes thinks, or until I am put in the penalty box at home. The kids are heading towards puberty at full speed and need attention. Slowly but surely, he seems to be short on time for anything at work. He finds himself rushing through everything to make it to the next appointment or activity. Instead of a catalyst that tracks down new initiatives and gets everyone excited about new projects, he's more and more the one putting the brakes on things, a delaying factor.

This all becomes even clearer to him during those two weeks in Corfu. The mental calm he felt on vacation is gone once he's back at the office, and this stifles all the creativity and new developments.

He doesn't even have time to think about all this either. He's back just in time for the Spoga trade show in Cologne the first weekend in September, still the world's largest B2B trade show for patio furniture. The prospects for Bukatchi are good; they can easily go to the show and pick up even more sales. This thought distresses Frank no end because he knows what this will mean.

The Cube Set in particular has been a huge hit. This is Bukatchi's first patented product. A complete six-piece wicker lounge set, it can be stacked in a box measuring only one cubic meter, making it perfect for shipping and for storing in the winter. They play a video on a big screen showing two charming young ladies setting up the set without tools, and neatly putting it back together again in no time at all.

Bukatchi's new collection meets with unusually positive reactions. Frank should actually be really happy about this, but mostly, he's just really worried. The idea of the huge amount of work that will be expected of him weighs heavily on his mind. In the next six months, he'll have to make another six trips or so to China and Indonesia to make sure everything goes smoothly. The wife and kids will just love this, Frank thinks. The puzzle they have to solve to get the financing arranged again is also getting more and more complicated. It's no longer a fun challenge, just a major task and burden.

Two weeks after the trade show, Frank takes the plunge and calls Marktlink. After a few brainstorming sessions, one conclusion emerges that is completely clear. Bukatchi is ready for another form of management. This is the only way for it to continue to grow and develop. They briefly toy with the idea of recruiting an experienced manager, so that Frank will be able to take more distance as the owner, and supervise the new employee in the daily activities. The longer Frank thinks about this, the closer he gets to the conclusion that this construction is doomed to fail.

"This will only work if the new manager gets all the freedom he needs to do the work his own way," he says to Tim, one of the Marktlink partners. "This makes sense; after all, everyone is different. But this means I will run the risk that someone else does it all completely wrong, and then imagine the risks of damage to my image as the owner."

"You can minimize these risks as much as possible, but you can't exclude them entirely," Tim informs him.

"It's just not appealing to me, Tim. I have worked like a madman for over six years building up this company. I can't let someone else mess that up, can I? I would constantly be getting in the way, looking over his shoulder."

"In that case, there's really no point in doing it, Frank. You'll be back at square one, and you might as well just keep running the company yourself in that case."

"Yeah, and that's no good either, and that's the reason we're sitting here now. I have seen way too many examples, even at healthy companies, where a new guy comes in and makes an incredible mess of everything. Sometimes, it was so bad that the company was teetering on the edge of the abyss within a year. And this includes companies in the patio furniture industry. This just isn't going to work, Tim. You all will just have to see if you can find a suitable party that is truly interested in investing in Bukatchi. This has to be in combination with an experienced manager, who wants to put their heart and soul into the company, and who has the skills to steer Bukatchi on to the next phase. A baby was born seven years ago, and it is slowly growing up. Childhood is over, and puberty is also partly behind us. The new parents will have to raise this big teenager to adulthood and will have to prove they're good at it. I want to be able to be proud when I drive past our building five years from now, because I will know that we made the right decision."

"I understand what you mean, Frank. You aren't the first person we've done this for."

"I want Bukatchi to be able to continue to exist on its own. I want it to have the chance to continue to grow, and for all the employees to keep their jobs. Not only in Hengelo, but also in China and Indonesia. That is a non-negotiable condition. And the investor can't get nervous if things don't go well one year; after all, we are dependent on the weather and the season. They have to have a strong financial foundation and know what they're getting themselves into."

"We get that too. We are going to be very specific in our search, so that the average Joe Schmoe doesn't even appear on our radar screen."

"Exactly. And will you also exercise the greatest possible caution and secrecy while you're at it? If any of the competition gets wind of this, they will use it against us. They can start all sorts of rumors among our customers, that something is going on at Bukatchi. This is the last thing we need of course. No one can know anything about this. This is also key for our business operations. It will only distract people from their work. The company just has to keep running the way it always does. I will set the example. I suggest that from now on, we meet and discuss things as often as possible in the evenings and on weekends. I really have to get started on the purchasing for the coming season, and the development of the new collection for 2013."

No fewer than 26 interested parties contact Marktlink. Frank is pleasantly surprised by this number. Tim tells him that it is a lot, but he had also expected it to some degree.

"There aren't that many healthy companies in the wholesale sector right now looking for an investor. Everything is perfect at Bukatchi. Great brand, good market position, beautiful collection and a really nice building. When you combine this with the good results from the past six years, it actually makes perfect sense."

"But where do we go from here?" Frank asks. "I don't have the time or desire to sit down at the table with all these people. We also have to be able to continue to do our work."

"Yes, you do. That's why we're going to screen them first. Then we'll make up a short list of no more than 10 parties, and we'll schedule two days during which we talk to all of them."

In January 2012, there are only three investors left with whom they engage in further negotiations. They all satisfy the profile that Frank has drawn up, one a bit more than the other, but he would actually be willing to take on the challenge with all three of them. Ultimately, one party jumps out, mostly because of their professional attitude. This is obvious from their presentation, their entire action plan, and their track record.

Antea Participates from The Hague may not offer the best terms, but they do bring the most knowledge and skills to the table, along with an extremely professional manager who is eager to take the leap to entrepreneurship in the SMB sector. He has worked in consumer electronics for almost 20 years, at Philips among others.

He is extremely well-educated and has lived all over Europe for his work. Frank is actually pretty proud that this combination of people has chosen Bukatchi. He expects that this will also give his colleagues a safe and good feeling, with a protective umbrella like this over their heads.

While this entire process is in motion and planned down to the minute, Frank gets an unpleasant phone call from China.

"Are you sitting down?" Flora asks.

"Why? A few days ago you said that everything was under control."

"It was. Not anymore. Eastco in Ningbo is about to go under. We have placed almost a million dollars' worth of orders with them and now they say they can't deliver. Their suppliers won't send them any more raw materials because they are worried they won't get paid."

"But this is a disaster! We've got deliveries to a large German and Dutch home-improvement chain that are depending on these orders. If they are too late, we'll miss out on those sales and will get slapped with a claim to boot."

Although this news has really unsettled Frank, he can't tell her that the sale of Bukatchi will be hanging by a thread if this doesn't get sorted out. This will mean a sudden gap of one million in the forecast, and this would be enough to scare off any investor.

Together with Flora, he goes over their options and alternatives. The bankruptcy of Compex is still fresh in everyone's memory. This has to be prevented now, at all costs.

After half an hour of brainstorming, they finally come up with a solution. Frank will transfer 50,000 dollars to China. Flora will fly to Ningbo together with Leo, Bukatchi's Chinese quality control manager, and visit all of Eastco's suppliers. Every factory that refuses to deliver will receive a cash advance from Bukatchi. This will be laid down in writing, in a simple contract. This is how they will have to regain their trust so that they resume deliveries to Eastco.

The two factories Eastco outsources the welding and color-coating of the frames to will also be persuaded the same way. Leo will remain there for two months and supervise the progress. He's wearing a money belt around his waist containing at least 20,000 dollars that he guards with his life. Every time they need oil to grease the wheels, he takes care of it. Production seems to be starting up again.

In February, Frank and the investor sign the letter of intent which contains the basic agreements and the further procedure. Frank is happy that he can rely on the specialists at Marktlink now and then, and on his right-hand finance man, Rodie. An incredible quantity of paper, contracts and legal documents, flies across the table. It dizzies him on a regular basis. This is no wonder, since he has insisted that all these activities take place in the evenings and on the weekends. During the day at the office, Frank still works full steam ahead, the way his colleagues have grown accustomed to from him.

In mid-February, Frank can't avoid another trip to China. He flies directly to Ningbo in the northeast of China to visit Eastco, together with Flora and Leo. Once again, production has been brought to a standstill. This time they can't get any more nuts and bolts, and the cardboard supplier refuses to deliver a single box.

Frank first changes clothes in the hotel; the temperatures are around freezing in Ningbo, and he knows the situation in the factories there. No heating and no office anywhere to warm up quickly. He pulls on his thermal underwear, laces up his hiking boots and pulls on an extra fleece sweater over his other sweater just to be sure.

Upon their arrival at Eastco, they find the owner at his wit's end; he no longer knows what to do to make things right. After talking for hours, they finally get their plans down on paper. They have him put his signature on the plans, and seal his commitment with the company stamp. The man doesn't speak a word of English, and Flora has to translate everything. He keeps either walking away or answering his phone, making it seem like an eternity before they can get any clarity about the situation. Frank feels the cold slowly seeping into his legs. In spite of all the layers he's wearing, standing still for hours in these temperatures is no party.

The next day they visit the two suppliers who are still refusing to do business with Eastco. Frank explains the situation, makes an advance payment, and manages to persuade them. A fat stack of bills does work wonders here.

Back in the Netherlands, all three of the major banks take turns listening to a presentation at Antea's office in The Hague. Frank is there too to tell his side of the story. In addition to ING and ABN Amro, "his" Rabobank has also been invited. It gives him a huge sense of pride to know that all three banks want to do their best to be allowed to participate in the deal. Ultimately, ABN Amro draws the longest straw. After nearly seven years, this bank is back in the patio furniture business.

In China, things are extremely tense at Eastco. Frank has had to transfer a second installment of 50,000 dollars to Flora. This will enable her to pay the suppliers, little by little. They will ultimately deduct this money from the amount they owe Eastco when the products are shipped. It's been a creative solution, but highly unusual. The customers' deadlines are rapidly approaching, and nowhere near all the lounge sets have been shipped. Frank is feeling the stress, and is in daily contact with his colleagues in China, worried that something could still go wrong at the last minute.

The most nerve-wracking part of the conversations with the investor is also beginning. The deal can still fall through at this point. He knows that everything is in order, and has complete confidence that it will all be fine in the end, but it still isn't 100% certain. All he has to do is think back to the Support Plus days to jolt him back to reality.

"We just assume it will fall through," he says to Tim. "That way, there are no negative consequences if something goes wrong."

Frank has already prepared everything for the audit, with Rodie's help. All the documents are in special binders that they have put together in the weekends leading up to this. The accountants at De Jong & Laan are busy with all their own preparations.

Once they get the green light for the audit in mid-March, they can get started immediately. A special room has been set up at De Jong & Laan where Antea's regular accountant can work. The transaction date has been set at March 26, 2012. This means they will really have to work hard until then, even though Frank is once again getting ready for another trip to the

Far East. He will be gone for nine days, and will fly back from Indonesia on Sunday, March 25th, just in time for the closing, the legal completion of the acquisition.

All the accountants' questions are able to be answered to their satisfaction, and the results of the extensive audit don't reveal any unpleasant surprises. Even all the lounge sets that Eastco had to produce under dubious circumstances are loaded into containers and shipped one day before the expiration of the deadline.

At Antea's attorney's office, the last little wrinkles are ironed out before the official documents are signed. A few hours later, the group goes to the notary's office. With a large stack of folders clutched under his arm, Frank walks into the prestigious building in the Zuidas section of Amsterdam. He sinks into very plush, deep-pile carpeting up to his ankles.

It's 4:00 in the afternoon by this time, and the spectacle can finally begin. Frank figures that all the documents will be signed within an hour. He is looking forward to the final meal, the "closing dinner". He has heard that a lengthy meal is standard after closing a deal like this. If the luxury at the notary's office is anything to go by, Frank has really high expectations for the restaurant they will be dining at later. But first, the notary has to look into a few things. It takes forever, and Frank's stomach is starting to rumble. He is also having trouble staying awake; thanks to jetlag, he feels like it's 1:00 in the morning. He looks at Rodie who is rubbing his generous stomach. He turns to Frank and whispers, "Wanna bet that that notary is sitting downstairs in the company restaurant, eating a pizza?"

"Great minds think alike," Frank says under his breath. "And we're sitting here, drinking water."

The last signatures are finally put to the documents at 8:30. It was a major ordeal, with entire binders full of contracts, every page of which had to be initialed. Once that is over with, the group raises their glasses and toasts the great deal.

"Here's hoping that it makes everyone very happy," the notary says. Frank cheerfully joins in the toast and thinks, finally, room to breathe. Everyone goes their own separate ways, and Frank and Rodie are left behind with their empty stomachs.

As he sinks into the passenger seat in Rodie's car a little later, Frank is happy he doesn't have to drive back. He is completely exhausted. The combination of all the stress, the jetlag and his empty stomach has taken its toll.

The last 12 years flash through his mind. He has finally been able to shake the label of loser and "master of disaster". Mostly, he has proven to himself that he really can do it, build up a successful company. He has come full circle. He is mostly relieved for his direct colleagues, even though some of them may have a hard time understanding his decision. Hopefully, they will eventually understand. Frank realizes that it will seem to come out of nowhere for them, but a word is enough to the wise. He just couldn't continue on in the current situation any longer. The risk of failure was just too high. With this transaction, the company will be relatively safe in the arms of a stable, strong and professional company, his 18 co-workers' jobs will now be a lot more secure, and they can continue to build on the future with confidence.

He is mainly relieved that he can finally work towards a life with more time for himself and his family. They have agreed that he will train his successor, Thijs, on a full-time basis for the coming year, and will transfer all his duties to him. After that, a new era will begin. As a fanatic soccer fan, Frank plans to go to many soccer matches abroad. He wants to see all the great stadiums of Europe. He also wants to focus on writing articles and blogs and learn a lot more about brand management at SMBs, a subject that fascinates him no end. This is still uncharted territory.

At the very top of his list is something he has been toying with for years, writing a book about his 12 years as an entrepreneur.

He wants to write about all the disasters and resurrections, the bankruptcies of Compex, Unimeta and Support Plus. He also wants to talk about the start of Bukatchi and the adventures he experienced there.

But first, they drive to the roadside restaurant in Stroe. It's on their way and they are both absolutely famished. By the time they get out of the car to go into the restaurant, it's 10:00. The restaurant is closed.

"Oh no, this can't be!" Frank cries. He looks at Rodie.

"Burger King it is; it's right next-door."

Right as they reach the door, an employee in the typical yellow and red uniform flips the sign in the window from "open" to "closed".

"Also closed," Rodie says sadly.

And so it transpires that two hours after Frank closed the deal of a lifetime, he is sitting at the Shell station in Stroe, trying to choke down an old cheese sandwich at 10:00 in the evening. He manages to wash it down with some creamy drinkable yoghurt. After this fancy "closing dinner", he stands with both feet firmly planted on the ground. Like a true Tukker.

Epilogue

SMOKE CLOUDS OVER NAIROBI

Zanzibar, August 2013. It has been a year and a half since Frank took the most rigorous step in his working life. He has finally set sail onto smoother waters. He spent the first year after he put his signature to all those contracts chugging away at work as if nothing had changed. They agreed that he would spend a full year training his successor. In situations like this, it's all or nothing for Frank.

After the year was up, he continued to work two days a week as an advisor. He has been doing this for a couple months now, and this gives him the time to fulfill a long-cherished desire, to write a book about his experiences. A book about the last few hectic years and all his unusual and often bizarre adventures. Frank has nearly completed it as he watches his children play from where he relaxes on his sun lounger.

In his mind, he can still see himself standing in the Unimeta cafeteria for the first time. Hard to believe that was 13 years ago. Five months later, a true inferno broke out in Enschede, during which his complete inventory of patio furniture was blown sky high. A year later, the biggest terrorist attack in human history took place. Frank can still hear the pilot say that he is going to dump kerosene, and still sees himself standing in the field next to that United plane. Five nights spent sleeping on army stretchers in the university auditorium followed, together with his 200 fellow passengers somewhere in a remote yet hospitable corner of Canada.

His thoughts then travel to the reorganizations he had to lead as a result of the growing competition from China. The copycats, some of whom even seemed impervious to lawsuits, and the phone call from his wife when she asked him exactly where he was in China.

Frank remembers the 100 hotheaded Chinese suppliers he gave the speech to in the hotel. To no avail, as it turned out, resulting in the bankruptcy of Unimeta. The darkest page in the history of his career; for himself, but also for all those employees who had deserved better.

He turns over on his sun lounger.

He can still clearly see Peter Groeleken's face, the man from ABN Amro's Special Credits division. They had sure had their share of squabbles. Peter had waited one day too long for Unimeta to be able to restructure. Everything seemed to be over at that point, but people can be very resilient.

Six weeks later, Bukatchi was born. Frank's brainchild, one that grew steadily. He had saved it from the parent company Support Plus just in the nick of time, right before it came untethered. It grew to become a fantastic company in the years that followed, super healthy and with enormous potential. Set up as a lean and mean machine, it had a gorgeous collection, a beautiful building and great results. With its offices in China and Indonesia, and a distribution center in Germany, it was actually a mini-multinational.

As he watches his children playing in the swimming pool, Frank realizes that all of this had stretched him to the limit. He took it to extremes, possibly excessively so, and at his own expense, that of his family and indirectly, also of his co-workers. Fortunately, they all stayed healthy all those years, otherwise he never could have gotten this far.

He remembers the call from Marktlink like it was yesterday, when they called to talk about Bukatchi's future. Just before that, he had pulled the biggest stunt of his career; ensuring that TiTaTuinmeubelen.nl became the main sponsor of De Graafschap. Frank can still see himself sitting there, seeing his company's logo on the jerseys.

Six months of blood, sweat and tears later, he was no longer the CEO and owner of Bukatchi, and with a dusty-dry sandwich as his final reward.

A smile curls around the corners of his mouth. Yes, that's how it all happened. And now he's lying here, at his exotic vacation destination. They don't have much longer here; they'll be leaving soon. The suitcases are already packed. They're flying home later, from Zanzibar via Nairobi back to Amsterdam. He scrolls down the Dutch news sites. One unusual report catches his eye.

Smoke clouds over Nairobi. Airport at Kenyan capital on fire.

The photos speak volumes. The terminal for international flights is ablaze, and the airport is closed until further notice. It looks like the airport is in a state of major chaos. Without even thinking about it, Frank switches to autopilot. First, he calls the travel agency they booked their vacation with. They will need at least 12 hours to get any kind of clear information on what will happen. He realizes that waiting this long will be disastrous for finding an alternate flight. He calls his business travel agency right away, the one he had worked with for years. Fortunately, they still remember him. The next possibility for flying back is via Dar Es Salaam, two days later. There are still nine seats left on that flight. Frank has the agent reserve five immediately. Next, he manages to make arrangements so they can stay in their African hut another two days. He hasn't told his wife and children what's going on yet. When they hear the news, they're taken by surprise.

They were supposed to be going home, weren't they?

Frank laughs, thinking about it.

They were supposed to, yes.

During the course of the afternoon, the consequences of the disaster at the airport become clear. No international flights for days. One complete terminal has been burned to the ground, and thousands of passengers are stranded. Mostly, there's just a whole lot of confusion about what to do now, there in Africa.

The travel agent finally calls Frank back. They're still not sure of anything, but maybe they'll be able to get a flight home in another five or six days. All the international flights for the next week are fully booked. Of course they are, Frank thinks. He tells her about the seats they reserved.

For a moment, there is silence on the other end of the line.

"It sounds like you have some experience with this," he finally hears.

Frank takes a deep sigh.

His insurance pays for their extended stay in Zanzibar. When he tells his children that they're going to have an extra two days of vacation, they cheer. His wife has already unpacked their suitcases again. Azure blue ocean, snow-white beaches, great food and cold beer. Frank stretches out on his sun lounger. Life's what you make it.

In der Beschränkung zeigt sich erst der Meister
(In limitation, the master reveals himself.)

Johann Wolfgang von Goethe

www.ingramcontent.com/pod-product-compliance
Lightning Source LLC
Chambersburg PA
CBHW071645200326
41519CB00012BA/2411